The
Lean
Machine

The Lean Machine

How Harley-Davidson Drove
Top-Line Growth and
Profitability with Revolutionary
Lean Product Development

Dantar P. Oosterwal

⁴AMACOM

American Management Association
New York • Atlanta • Brussels • Chicago • Mexico City • San Francisco
Shanghai • Tokyo • Toronto • Washington, D.C.

Special discounts on bulk quantities of AMACOM books are
available to corporations, professional associations, and other
organizations. For details, contact Special Sales Department,
AMACOM, a division of American Management Association,
1601 Broadway, New York, NY 10019.
Tel: 800-250-5308. Fax: 518-891-2372.
E-mail: specialsls@amanet.org
Website: www.amacombooks.org/go/specialsales
To view all AMACOM titles go to: www.amacombooks.org

This publication is designed to provide accurate and authoritative information in
regard to the subject matter covered. It is sold with the understanding that the publisher
is not engaged in rendering legal, accounting, or other professional service. If legal
advice or other expert assistance is required, the services of a competent professional
person should be sought.

Library of Congress Cataloging-in-Publication Data

Oosterwal, Dantar P.
    The lean machine : how Harley-Davidson drove top-line growth and profitability with
revolutionary lean product development / Dantar P. Oosterwal.
        p.   cm.
    Includes bibliographical references and index.
    ISBN-13: 978-0-8144-3288-4 PB
    ISBN-13: 978-0-8144-1378-4 HC
    1. Harley-Davidson Incorporated—Management.   2. Product management.
3. New products.   I. Title.
    HD9710.5.U54H3752   2010
    658.5'75—dc22

                                                                    2009019982

Printing number

10   9   8   7   6   5   4   3   2   1

To my girls: Kathey, Audrey, and Eva.

To the Harley-Davidson family,
past and present, who made
the learning possible and without whom
the journey could not have happened.

To Dr. Allen Ward,
in acknowledgment of his contribution and
appreciation of his
friendship.

Contents

Acknowledgments   xi

Introduction   xiii

1   **Working Hard**   **1**

   Springtime in Paris   2
   The Concurrent Product Development Process   4
   A Reality Check   7
   Unexpected Competition   8
   Problems Late in the Development Process   10

2   **The Harley-Davidson Environment**   **25**

   Harley-Davidson Was Different   27
   Consensus Decision Making   30
   We Fulfill Dreams   30
   Lessons from the Dark Days   33
   The Circle Organization   36
   Consensus-Driven Organization   38
   Managing Conflict   39
   The Harley-Davidson Business Process   39
   Organizational Learning   41

CONTENTS

3   **Harley-Davidson's Product Development Leadership
    Learning Team   43**

   The PDL²T Journey   46
   Learning Organizations   47

4   **The PDL²T   61**

   Systems Thinking   64
   Learning to See the Product Development System   67
   Learningful Conversations   70
   Creating Shared Vision   75

5   **Firefighting and the Tipping Point   80**

   The MIT Connection   81
   Firefighting   82
   The Tipping Point   83
   Past the Tipping Point   84
   Lessons from Beyond the Brink   91

6   **Cadence and Flow, Bins and Swirl   94**

   The Outstanding Corporate Innovator   97
   Product Development Flow   99
   Product Development Cadence   100
   The Application of Cadence and Flow   104
   Bins   107
   Heuristic Rules of Thumb   111
   The Innovation Swirl   113

7   **Supply and Demand   116**

   The System Dynamics Model of the Motorcycle Business   122
   A Soft Landing by Reducing Shipments   126
   Generating Product Demand   126
   Developing New Products   128

CONTENTS

8   **A Left Turn: Implementing Lean Principles in Product Development   131**

Don't Bring Lean Manufacturing Upstream   133
The Roots of Knowledge-Based Product Development   136
The Systems Approach to Flight   138
Work Smarter, Not Harder   143

9   **The Product Development Limit Curve   145**

Haste Makes Waste   147
Bad Systems Beat Good People   150
Design Rework Loops   152
Product Development Is Predictable   153

10   **Integration Points and False Positive Feasibility   158**

False Positive Feasibility   162
Design Cycles and Integration Points   164

11   **Learning Cycles   167**

The Learning Cycle   170
Set-Based Product Development   174

12   **Set-Based Design   179**

A New Framework for Product Development   183
The Second Piece of the Limit Curve Puzzle   184

13   **Leadership Learning and Pull Events   193**

The Leadership Learning Change Model   194
Early Pull Events   199
Creating Leverage Through Pull Events   203

14   **Quickening Product Development   206**

Railroad Planning versus Combat Planning   207
Establishing and Using Help Chains   210
Using Visual Management   212

CONTENTS

15 *Oobeya* **217**

Collaboration Using the *Oobeya* Process 217
The *Oobeya* Process 221
The Wall 226
Quickening the Pace of Innovation 230

16 **Knowledge-Based Product Development 234**

Indications of Success 237
Creating Change 241

Notes 245

Index 249

Acknowledgments

I am very grateful that my career intersected with the rich and storied history of Harley-Davidson, which made the learning journey shared in this book possible. It is impossible to credit everyone who contributed on the trip, other than to acknowledge the Harley-Davidson family—it was a pleasure and a privilege to work with you all. There are a number of individuals in particular, some of whom are mentioned in this story, who deserve special thanks and recognition due to the contribution of their thoughts, insights, support, and energy including: Garry Berryman, Willie G. Davidson, Pat Keller, Don Kieffer, Kerry Luczak, Jim McCaslin, Louie Netz, Steve Phillips, Anthony Reese, Ken Sutton, Hugh Vallely, Earl Werner, and Tony Wilcox.

Beyond the Harley-Davidson family there are a number of people who deserve specific mention because they contributed directly to or significantly influenced the destination of the learning journey. These include Nelson Repenning, Peter Senge, John Shibley, Durward Sobek, John Sterman, Takashi Tanaka, and Allen Ward.

I would also like to acknowledge Michael Kennedy for prodding me to share my thoughts and experiences so others could learn from my journey, and Tricia Moody, who thought it was a good idea and enthusiastically supported this effort from our very first phone conversation.

Introduction

Learning is not compulsory . . . neither is survival.

W. Edwards Deming

This book is written with one purpose in mind: it is intended to help you improve the effectiveness and efficiency of your product development system. The objective of this book is to provide you with the insights necessary to develop more new products of higher quality in less time with your existing organization. This is the story of my personal journey of learning and discovery and is intended to encourage you on your improvement journey, or perhaps persuade you to embark.

In 2003 Harley-Davidson was awarded the Outstanding Corporate Innovator (OCI) award by the Product Development Management Association (PDMA). The OCI award was won based on conventional phase gate thinking.[1] Through the application of lean principles to product development, the same organization reduced their development time by half and quadrupled new product development throughput. This book provides the organizational learning practices and the knowledge-based development principles to enable your organization to achieve similar or better results.

This is a true story, not a novel. Some poetic license has been taken in the chronology of events to make the story meaningful to the reader because, as with any good road trip, the learning journey does not necessarily happen in a neat and orderly fashion. Any learning journey has its fair share of wrong turns and dead ends. To convey the message in a readable fashion our experience is abbreviated and presented more linearly than it actually happened. All of the people in the story are real people. In some cases real names have been used to recognize and acknowledge their contribution. In other cases names have been changed to protect identities.

All of the information presented in this book is actual data. If the information is discoverable through publicly available sources, then the actual numbers are presented unchanged. However, if the actual numbers are not generally available through public means, then the numbers have been modified to convey the message without providing actual values to maintain confidentiality.

Overview

The story has three parts: The current state of product development, the learning environment and organizational learning fundamentals, and the principles of knowledge-based product development. The book is structured to first allow you to see product development as an integrated system and recognize that improvement of the system is only achieved through a learning journey, then provide you with means to take the journey for yourself.

In Chapter 1 the story begins with the current state of product development, based upon firsthand experience working at a car company I've chosen to call "Roaring Motors." It is the way I was taught to develop products. It is the way almost everyone I know learned to develop products. It is what I see at nearly every company I visit. The current state of product development lays the foundation for frustration, and subsequent motivation to find a way to work smarter rather than harder.

Chapters 2 through 7 describe the learning environment that was present at Harley-Davidson and which allowed this journey of discovery. These chapters present principles of organizational learning necessary to improve product development. They describe how system dynamics and organizational learning enable continuous improvement in product development. The foundational elements for effective product development necessary to build a knowledge-based development system are also described in these chapters.

Chapters 8 through 16 describe the learning and discovery journey in the application of lean principles, which resulted in knowledge-based product development. These chapters describe the principles necessary to make product development effective and the improvement outcome you should expect.

The Importance of Product Development

Product development is the lifeblood of our companies and it fuels the economy. Product development is the road that innovation travels on the way to market. It is the key which unlocks dreams and the spark which ignites the future. A recent survey by the Product Development Management Association (PDMA) identified that the top performing quartile of companies in their study derive nearly 48 percent of their sales revenue from new products and nearly half of the company's profits from new products (products in the market five years or less).[2] As the effective life span of products and services in today's market decreases, it drives the need for shorter product lifecycles. In some cases the development time for new products exceeds the life expectancy of the product in the market. The innovation rate necessary for a company to be successful is rapidly accelerating. The driver for business success is evermore becoming a company's ability to innovate.

The Boston Consulting Group (BCG) conducts a global survey of senior business leaders annually to identify the strategic direction of firms. The results reinforce the importance of innovation; recent findings from these surveys indicate that innovation is consistently a top strategic priority. In 2007 the BCG survey polled 2,500 senior executives from fifty-eight countries across all industries and found that 66 percent of the companies identified innovation as one of their top three strategic initiatives. The study also determined that over 50 percent of the senior executives polled believed that their company did not innovate well in spite of this strategic focus. Most of the respondents indicated that their company did not receive the return on investment of innovation they expected. A similar study by the Economist Intelligence Unit sought to understand the connection between innovation and company success.[3] In this study, 87 percent of the senior executives polled identified innovation as either important or critically important to the success of their company. The study identified that the beneficial impact of innovation efforts goes far beyond corporate performance and actually drives the national economy. The development of new products and services is increasingly being identified as the engine for growth and prosperity.

Former Commerce Secretary Carlos Gutierrez has said, "Innovation is a driver of our economy."[4] The role that innovation plays in the economy is so important that the United States Commerce Department has made the creation of a universal system of metrics to evaluate the impact of innovation on the economy their top priority. The importance of innovation is echoed in a recent Council on Competitiveness report, which identified that as manufacturing capacity becomes globally available at low cost, the competitive value of manufacturing declines.[5] This global competitiveness study emphasizes that innovation is now the primary source of value for United States companies and American workers. The president of the council, Debora Wince-Smith summarized the report by saying, "The only driver for productivity growth for the U.S. is our innovation capacity."

The need for innovation to drive economic growth goes well beyond the United States or the primary developed nations. China and India have recognized the importance of innovation and are beginning to break out of their position as members of the underdeveloped world through investment in knowledge creation and innovation. These countries are embracing a culture of new product development by establishing favorable laws and regulations promoting learning and product development. China has recently become the second largest investor in R&D spending, surpassing even Japan. Only the United States continues to outspend the rest of the world as a single nation.[6]

According to Dirk Pilat, head of the Organization for Economic

Co-operation and Development's (OECD) Science and Technology Policy division, "The rapid rise of China in both money spent and researchers employed is stunning. To keep up, OECD countries need to make their research and innovation systems more efficient and find new ways to stimulate innovation in today's increasingly competitive global economy."[7]

Innovation has become the driver for productivity and growth for every developed nation, as well as for every company that is attempting to grow its business and control its own destiny. Whether country or company, innovation is the differentiator for success. Those who do not innovate will fall behind and will have their fate determined by those who do. This book shares lessons and principles to allow your organization to bring more innovation to market faster with fewer problems through a more effective and efficient product development system.

For more information about the principles enunciated in this book, see www.theleanmachine.org.

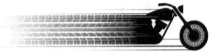

CHAPTER 1

Working Hard

No flying machine will ever fly from New York to Paris . . . [be-cause] no known motor can run at the requisite speed for four days without stopping.

Orville Wright

I returned to my office after lunch and noticed the message light on my phone was on. No surprise—it seemed to always take at least an hour in the morning and another hour after lunch to get through all of my messages. I picked up the receiver, punched in the password to my voicemail and settled in for what was sure to be a long review of messages. The first message was from Gene, my manager: "Guys, listen to the attached message from the boss." Gene was passing along a message he had received about the previous year's engineering department's performance. After a few additional forward introductions, I finally got to the original message from Jack, the vice president of engineering. Jack had made it through all the business and budget reviews that customarily followed the closing of the fiscal year and he was diligently sharing the information with his reports. My mind drifted off somewhere in the message but I snapped back to listening as Jack got to the conclusion of his message and the performance numbers. "Well, I'm sorry to say that we missed our targets again this year.

We overspent the budget by 15 percent and we didn't even deliver what the organization expected. Overall, 26 percent of our projects were delivered late, and we ended up canceling 23 percent of the projects we started," Jack said. "I know that this is a highly dedicated and talented group of people," he emphatically said, but "I know that all of you can do much better. I want you to recommit yourself to doing better. We need to work harder! I need you to redouble your efforts to deliver the projects we have committed and that the organization is expecting from us . . ." Jack continued on with his pep talk, but my mind drifted off again as I hung up the receiver. I was already working nearly fourteen hours per day. I didn't know how I or anyone on my team could possibly work harder, or give any more effort. Work *harder* or work *smarter?* I asked myself as I spun my chair around and propped my feet up on the windowsill of my office to contemplate the message.

Springtime in Paris

It was that time of the year when it wasn't really winter anymore, but spring had not yet arrived. It was messy, rainy, cold, and wet. I lived in a small town on the outskirts of Paris. My office was located in a beautifully landscaped industrial park next to Charles de Gaulle airport. I was living my dream, or so I thought. For as long as I could remember I had wanted to work for a car company, designing cars. Now I was a new engineering manager for Roaring Motors. I had been sent to Paris to help set up a European technical center for the company. I had not been at the Paris office long before I learned the fitting nature of the close proximity between the office and the airport. My time was largely spent resolving production issues in plants across Europe or visiting customers to resolve development issues. My *official* job was to hire, train, and develop a local team of engineers to support and grow our European customer base with new products, but fixing production problems and fixing customer relationships was where I seemed to spend my time. The past year had been particularly difficult, so I was ready for the arrival of spring, with its promise of change and new beginnings.

After weeks of clouds and rain, the battle raged on between the sun and clouds for supremacy in the skies over France. Over the previous few days, the sun had begun to break through the dark gray clouds that dominated the winter months a bit more often. But on this day, the sun periodically fought its way through the grey and at the moment aligned with a small hole in the clouds. A narrow beam of sunlight found its way through my office window. The light shone brightly and splashed off my desk, filling the room with warmth.

I positioned myself in the path of the sun's rays to soak them up. With my feet propped on the window ledge I took a momentary respite from the voice mail messages waiting for me and the phase exit review that was coming up in a few minutes.[1]

As I gazed out my window, the airplanes landing at Charles de Gaulle airport caught my attention. For the first time I noticed the predictable cadence at which the airplanes landed. Initially I noticed it was the predictability of the trajectory that the planes took on final approach. Perhaps the pattern caught my attention because I was deep in thought, wrestling with the idea of working *smarter* rather than *harder* and staring into the nothingness, or perhaps it was the contrast of the bright landing lights against the darkness of the clouds, or perhaps it was just the way I was sitting. From the way my feet were propped up on the windowsill, each airplane appeared to skip across the tip of my shoe in sequence as they came in to land. At first it seemed coincidental that the planes passed this point, but as I watched a few planes go by I realized the uncanny accuracy of each airplane's trajectory.

Looking to my left in the sky, I could see a series of airplanes silhouetted against the gray clouds. The landing lights revealed a pattern of six airplanes lined up on a trajectory for final approach. As the formation of airplanes approached, each one in sequence followed a course that skipped across the tip of my shoe as the plane came closer to the ground, and then passed through a point where the roofline of the building across the street intersected with a poplar tree in the park. Each airplane passed through these points at an even time interval. It dawned on me that each airplane, regardless of size, distance traveled, country of origin, nationality of the pilot, experience of the crew, or any other attribute, followed exactly the same identical, predictable pattern when it came in for a landing. Even when the supersonic Concorde occasionally interrupted the pattern of conventional airplanes, its engines growling low and nose tilting, it also followed the same trajectory, adopting the same flow, interval, and cadence as every other airplane when it came in for a landing.

The high-pitched whine of a motorcycle engine and the sight of a sport bike streaking across my window abruptly brought me back to reality. All thoughts of airplanes with their rhythmic cadence and notions of working harder or smarter were all gone in that instant as I dropped my feet from the window ledge and turned my attention back to the Gantt chart on the wall of my office. The Gantt chart represented the most recent improvements to the corporate development process established by headquarters. The chart described the sequence and timing for the proper method for developing products.

Several years before, someone at headquarters had convened a team of experts from each of the divisions to create a common corporate product development process. This initiative had been our answer to address the widening gap in competitiveness the company faced in developing new products. The effort was well intentioned and seemed like the right thing to do. I remembered my enthusiasm for the initiative when I had first learned about it.

As a staff engineer, I led a team of engineers responsible for designing and developing products for a variety of customers. I applauded a uniform process that laid out the requirements for a project in advance. When I had been a project engineer, one of the most challenging aspects of my job was figuring out what needed to be done and planning out the work to bring products to market. A manual describing specific steps to follow to develop products more effectively would be a great tool to give to my development teams.

The Concurrent Product Development Process

The Concurrent Corporate Product Development Process (CCPDP) initiative had been prompted by our failure to win new business that we should have won easily. At first, not winning contracts was a business inconvenience, but the inconvenience quickly became a problem as more and more of our traditional customers went elsewhere. It became increasingly more difficult to get new business. Our products had become expensive and outdated. It took us too long to develop new products, and we were establishing a reputation for being unreliable. When we did win a contract we often missed our commitments. We missed internal project commitments, we missed our cost projection commitments, we missed our timing commitments, our test commitments, and we missed key customer project milestones. We were forced to go back to our customers with cost increases and requests for time extensions because we were unable to meet our performance objectives.

In an attempt to stem the tide, company leadership decided that each division of the company would send their best and most experienced project leaders to headquarters for a special assignment. These experts would collaborate and improve the current corporate research activity process with a new phase gate-based concurrent development process. With their deep knowledge of product development, they would include the latest techniques of cross-functional concurrent product development methodology, stating exactly what, when, and how everything required to successfully develop a product was to be done. The issues with the existing development process were well known. Product development took too long and the output was unpredictable. When products launched, they were expensive and quality was poor. Because the process took so long, the market often changed by the time products were introduced, resulting in lackluster sales and poor returns on investment. The new concurrent corporate development process would incorporate the latest phase gate methods, and we would finally be able to win back the business that had eroded so quickly and was now cutting into the bottom line performance of the company.

The objective of this new development process was to drastically cut the development time of new products to just over four years. This would be a phenomenal improvement since it was not long ago that our development lead time was eight years. We had all heard rumors that Japanese manufacturers at the time managed to develop a new car in just over two years, but experts at Roaring Motors knew this was impossible. Experienced engineers at Roaring Motors knew that new cars required four seasons of design validation testing to ensure quality before they could be launched. By definition, four-seasons testing took a year to complete. Four-seasons validation testing could not begin until the designs were completed and prototypes built, otherwise the final products were not really being validated. It was unthinkable for the design and prototype build as well as any evaluation testing and design iterations to be completed in twelve months. Just the competitive bid process to identify suppliers took months to complete. Our internal experts advised us that by definition, two years to develop a vehicle was impossible. The rumor of a two-year development process was an obvious ploy planted to lure us into creating a process that would rush the development process resulting in inferior designs and poor-quality products. Roaring Motors was too smart and too experienced to fall into a trap like that. The leadership was perfectly happy with the prospect of developing vehicles in four years rather than eight or ten years, so the team set an aggressive target to cut development time in half for the new CCPDP process.

A year earlier when my package had arrived from the special product development process task team, I had opened the package with great anticipation. My sleepless nights worrying about project deadlines and quality problems would finally be gone. I admired the wisdom of Roaring Motors' leadership. It had been a grand plan.

When I had first opened the CCPDP manual, I thought it was beautiful. It clearly identified 863 statements of work necessary according to the new corporate standard for the development of new products. The team had thought of everything. At first, 863 specific tasks seemed a bit excessive, but since they were built within the four-year time scale, it really didn't matter. The manual was thought to be a competitive advantage. It defined and scheduled the tasks necessary to successfully develop a new vehicle or a new component in advance, greatly reducing project risk, while also reducing development time.

The CCPDP intended to provide management oversight and improve delivery success by incorporating the latest thinking for phase gate methodology. The entire four-year development process was divided into six phases. At the end of each phase, the development team scheduled a meeting with senior executives for a review of the project, and requested approval to exit the current phase and enter the next phase. To reduce risk, the project team would present the status of their project according to a checklist defined in the CCPDP manual. The executive committee then compared what the team presented against the manual and subsequently determined if the project could proceed through the gate to the next phase of development. The check sheets for phase gate reviews made their job much easier. When a project came to a gate review, leadership simply needed to see that the tasks identified for the phase were completed, and the project could progress through the gate.

A Reality Check

My thoughts returned—somewhat despairingly—to the Gantt chart on my office wall with the list of the 863 statements of work representing the CCPDP development process. At that moment, the enthusiasm and the hopes I had for the new process were shattered. I had been sent to Paris to help create a technical center in support of our European customers. I supported plants located in England, Spain, and Italy with customers and potential customers spread across all of Europe. Our plant in England was teetering on the brink of extinction after losing some business we had enjoyed with a longstanding customer. We just had been notified that the new contract was awarded to a small upstart company from Germany that had been more creative, more nimble, and more responsive to the customer's needs than we had been. This product line represented the single largest component of business in the plant and without it the remaining products could not absorb the overhead. We would have to raise prices on the remaining products. Raising prices would certainly kill the remainder of the business.

I was expecting a call from Stephan. Stephan was one of those guys you just could not help but like. He was a young engineer who understood the products well and was enthusiastic about everything he did; his attitude was contagious. Earlier in the day Stephan had called me from the German sales office. He told me that he had gone over to make some final arrangements for the weekend's mountain biking trip with one of his engineering friends who worked for the customer, and his buddy hinted that not everything was going well with the new supplier. Before long Stephan's conversation with his friend changed from biking to development issues with the new product. His friend let it slip that the new supplier was having difficulty delivering on the project commitments. After a while a few more engineers joined in the conversation, and then their managers joined in. By the time Stephan left the development center, he had been asked "confidentially" if we could step in again and supply the product for the new vehicle. The catch was that the new vehicle was completely redesigned, and to meet production we would need to develop the new product in thirty weeks. This opportunity could be the saving grace we needed for our plant in England. At that moment reality hit and somehow the new CCPDP process was not nearly as attractive to me anymore. I had asked Stephan to give me until the end of the day to figure out how we might pull off this request and my time was running out. I anticipated a call at any minute from Stephan looking for my answer and I had still not figured out how to fit our 863 statements of work into a thirty-week development program.

Unexpected Competition

Fulle was a small family-owned metal tube manufacturing company located in northern Germany that had won the business. The company was known for fabricating simple tubing products such as railings, overhead luggage racks, and a variety of other items for the German railroad. They had seen an opportunity several years earlier to expand their business into the high-volume automotive industry by producing simple tubular components as a tier two or tier three supplier. Fulle supported this effort with a small product engineering and test department, so they had extremely low overhead. When the opportunity to expand their business by reaching further up the value stream came along, they bid on the business. Due to their low cost structure and flexibility in working with the customer, they presented a very attractive proposal to the customer. We had never seen them as a threat to our business. Now they had developed a prototype and taken our business—a business that had been very lucrative for us. It was a business that we counted on, but that we spent very little effort on maintaining. The product design hadn't changed much over the years and we were certainly in no hurry to drive change. The products worked relatively well (most of the time) and the customer bought them. In hindsight, it was a business we had taken for granted.

Fulle had little experience in the new products, but the design seemed simple enough, so they won the business based on a very attractively priced proposal and an aggressive development plan. They had produced a few sample prototypes for the customer. Initial testing by the customer indicated that the design was feasible. Now several years into the development process the issues with the new design were becoming apparent. Fulle had slipped up on the delivery of the project due to "design complications." As the development of the vehicles progressed, the relationship was becoming increasingly strained as the customer lost confidence in Fulle's ability to deliver the design for their vehicle. The product samples were no longer passing the customer's test and the test failures were beginning to slow down progress of overall vehicle development.

Fulle had abruptly won the business and we were out without any warning. The plant in England, with the volume loss, was no longer competitive. The loss of this business created a huge overhead burden that could not be spread without making all the other products uncompetitive. There was now a small window of opportunity to win back the business if we could step in with a new product in just thirty weeks. How could a small team of inexperienced engineers possibly deliver an entirely new product in thirty weeks when the experienced home office delivered a "rush" job in three *years*? The new development process that hung on my wall was intended to be the answer. The more I thought about it, the less this new process looked like the saving grace it was intended to be. Unfortunately, the very same issues that Fulle faced with the German customer we were also facing with one of our new customers in Sweden, and the request for a new product in thirty weeks fell on top of that.

Problems Late in the Development Process

Although I didn't realize it at the time, the problem I faced with the new customer had actually started years earlier. The problem was totally preventable and was the unintended consequence of a decision made early in the development process. It just had not shown up until late in development. The division of Roaring Motors I worked for had been given a mandate to increase component sales from outside the parent car company. Someone had come up with a novel design twist to our traditional products that had been in production for over twenty years. With the push for new business, sales had quoted it on a new account.

The products that the division made had two primary functions: 1) To transmit torque from the steering wheel to the front wheels of the car so that when you turn the steering wheel, the front wheels turn, and 2) absorb energy in a car crash to protect the driver during a collision. The first function of transmitting torque is quite straightforward from an engineering perspective. Based on the weight of the car and the steering geometry a certain amount of torque needs to be transmitted. Most every product the company produced met similar requirements for strength and durability. Other than the length, the design attributes for torque transmission did not change much and the design issues were well understood.

The design attribute for absorption of energy in a crash, on the other hand, is highly variable and the solutions are very much dependent on each specific vehicle application. Every car has a unique crash pulse that creates different requirements to protect the driver in a collision. The mounting position in the vehicle, the seating position of the driver, the way the mounting structure of the car bends during a crash, the interaction with the air bag, and the space available under the dash all greatly influence the energy absorption capability of each design. The new design changed how energy was absorbed during a crash, and initial testing showed great promise for the new design compared to more traditional products.

The new design was easier and less expensive to build, and absorbed energy better than the old design. The dilemma with the design was that it required a unique vehicle application for it to function. With the push for new customers, it wasn't long before sales sent in a design request from a new customer that had a perfect match for the new design. Some quick feasibility testing to the customer's design requirements verified that the design could work, so sales quoted it to the new customer. The project had been kicked off with great optimism, but it wasn't long into the development program before issues started to arise. During the second round of crash testing, the issues turned into serious problems. The prototype parts failed the tests. They did not absorb enough energy during a crash and we were at risk of being kicked out as a potential supplier. I was in Germany visiting a customer when my boss, John Rock, tracked me down.

"We've had some problems with the supplier evaluation testing at the new customer in Sweden, and I need you to go over and take care of it," he said. John was a very traditional action-oriented command-and-control manager; like a general commanding troops, bellowing out orders in the heat of battle. He loved nothing more than fixing problems. The bigger the problem, the brighter he shone. Somehow, he seemed to quietly create his own problems, then publicly solve them in dramatic fashion. I often thought of him as a firefighting arsonist. John had built his career fighting fires.

"I know it's not your project, but since you're in the area anyway," John went on, "I need you to stop by Sweden on your way home and see what's going on. All I know so far is that our parts failed the crash tests and the project engineer over there in Europe is an idiot and needs help. The customer has stopped all further testing with our parts until we assure them that we've fixed it. I need you to go over there and fix the problem. I'll make sure that Gertrude meets you at the airport and introduces you to the customer."

I had briefly met Gertrude at our European sales office, but had never worked with her. She was the salesperson on the account, and she briefed me on what she knew of the situation on the drive to the test center after picking me up from the airport in Gothenburg the following day. It wasn't long before I was crawling around the twisted metal carcasses of crashed cars. But even after a review of the high-speed films of the crash tests, the solution was not apparent. The customer was on a tight evaluation test schedule, but was willing to shuffle the test sequence, and give us two weeks to resolve the issues and replace the test samples. The test center time was expensive, so if we missed the two-week grace window, we would be eliminated from the bid process.

After a day in Sweden, Gertrude dropped me off at the airport with my luggage and all the failed parts I could carry. The flight back to the United States gave me plenty of time to contemplate why we always seemed to end up in this kind of a predicament no matter how optimistically a project started. When the plane landed in Detroit Friday afternoon, I still had not figured it out but it was time to get busy fixing the problem.

John arranged for the design team and someone from the proto-type shop to work over the weekend, so at 6:00 Saturday morning I walked in with a box of doughnuts under my arm and plenty of coffee. Doughnuts and coffee were the requisite bribe to get engineers or tech-nicians to do anything on a weekend. They had all finally straggled into the conference room by 7:00, sleepy-eyed, groggy, and in no mood to give up their weekend. We started with a review of the issues as the team understood them and the challenge we had in front of us. As we went around the room, each person shared what they knew. As I wrote the comments on a flip chart I thought to myself, "All things consid-ered, this is a pretty good team to be tackling this problem." I had known each of them for a long time, and knew their strengths. 7:00 A.M. on a Saturday was not their time to shine, but each one of them was highly committed to fixing the problems. They were as disap-pointed as anyone else with the outcome of the latest test results, and didn't understand what had gone wrong.

After everyone's input had been captured on the flip chart, Lenny, the lead engineer, rolled out the drawings for the design. He led a review of the test parts I had carried back on the plane from Sweden against the drawings. Then the test engineer reviewed his internal test data and compared it to the customer's results. We weren't very far into the doughnut box before the conference room was full of parts and the walls were covered with drawings and test reports. Until this series of tests, every test that had been run on the new design had passed.

It wasn't until the test engineer compared the high-speed film from the customer's tests to his old test pictures that an anomaly showed up. While carefully reviewing the customer's films, looking for clues, one of the team members pointed out that as the car crushed it buckled, changing the angle at which the test dummy hit the air bag. As the car buckled, the mounting points changed, creating an angle higher than anything the team had tested. The feasibility testing had been done to the angle the customer had specified, and the design had passed. All of the other products we had in production were not very sensitive to such a change in angle, but with no other leads it was decided to test at an angle that we thought represented what we saw happening in the films. Bill, the test technician, worked with the prototype shop and quickly cobbled together a test fixture that represented the deformed angle in the customer's test. By midafternoon the tests had been run and Bill came back with the results. The new tests at the deformed angle mirrored the customer's results. Every test failed.

Bill went to the board in the conference room and wrote two headings: Test Number and Energy Absorbed. Then he pulled out his test folder for the project and began to write down the results from all the tests that he had conducted for everyone to see (Figure 1–1):

As he finished recording the information he spoke. "Look, the lowest energy we have seen on any test until today was 1144 joules of energy," he said, circling test number 14 with the marker for emphasis. Then he wrote down the latest results: 150 and 122 joules. "I couldn't believe the results on the first test run," Bill said, "so I decided to run it again. The second one was even worse. Our goal for this car has been to absorb about 1000 joules. A bit more if we can, but at least that much. This design clearly does not work." Bill sat back down in his chair glaring across the table at Lenny, the lead design engineer.

Figure 1.1

Test Number	Energy (joules)	Test Number	Energy (joules)	Test Number	Energy (joules)	Test Number	Energy (joules)
1	1235	10	1295	19	1126	28	1261
2	1220	11	1163	20	1286	29	1206
3	1208	12	1216	21	1353	30	1274
4	1251	13	1369	22	1229	31	1187
5	1261	14	1144	23	1367	32	1329
6	1145	15	1356	24	1308	33	1207
7	1288	16	1182	25	1310	34	1390
8	1248	17	1187	26	1240		
9	1195	18	1226	27	1164		

Bill always liked to taunt the design engineers. He thought that the engineers who came into *his* lab were prima donnas, so he reveled in the fact that he had found a problem.

After a quick review of the data it was clear that Bill was right. Within the range specified by the customer, which was the range of angles that the feasibility testing had been conducted at, the new design worked very well. But at the actual test conditions, the design didn't work. The team was dejected. They had hoped to find a problem with the customer's testing. The problem was not with the test, but how the car performed during the test. The act of conducting the vehicle crash test had changed the intended test conditions. We had just verified that our design did not work. The car was not going to change—so if we wanted the business we needed to fix the design and have parts in Sweden within two weeks.

It was late in the afternoon and the team clearly needed a break. We decided to leave everything where it was and sort out what we were going to tell John Rock in the morning. He was not going to like what we had found. He was a man of action.

"Stop wasting time," he would shout. "Just pick a solution and make it work!"

We would clearly need the better part of Sunday to develop our story and PowerPoint presentation for John on Monday. The team left for the day and I took the thick binder of test reports that Bill had left on the conference room table back to my desk. I mindlessly flipped through the pages of test reports that Bill and the other technicians had written. Each of the tests had at least five pages of written analysis. The techs were always complaining about all the writing that they had to do for each test request the engineers submitted because it always seemed to take the greatest amount of time. Bill would say, "If it wasn't for all those damn reports my team could get three or four times as much testing done! I wouldn't need half the staff! Every one of the guys hates it when John makes them come in on the weekends to clean up the backlog of test reports. We're test technicians, not authors!"

As I flipped through the pages of the binder, the chart that Bill had drawn on the conference room board came to mind. Every one of the tests that we had run had been above the 1000-joule target we had set for the program. Individually, every one of the tests had passed, until today. At this stage of the project, the team had done more testing with better results than on any other project to date. John had confided in me that this was the best project he had ever seen—until this disaster.

"Lenny must have screwed something up," he had told me. "I think I need to can the guy."

Bill had put two headings, "Test Number" and "Energy," on his chart in the conference room to highlight the disparity between the previous test results and the ones he had run that day. But as page after page of test report flipped past, I recognized the depth of information in every report. Engineers always got the full report back after a test, but the summary was generally all they ever looked at unless there was a problem. The cover sheet of the test report summarized the information in the test report. It identified who had run the test with some basic test conditions and the high-level results. Across the top in bold red letters they would be stamped "Passed" or "Failed." If the top of the summary sheet said "Passed," the report rarely got read. All the pages of analysis the technicians spent so much time typing scarcely got a glance.

I picked up the binder and went back to the conference room.

"There must be some variable that we are not accounting for," I thought to myself. As I flipped on the lights to the conference room, I realized that the variable that we had changed that day was the angle of the test fixture. The test report binder had the fixture angle recorded for every test, so I erased the number sign in the heading on the whiteboard and replaced it with "Angle," and then began leafing through the test report binder to document the new information. When I finished transcribing the information onto the board, it didn't look a whole lot better (see Figure 1–2). I'd had it for the day, and it was really getting late so I turned off the lights and went home.

The next morning when I rounded the corner of the hallway to the conference room, I saw that the lights to the room were already on and someone was in the room. As I opened the door and entered the room, Lenny turned and said, "I see you've been messing with Bill's numbers and going through his stuff. You know Bill gets upset when you touch his stuff." "Yes," I told Lenny, "but it was really bugging me last night. I really don't want to tell John that we have to pull our quote. John really wants us to win this one. I think he's already told the CEO that we have the business given how well the initial tests went. John told me the customer committed to give us the business if we passed their tests."

Figure 1.2

Test Angle (°)	Energy (joules)	Test Angle (°)	Energy (joules)	Test Angle (°)	Energy (joules)	Test Angle (°)	Energy (joules)
23	1235	15	1295	27	1126	15	1261
15	1220	23	1163	15	1286	20	1206
27	1208	25	1216	0	1353	20	1274
20	1251	0	1369	25	1229	20	1187
20	1261	27	1144	0	1367	0	1329
25	1145	0	1356	0	1308	25	1207
0	1288	23	1182	15	1310	0	1390
23	1248	27	1187	15	1240		
27	1195	23	1226	25	1164		

"Wow, I hadn't heard that yet", Lenny said, as a worried look came across his face. He walked over to the table and held up a piece of paper for me to see. "I couldn't sleep last night either, so I came in early this morning," he said. "When I saw all this stuff on the board I graphed the numbers. It's really interesting when you see all the information from the different test reports on one graph." I looked at the graph that Lenny was holding (Figure 1–3). On the horizontal axis Lenny had labeled "Test Angle," and on the vertical axis he had labeled the output in joules. He had plotted all the data from the board, and then had also put an X at the locations for the test Bill had conducted the day before.

"Look," he said tracing his finger across the points on the graph from left to right. "The test we ran yesterday should have been here," jabbing his finger at the paper at a point just above 1100 joules on the chart. "The results we got are down here. Obviously there is something going on with the internal energy absorber so it doesn't work at the

Figure 1.3

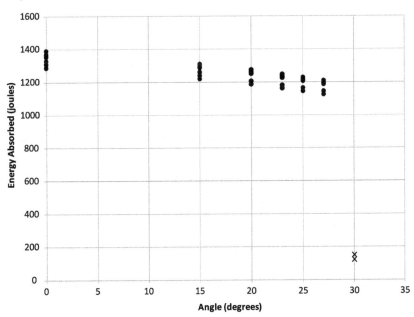

higher angles." Lenny was right—just beyond the range that had been tested, the product behaved drastically differently. This new design behaved different from everything else in production and in a way we neither understood nor expected.

Just then, the rest of the team came into the conference room and started picking through the remnants of day-old doughnuts on the table. When Bill saw that we had been working with his test report binder without him, he was upset, but once he realized how the connection between all the various individual test reports painted a picture of the issue he was eager to move on.

Lenny brought the team up to speed with the data by redrawing his graph on the board. There seemed to be a collective understanding that came over the team as they "saw" the problem we needed to address. Visually seeing the problem we needed to solve brought tremendous clarity and focus to the team. One of the engineers spoke for the group when he said, "Yesterday when we left here, I thought we would be working on a PowerPoint presentation for John Rock showing that the design doesn't work; now I think we can figure this out. I'd like to spend the day working on understanding *why* the design doesn't work."

I knew that not having a presentation for John on Monday morning was suicide, but then, telling John that we didn't have a solution and that we needed to pull our quote was even worse. "All right," I said, "John asked us to fix it. Let's find a solution."

This was something new. It seemed that our products were always developed based on rules of thumb or "black art." We developed products with a "make it and break it" mentality. I remembered more than once telling John that a part had failed a test and John slamming his fist on the desk and firing back at me, "Damn it, I know that part's good! Go test it again!" Now we were going to figure out why the design worked and didn't work.

"Well," Lenny began, "The plant has been giving us a hard time over the number of parts we keep making them build, stock, and use, so we decided to use an existing energy absorber in this design. We really didn't think we needed a unique one given how well all the feasibility testing had come out. We haven't explored any alternatives to this standard design at all. I think that if we changed the energy absorber we could influence the performance at higher angles."

In just an hour of brainstorming the team had identified about a dozen viable design alternatives. As was customary, particularly when there was a time constraint (and there was always a time constraint), the team picked the most likely solution out of the brainstormed list. Then we turned to Ray, the experimental build mechanic on the team, to see how quickly he could fabricate the new design. "Well," Ray stated, "if I work through lunch I can have a sample of that particular design built for you by one o'clock. I can probably have a couple more samples by the middle of the afternoon."

Ray worked quickly and had the first sample finished by 12:30. Bill had worked with Ray long enough to know he needed to be ready with his test fixture, so by the time the rest of the team was back from lunch at 1:00 to check on Ray's progress, Bill came bounding into the conference room with the first test results. Looking at the spring in Bill's step and the smile on his face, I knew he had good news. "OK, Bill," I said, "why don't you share with the rest of us what you are smiling about." Bill went up to Lenny's graph on the board and circled the location for the data from the latest test. A collective sigh went up from the group, and everyone seemed a bit more relaxed. "That's more like it," Lenny exclaimed. "That's what I expected; it looks like we're done."

Bill was the first one to speak up. "I don't think so," he said. "I've always looked at the tests you guys sent me as pass or fail. Looking at the data as a collective set, I think we should do more testing. You guys know I'm never one to look for more work and I can't even imagine what this test write-up is going to take to complete, but I think we need to find out how this modified design functions as the angle continues to change."

Lenny had already stood up and was busy packing up his things to go home and enjoy what was left of a sunny Sunday afternoon. He let out a groan and sat back down realizing that Bill was right. I turned to Ray and asked him how quickly he could get us some more samples. "Well," Ray remarked, "I did say I could get a couple of them done through the afternoon. I finished a second one while Bill was testing, and if you give me one of the test technicians I think I can keep up with Bill's testing." "OK," I said to the group, looking at the clock, "It looks like we can get about five more tests in this afternoon. Which angles should we test?" The team worked out a variety of angles as Ray took a test technician to go build more samples.

By 4:30, the team was exhausted, but we had five additional data points to work with. The graph on the conference room wall evolved as the day progressed, one data point at a time. When the sixth and final test of the day was completed, we had a very different picture than the one we had started with in the morning (see Figure 1–4). We had a new understanding of the problem we were trying to solve, and grasped it in a way that we had not imagined that morning.

Bill went to the board and added the final circle on the graph for the day completing the chart. "Well," I started, "Great work, you guys. How does everyone feel? Tired and ready to go home?"

Figure 1.4

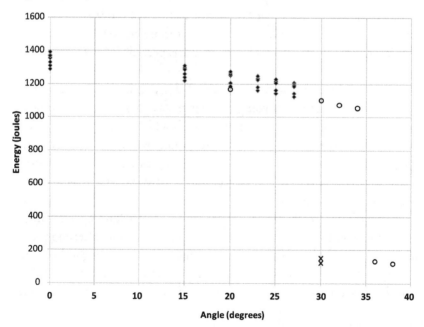

"Yeah, I'm out of here," Lenny said, picking up his briefcase as he bolted for the door. The rest of the crew followed Lenny out the door. Bill paused at the doorway and turned. "You're not going to make me have all these tests written up before your meeting with John in the morning, are you?" he asked, glaring at me. "No," I said, "Thanks for all your help. Don't worry about writing up a test report. I'll take the data from the board and put something together for John. Just put a report together to record the test conditions and attach the graph when you get a chance next week." Bill disappeared before I finished my sentence.

I was in no mood to prepare a fancy presentation for John that night. But I knew a presentation was the proper protocol. The simple graph had all the information necessary, and it would be so much simpler just to show John the graph, I thought to myself.

Monday morning I walked into John's office with the graph I had copied off the board the night before. "Well," John began, "Did you guys fix Lenny's screwup?" "I don't think it was really Lenny who caused the problem," I started. "I think the problem comes from the way we design our products," I said.

"What the hell do you mean!?" John fired back at me. John was clearly offended by my remark. John was the boss and any suggestion that there might be an issue with the process reflected poorly on him. John had been managing this department for years and he ruled with an iron fist.

I felt convinced that what we had learned over the weekend was important even though it was not the way that we normally did things. "Look," I said putting the graph on his desk so he could see. "By the end of Saturday we thought that we had an unworkable design. I planned to come in here today and tell you that we need to pull our quote." I could see John getting red in the face and I was clearly in a place I didn't want to be. "Like hell I'm going to pull our quote!" John blurted. "I've already committed this contract in our business projections. If you can't get this thing to work, then I'll find someone else who can!"

"Yes, I understand," I told John. "Fortunately, Lenny graphed the data in a way that we were able to see the problem rather than individual test results. Graphing the data led us to a solution that will work for us." "Great!" John said as a more normal color returned to his face, "What is it?" I pointed to the graph on his desk and said, "Look, the original design was trying to minimize the impact of part count in the plant. It used some fairly standard subcomponents and it worked well in all our testing, so we made a proposal based on that design. It turns out that the actual test conditions are different than what the customer specified. Our original design binds up right here." I pointed to the graph to indicate the angle where the original design failed. "Once we realized that," I went on, "the team modified the design so it would work. To make sure we understood it, we also decided to figure where the modified design works and doesn't work."

"Don't bother me with what doesn't work!" John interrupted. "How are you going to fix it?" I began to explain to John what the team had come up with for a solution, but could tell that John was really not interested in the details. John preferred PowerPoint slides with an overview of the solution, but I was excited about the work the team had done. More importantly, the customer's testing had uncovered issues with a simple variant of the proposal. I was concerned that as we got into more complex variants that we would run into even more severe issues. I wanted to convince John that we needed to investigate other attributes of the more complicated product variants with similar testing immediately.

John was quickly losing interest so I jumped to my proposal. "Look," I said to John, "This testing and the way the team worked to understand the design limits by graphing the information has made me realize that we may have additional issues with the more complex product offerings for the customer. I know that this is not my project and that you just asked me to help out, but I think we need to quickly get into additional testing of design variables on the other product variations in the quote." I could see the red coloring return to John's face. Clearly this was not the way things got done in John's department, and I was offending him by suggesting that we may need to do things differently. "Why the hell would I waste time testing things that I don't even know are a problem? This department has got enough problems to worry about. There is no way that I'm going to use any lab time working on some concern you think *might* be a problem. I've got enough fires to fight. The plants are crying about products that don't work and assembly concerns. Customers are constantly on my back with design modifications. No way am I going to divert any test resources from a department that is already stretched to chase something that might be a problem. We have a system that works around here, and that's the way it is!"

I got up to leave knowing it was best to get out of John's office as fast as I could. This meeting was not going as I had intended. "By the way," John added as I headed for the door with my graph, "You should have stopped after the first test yesterday when you had the problem fixed. I'm already over budget in the test department and you just added to it! You've got a lot to learn about how things get done around here."

For the first time I was on a project where we understood the design issue, how to fix it, and what the design limitations were. John had looked at the graph and chastised me for wasting test resources. John felt that once the team had solved the issue of the angle, we should have stopped and spent the time building samples for the customer rather than exploring the limits of the design.

The next week, the technicians built the samples based on the design modification that the team had come up with over the weekend. The samples performed well and passed the customer's tests. They performed just like the graph predicted, and the team won the business. Now a few years into the development program, I was in a new role. I was in Paris and inherited responsibility for the project, which was now late in the development program. As the team got into the more complex variants of the product, we once again faced design problems. The problems we uncovered with the more complex variants were much more difficult to resolve than the initial performance issues. We had the contract, but the design problems kept coming as the design team cycled through redesign loops to fix them. We were consistently on the customer's top ten issues list for delaying the new vehicle's launch. We were in no better shape than Fulle.

My office phone rang. It was Stephan from the German sales office. "Well," he asked, "are we going to take on the German job or not? I need to give them an answer today."

My assistant, Steffanie, who actually ran the place, came into my office and interrupted me before I had a chance to respond. "They're waiting for you in the conference room for the phase exit review. You better hurry before they decide you're not coming and they all leave. If they do that, you know you'll never get them back together for another phase exit review any time soon."

I told Stephan that I'd have to call him back after the phase exit review and I hung up the phone. At that moment I resolved to myself that I would figure out how to work smarter rather than harder. Deep down, I knew it must be possible to get more done with less effort if I could only figure out how. But at that specific moment, Steffanie was glaring at me in a "hurry up" sort of way, as she tapped her foot on the floor impatiently. I quickly grabbed the papers spread across my desk and stuffed them under my arm, following Steffanie's quick and deliberate march down the hall.

CHAPTER 2

The Harley-Davidson Environment

You are a product of your environment. So choose the environment that will best develop you toward your objective. Analyze your life in terms of its environment. Are the things around you helping you toward success—or are they holding you back?

Clement Stone

L oyalty and dedicated service were ingrained in me from an early age. "Study hard so you can get a good job, so a good company will hire you," I was taught. I did just that. I studied hard and got a good job with a great company. I had dreamed of working for Roaring Motors for as long as I could remember. I just assumed I would retire from Roaring Motors. I was brought up to believe that's what people do. You find a good company, commit yourself to the company, and work hard. If you are smart and work hard enough, you get rewarded by getting promoted. After a number of years of faithful service, you get rewarded with a pension. The new blood in the company takes over and the company takes care of you.

But people and companies have a way of changing over time. The need to learn, grow, and evolve is a fundamental human trait and is vital for the survival of both people and organizations. Yet in spite of its employees working harder, Roaring Motors struggled. The employees were committed, loyal, and dedicated to the company. They worked harder and harder to make the company successful. But regardless of how hard the employees worked, the products they produced seemed to be less and less desirable. Other companies began to offer more desirable products at lower prices and Roaring Motors suffered.

Roaring Motors had been born in the industrial age. It grew to prominence based on industrial-era thinking, and it prospered based on the attitudes, values, and business principles that were ushered in as the industrial revolution changed how people worked and how business was managed. Although Roaring Motors had pioneered many of the industrial-era business practices, the work environment had changed— but the company had not. It held tight to the core beliefs that had made the company great. Understanding and adapting to the changed environment could only come through a struggle of thought and a challenge to the ideals, core beliefs, and philosophical values upon which the company was based. Roaring Motors was ill-prepared and slow to adapt to the new demands brought on by socioeconomic change. The changes required for survival were counterintuitive to the traditional point of view and the leadership was blind to them. The changes Roaring Motors faced were impossible to conceptualize with an industrial-era mindset. Leadership clung to the beliefs that had served the company so well for so many years as the workers worked ever harder, despite an environment that had changed around them.

The business leaders at Roaring Motors had been brought up and schooled in industrial-era thinking. They had built their careers on traditional industrial principles. But the changes that were necessary required that these principles be challenged, unlearned, and replaced with fundamental new ways of thinking. Creating these new frameworks for the evolving world required challenging the underlying assumptions that supported their traditional intellectual constructs. But changed and replaced with what? This was a question they did not want to ask or know how to ask.

The changes necessary required a dispersion of power; that is, managers who lead by empowering knowledgeable workers to contribute through shared decision making. It required a leadership characterized by the notion of leaders as teachers, a willingness of leaders to say "I don't know," and a desire to create an environment of learning and discovery. The necessary changes challenged the very essence of stability that the traditional managers at Roaring Motors relied upon and took comfort in.

It was once unthinkable that Roaring Motors could someday not exist, but this was becoming a reality. The environment had changed and the very survival of Roaring Motors was at stake. Based on the industrial-era belief system, survival of Roaring Motors required shedding many of the parts of the company that had once enabled its rise in prosperity. Divisions that were once thought of as assets to success had become a burden and were dragging the company down. Employees who had worked enough years and were able to collect their pensions under Roaring Motors policy did so. Some employees stayed because they had no place to go, and others clung to their ingrained beliefs, unable to accept the changes happening around them.

The changes to Roaring Motors forced me to change my way of thinking. The company had been very good to me and had rewarded me very well. I was a lone individual caught in a sea swell of change. I struggled to let go of my core belief that commitment to a company and working hard resulted in mutually beneficial prosperity. The business environment had changed and my environment had changed and I began to see that my division would soon be spun off to better enable survival of the company. It was time to go.

Harley–Davidson Was Different

The environment is a very critical factor which determines how you think, the decisions you make and the roads your journey takes. Sometimes the environment occurs by happenstance and sometimes by design. I did not recognize how much my environment had shaped my perceptions of the world around me, how it had influenced my development and my behavior—until it drastically changed. From a cursory view, Harley-Davidson seemed similar to Roaring Motors. They both produced mechanical devices that provide transportation: rubber-tired vehicles that burned gas and oil. Yet Harley-Davidson was vastly different from Roaring Motors. Initially, I imagined a company made up of the stereotypical hardcore biker—bearded, heavily tattooed, beer-bellied men with long hair and black leather jackets. Rugged individualists and rebels living their lives their own way, by their own rules, not following the crowd, offering only disdain for the rest of world. Yet Harley-Davidson's business performance eschewed this image of lawlessness.

When it was time to leave Roaring Motors, I called my friend Earl. We had worked together at Roaring Motors. Earl left a few years earlier to become the vice president of engineering at Harley-Davidson. "Sure!" Earl had said to me when I finally got through to him on the phone. "We're hiring and we've got a place for you."

The contrast between Harley-Davidson and Roaring Motors was stark. My first visit laid to rest the notion of outlaw bikers meddling in business as I recognized that a bar and shield tattoo was not a requisite for employment. In contrast to Roaring Motors, Harley-Davidson was vibrant and alive with enthusiasm. I sensed a passion for the products, a commitment to clearly stated corporate beliefs and values, an energy and zeal for the company that had long ago fled Roaring Motors. I realized the leadership behaved differently than what I had grown accustomed to at Roaring Motors. The leadership was engaged and involved with both the products and the customers.

Harley-Davidson executives proclaim with pride, "We ride with you!" And they do. At Roaring Motors a gas truck would go through the parking lot twice a week to put gas in executive's cars so the executives wouldn't get gasoline on their suits. At Harley-Davidson the executives wore jeans and boots stained with bugs from their ride to work. Harley-Davidson executives are close to the customers as they actively attend motorcycle rallies, Harley Owner Group (HOG) events, and cross-country rides.

At Roaring Motors we built beautiful offices first and then filled them with people. My first visit to Harley-Davidson's headquarters in Milwaukee, Wisconsin, was a shock. The corporate headquarters of this great company was a simple industrial-era red brick former factory. Just a few years earlier, fenders and engine parts were still produced on some of the floors. The building was bursting at the seams with people and parts. Photos of motorcycles and of people on motorcycles covered the walls. The parking lot was an obstacle course with chunks of asphalt and concrete littering the premises; signs, orange traffic cones, and potholes made it difficult to navigate by car.

When I checked in at the main reception, I was personally escorted to Earl's office, not for security reasons but because there was no way for the receptionist to describe how to reach it. It was shoehorned into a corner of the building with some partitions and old file cabinets arranged to obstruct the view and muffle the noise from other conversations. His chair and the guest chairs by his desk were clearly from two different and long-gone eras.

In contrast, Roaring Motors' very specific guidelines for offices were an intricate part of the reward and hierarchy system of the company. Office size was clearly specified in corporate policy and reflected stature in the organization. Enclosed walls and a working door had replaced cubicle partitions many years ago for Earl at Roaring Motors. Even the office furniture at Roaring Motors proclaimed stature. Depending on one's level, office furniture was made from metal, oak, or cherry. Even cloth or leather covering on the chairs publicly proclaimed pay grade and stature. Earl's arrangement would be unthinkable at Roaring Motors. Harley-Davidson's headquarters at 3700 Juneau Avenue in Milwaukee certainly did not fit the picture I had for the headquarters of a profitable company.

At Harley-Davidson, people wore jeans and T-shirts to work, or anything else they felt comfortable working in, but at Roaring Motors, a suit and tie was always expected. Not long ago auto engineers only wore white shirts, and never another color that might make them stand out from the crowd. To my untrained eye I had no way of knowing someone's stature in the organization when I met them at Juneau Avenue. I found it confusing. At Roaring Motors manual laborers wore jeans, while everyone else wore a tie. Attire and office décor reinforced organizational hierarchy.

Harley-Davidson people talked about company values reflected on plaques mounted on the conference room walls. But the company values transcended the plaques, because people talked about them openly and could identify what the values meant personally to them. There were five company values:

- Tell the truth.
- Be fair.
- Keep your promises.
- Respect the individual.
- Encourage intellectual curiosity.

Consensus Decision Making

Over a year passed from the time I first talked to Earl on the phone to when I actually joined Harley-Davidson. It wasn't until I worked there that I learned why. Harley's hiring process was my first exposure to "consensus decision making." Consensus decision making is a process in which everyone has a say in the outcome of a decision before it is made, a process I became all too familiar with and dreaded for being agonizingly slow and cumbersome. But this process also results in remarkably quick adoption and unparallel support and commitment for a decision. Harley-Davidson was slightly older than Roaring Motors and it had already stared down the precipice of extinction. Harley had faced the abyss and survived. The courage and leadership that turned the company around established a rich and fertile environment for learning, growth, and development—an environment different from any I had experienced before. It was an environment foreign to my industrial way of thinking, and it was this environment that enabled the learning, development, and implementation of lean principles to product development, resulting in Knowledge-Based Product Development.

We Fulfill Dreams

It was 1903 when three brothers and a friend built their first motorcycle in an old shed behind their house with the words "Harley-Davidson Motor Company" scrawled across the door. Now over 100 years old, steeped in tradition and mystique, Harley-Davidson has become one of the most recognized brands in the world. The name Harley-Davidson has become synonymous with freedom and the open road; it evokes passion and emotion.

In many ways Harley-Davidson is a dichotomy. While customers, including an ever increasing number of women and new riders yearn for the products, communities are enacting stricter laws and restrictions regulating motorcycles in their neighborhoods. Society seems to have a love-hate relationship with motorcycles and Harley-Davidson, as the brand which embodies the rough-and-tumble biker image, traditionally bears the brunt. And yet, Harley-Davidson is greatly admired professionally, although society does not always appreciate the products in their community.

Harley-Davidson's mission statement begins, "We fulfill dreams through the experiences of motorcycling . . . ," which reflects the business model that drives the company. In this context there are two elements for business success: manufacturing customers, and manufacturing products to sell to customers. Harley-Davidson customers are manufactured through creating dreams. Dreams and the irrational yearning to own the beautiful works of art expressed through rolling curvaceous metal sculptures; the feel of leather and steel, the sweet melodic rhythm and vibration from the V-twin engine. The Harley-Davidson product line encompasses an ever expanding line of motorcycles, branded apparel, motorcycle-related services and a whole host of licensed apparel. The strength of the brand has spawned a myriad of products that sport the Harley-Davidson logo, ranging from pool tables, beer, and pick-up trucks to T-shirts and lingerie so people can dream and show their colors even when they are not riding.

Business success under this model is built through a self-perpetuating cycle of dreams and new products. Dreams are created by new products that stimulate the imagination and drive a yearning. New products may reach back into the long lineage of motorcycles drawing on heritage for inspiration or they may reach forward to test the limits of the brand. All new products invariably link to the rich legacy of the company and are different enough to create the desire to trade up or

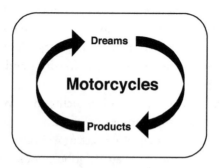

expand the collection of Harley-Davidson products. The flow of new products drives the cycle of dreams and products. It is this cycle of a reinforcing loop that powers the growth and success of the company. The flow of new products is the lifeblood of Harley-Davidson, just as with any other successful company. For Harley-Davidson, at the heart of this cycle is the motorcycle.

The real Harley-Davidson, beyond the public's purview ("The Motor Company," as it is affectionately called internally), is in fact a dichotomy in many ways. Behind the tough macho facade of The Motor Company that consistently delivered accelerated revenue growth since going public in 1985 and maintained double digit earnings for over twenty years, is a professional, well-managed, paranoid company competing with passion, heart, and soul in an extremely competitive international motorcycle market. Harley-Davidson learned the lesson of complacency in the 1970s and 1980s. The experience left a sense of paranoia and paranoia is a terrific antidote to complacency.

To understand Harley-Davidson's success is to first recognize that lawless beer-bellied, blacksmiths do not wield hammers and torches to beat iron into submission and shape steel into art one motorcycle at a time, as the chopper shows on TV would have us believe. Harley-Davidson's success is the result of a seasoned management team deeply committed to and in tune with their customers' dreams, leading a very passionate, progressive organization based on a solid system of core beliefs and values. It is this environment that instills success.

Lessons from the Dark Days

By the time I joined The Motor Company, the dark days of Harley-Davidson's history, when thirteen executives bought back the company from AMF, were already behind them. Those years may have been in the distant past for many, but the scars brought on by the events were still clearly visible if you looked. There were two groups within The Motor Company—those who were there and endured, and those who came after.

In the 1980s Harley-Davidson needed tariff protection and successfully petitioned the U.S. government to restrict foreign (Japanese) manufacturers from dumping unsold motorcycles onto the U.S. market. It was a very difficult experience for Harley-Davidson and an experience that Roaring Motors would perhaps still need to experience. The lessons learned in the tough times are clearly etched in the foundation and forged in the framework that supports The Motor Company. The turnaround years may be what Harley-Davidson is best known for in business circles, but it is the management principles that the leadership dared to instill during the turnaround years that have continued to power success of The Motor Company. They were daring and bold changes to a deeply entrenched way of management that Roaring Motors could not and would not entertain.

The Harley-Davidson Motor Company began when three brothers and a friend attached a small motor with a soup can for a carburetor to a bicycle to create their first motorcycle. They sold three motorcycles the first year. As the company grew, the founders quickly recognized the importance of quality and prided themselves in the reliability of their machines. They proved their worth by winning endurance races and the company grew in spite of two world wars and a depression that eliminated all but two American motorcycle manufacturers—Harley-Davidson and Indian. Then the Indian Motorcycle Company gambled and lost their company over a strategic product development decision to introduce in-line four-cylinder motors in place of V-twin motors across their entire product line at once. When the Indian Motorcycle Company met its demise in 1953, Harley-Davidson remained the sole American heavyweight motorcycle manufacturer. AMF bought Harley-Davidson in 1969 to bolster their portfolio of leisure and recreational products companies. However, a remote management team out of touch with the needs of the business and the dreams of their customers was lured by easy money into increasing production volumes. Increased production volumes with neither appropriate quality controls in place nor a stream of new products to drive demand resulted in a glut of undesirable, poor-quality products that no one wanted.

By the late 1970s Harley-Davidson's short-term profit potential had been exploited and the company was back on the block. The need to sell was a direct result of a sharp reduction in sales due to poor-quality, ill-conceived products. With no one interested in the depleted hulk of a company, thirteen Harley-Davidson executives who believed in The Motor Company leveraged their personal assets and purchased the company back from AMF in 1981. The road to recovery was more tumultuous than anyone anticipated and shortly after the purchase an overall slump in the motorcycle market drove additional production cuts, resulting in 40 percent of the work force being eliminated. By 1985 Harley-Davidson was nearly bankrupt. CEO Vaughn Beals convinced the banks to accept a restructuring plan that included the application of "Japanese management principles." These practices, such as Just-In-Time (JIT) manufacturing and quality circles, have evolved into what is now "lean manufacturing." The principles had been pioneered by Henry Ford and Taiichi Ohno, promoted by W. Edwards Deming and Phil Crosby, and adopted by Toyota even while they were rejected in America. The application of lean manufacturing principles coupled with the adoption of new management theories and a temporary tariff on large imported motorcycles created a brief window of opportunity for a turnaround—and the rebirth of Harley-Davidson.

The team of Vaughn Beals, Rich Teerlink, Tom Gelb, and Ron Hutchinson provided just the visionary leadership the company needed. The changes he instituted were bold and magnanimous beyond the normal confines of an existing business structure. The daring plan worked and in 1987, one year before the five-year temporary import tariff was scheduled to expire, Harley-Davidson announced that they no longer needed tariff protection to compete. They petitioned the International Trade Commission for early termination of its tariff deal. Between 1985 and 1987 the company had increased inventory turns from five to twenty, reduced inventory by 75 percent, reduced scrap by 68 percent, increased productivity by 50 percent, and reduced manufacturing space requirements by 25 percent.[1]

Although the tariffs helped Harley-Davidson, they did not save Harley-Davidson. Harley-Davidson saved itself when it addressed its manufacturing woes, created cool, exciting products that addressed the quality issues, leveraged the power of the Harley-Davidson brand, and revamped its management approach. Harley-Davidson may have initially conquered its toughest business challenge with a hierarchical leadership, but based on the leadership's belief in the power of people it moved to establish an empowered workforce with decentralization of decision making. In 1993, under the leadership of Rich Teerlink and guidance from Lee Ozley, a new and unique Circle Organization structure of management was created. This unique leadership structure was derived from the principles of self-directed work teams in the factories.

Harley-Davidson's fabled turnaround led to an open, participative culture of trust where passionate people give their best. Rich Teerlink believed in people and believed that people should feel passionate about coming to work. He believed that people should work at Harley-Davidson because they want to. He also believed in empowering employees by making people feel they have the freedom to do what they think is right within the company's value system. Rich committed himself to lead Harley's difficult journey from a traditional "command-and-control" culture to an open, participative organization, where employees had new levels of responsibility for charting their course and developing a culture built on trust. To enable this philosophy, it was critical that the organization's strategy and values were shared by people at every level. So to supplement the Circle Organization structure, Rich instituted a structured, formal business process further supporting his belief that corporate culture begins with employee engagement in and their understanding of company values, organizational direction, and purpose.

The Circle Organization

The circle organization that Rich Teerlink championed reflected his belief in people and the notion that business has two primary functions: to manufacture customers and to manufacture products. In order to focus on these key aspects for the business, Harley-Davidson was divided into three broad business areas called "circles." Similar to self-directed work teams, these leadership circles focused on manufacturing customers, manufacturing products, or providing the support these two areas required. These circles were called the Create Demand Circle (CDC), the Produce Products Group (PPG—the PPC acronym was already used for the Product Planning Committee), and the Provide Support Circle (PSC).

Each circle was comprised of the leaders representing the specific functions within the business objective of the circle. Collectively, each circle had functional responsibility for the area the circle title indicated. The CDC had responsibility for the rate at which customers were manufactured. The PPG had responsibility to design, develop, and manufacture products. The PSC had the responsibility of supporting the CDC's and PPG's ability to focus on manufacturing, customers

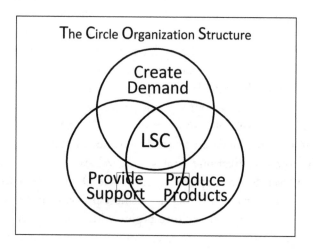

The Circle Organization Structure

and products through addressing human resources, legal, finance, information systems, etc. for the company. The leadership represented by these three circles was referred to as the Functional Leadership Group (FLG).

At the intersection of the three circles was the Leadership and Strategy Council (LSC). The LSC functioned as the body to set policy and strategic direction for the company. The LSC was made up of the CEO, the President and COO, the General Council, the Chief Financial Officer, the vice president of strategic planning, the vice president of Human Resources and two representatives from each of the three circles. The Circle representatives were elected by the circle members and served on the LSC to represent their particular circle for two years. There was no formal stature or status change as a result of being elected to serve on the LSC. Additionally, the CEO had the authority to appoint other FLG members to the LSC to assure appropriate cross-functional representation as situations dictated.

The circle organization came about because Rich believed that if manufacturing personnel could operate as self-directed work teams, senior executives could also. This revolutionary leadership structure was intended to better support individual growth and to develop interdependence and cross-functional collaboration as a norm. The changes imposed by the circle structure resulted in a flatter organization in which functional leaders were forced to collaborate to provide leadership and direction. The structure proved invaluable in developing leaders and in improving shared decision making. It positioned the company to continue meeting business challenges and focus on the two most pressing issues at the time—improving quality and increasing motorcycle production capability.

The creation of the circle organization structure did not come without significant pain and agony. Building and operating in the circle structure environment required trust and unprecedented levels of collaboration. Extensive coaching and development was invested on the FLG personnel. Decisions did not necessarily happen quickly. Operating the company through the circle structure also required exceptional skill and a unique leadership style.

Consensus–Driven Organization

As Rich established employee empowerment and people were given the freedom to do what they thought was right within the company's value system, the traditional command-and-control culture was transformed into a participative organization. A participative organization is highly dependent on consensus-driven decision making and "clear fences" of individual authority. Initially, consensus-driven decision making appears slow and cumbersome. Every employee involved in a decision feels the need to be part of the discussion and provide input on the decision before it is made, vastly protracting the decision process. But although the initial decision-making process is painstakingly time-consuming and arduous, the payoff comes in the implementation of decisions. The consensus-building process creates buy-in and commitment as it vets the alternatives and the constituents become personally committed to success. As employees work in a consensus decision-making environment they build ownership and commitment for change because they have been an integral part of the decision.

With the new level of freedom and empowerment of consensus decision making came the responsibility to clarify how to make decisions. It was important to clarify who was involved and who was not involved in decisions. In order to develop the culture of trust, the organization educated employees on what consensus decision making meant. The organization identified three types of decisions: type 1 (individual), type 2 (shared), and type 3 (group).

In type 1 (individual) decisions, one individual makes the decision alone using available information in isolation. They may request input from others, but the decision is solely the responsibility of one person. In type 2 (shared) decisions an individual shares the problem, questions, and situation with others. These may be subordinates and/or peers that are gathered together for their suggestions and input. The individual then makes the decision that may or may not coincide with the group's input, suggestions, or feelings. In type 3 (group) decisions, an individual shares the decision situation with others and they assist in generating and evaluating alternatives. In a type 3 decision the individual tries not to influence the group through use of authority and must be willing to accept and implement any solution on which the group reaches consensus.

Managing Conflict

The unique nature of the circle management structure required a mechanism for managing conflict. When individuals within a circle could not resolve an issue, the expected process was to assemble the circle and work toward a consensus of the group and bring in resources as required in an effort to achieve consensus. Constructive conflict was an intended positive force that was encouraged and expected among circle members. Constructive disagreement was encouraged over universal "group thinking." If a circle was not able to reach consensus, the president or the CEO was brought into the process. As an alternative, a circle could use the LSC to work toward consensus.

The Harley-Davidson Business Process

The circle organization established an unprecedented level of empowerment and harnessed the collective intelligence of the senior leadership to the extent it had never been done before. To empower the entire organization and fully harness the energy of the workforce, Rich established a structured, formal business process to further support the belief that corporate culture is founded on employee engagement. To engage the entire organization, they needed to believe in, understand, and commit to the company values, organizational direction, and purpose.

The Harley-Davidson business process was initiated to compliment the circle organization structure in 1993 and became the backbone of Harley-Davidson's management system. The business process is anchored with three overarching "umbrella" constants: values, issues, and stakeholders. These constants establish the foundation for expected behavior and serve to guide the decision process. These three constants are ever present as a constitution to the company. They define why the company exists, priorities, and the decision protocol. These constants do not change over time and are ingrained in every employee.

The Harley-Davidson values are the credo by which the company—as a corporate entity and as individuals who work there—lives and operates. These core values are: tell the truth; be fair; keep your promises; respect the individual; and encourage intellectual curiosity.

Harley-Davidson Business Process

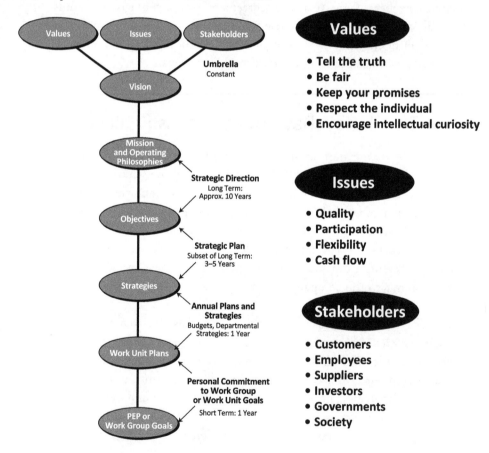

Values

- Tell the truth
- Be fair
- Keep your promises
- Respect the individual
- Encourage intellectual curiosity

Issues

- Quality
- Participation
- Flexibility
- Cash flow

Stakeholders

- Customers
- Employees
- Suppliers
- Investors
- Governments
- Society

The issues are those aspects of business that are paramount for company viability. They provide a focus for what is important in driving business success. The Harley-Davidson issues are quality, participation, productivity, flexibility, and cash flow.

Stakeholders are the people for whom the business exists. Harley-Davidson makes it clear that stockholders are not the sole beneficiaries of the company's existence and that long-term success is achieved through balancing the needs of all stakeholders—customers, employees, suppliers, investors, governments, and society.

Every conference room at Harley-Davidson has three plaques representing the values, issues, and stakeholders. When I first joined Harley-Davidson, I was not surprised to see the plaques on the walls. Many companies have company statements or slogans posted. I was, however, amazed the first time a meeting was interrupted and the attention of the meeting was redirected to one of the plaques and the meeting focus shifted to how the potential solutions being debated fit in the context of the company values. Meetings were frequently stopped by someone pointing to the stakeholders on the wall, and asking if we were properly taking into account *all* the stakeholders and whether we had struck the proper balance. Harley-Davidson is a company built on heritage, driven by strong values, principles, and camaraderie. Perhaps these are principles borrowed from the credo of the open road. Coming from Roaring Motors, I found them refreshing. I even found myself often referring to the company values, issues, and stakeholders in making decisions.

Organizational Learning

The Harley-Davidson environment is an essential aspect of the company's success. The environment is an outgrowth of the turnaround experience that resulted in the circle organization, the business process, adoption of corporate values, and a corporate belief system. This environment established fertile conditions for collaboration and dialogue. As a whole this environment produced the opportunity for unique introspection of how product development functions and an opportunity to explore how to improve it. New product development is a crucial business process. New product development was important to Harley-Davidson's resurgence and remains the fuel that powers revenue growth. New, exciting products attract new customers to the Harley-Davidson brand and are the reason customers come back to trade in and trade up, or add to their collection.

The ability to innovate and the tone of product development are largely set by the environment in which product development operates. The social, physical, and political environments establish the norms of behavior and the protocol in which work is accomplished. Harley-Davidson became the successful company it is today in large measure because its leadership recognized and valued the importance of the environment. Within this unique environment, Peter Senge's work related to organizational learning greatly influenced progressive members of the FLG, resulting in the creation of various learning teams. The PPG sponsored the creation of a learning team to improve Harley-Davidson's product development process, called the Product Development Leadership Learning Team (PDL^{2}T). The PDL^{2}T became an important incubator for understanding and improving product development.

CHAPTER 3

Harley-Davidson's Product Development Leadership Learning Team

Now, it is not only necessary to do the right thing, but to do it in the right way and the only problem you have is what is the right thing to do and what is the right way to do it. That is the problem.

Dwight D. Eisenhower

John Shibley knocked on the doorsill of my office to get my attention as he walked through the open doorway. "Ready to go over the PDL²T agenda for tomorrow?" he asked while making himself comfortable in one of the chairs in my office. I had just started a new assignment. I had applied for a chief engineer position that had been posted but I didn't get it. Instead I got caught in the rotation of job changes resulting from backfilling vacancies.

In the shuffle of jobs, Earl offered me the opportunity to lead the

Product Development Office. I was thrilled to do it and I jumped at the chance. As a part of the new role I inherited leadership of the Product Development Leadership Learning Team (PDL²T). I had heard about the PDL²T but never experienced it before I took the job. Everyone involved with product development at Harley-Davidson had heard about the PDL²T but very few people really knew what it was. The team was modeled along the principles of the circle leadership structure of the company, so it included all the cross-functional leaders involved in product development. The storied group included about twenty people from the engineering, marketing, sales, service, finance, and manufacturing departments. Once a month all of the product development leadership met for a day to discuss product development.

With product development void of leadership one day per month and no information other than "I was at the PDL²T," stories emerged of a secret society. Rumors circulated of druids, special bonding rituals, and secret handshakes. It was even rumored that there was a special tattoo for members. The PDL²T was referred to reverently by people outside the meeting, because no one seemed to know exactly what it was, or what the group did, although everyone wanted to be a part of it. Rarely was anyone other than the leadership group invited to participate. If non-members were formally invited to the meeting, they came in for a very specific purpose and then left. They never attended the whole meeting. This added to the mystique and intrigue of the group.

PDL²T members didn't talk much about what went on in the meetings in public. No specifics were ever discussed. No reports came from the meetings. There were no minutes. There were "Reflective Notes" from the meetings kept online, but they required a password to access.

When I joined the group I was relieved to learn that there was no secret handshake and no special initiation ritual. I quickly learned to appreciate the power of the PDL²T as a learning forum. Based on the sponsorship of some progressive Produce Product Group leaders, the PDL²T was attempting to employ systems thinking and organizational learning principles to better understand how the product development system worked and how to improve it. The importance of secrecy became readily apparent at the first meeting. This small group had been given a unique safe haven to experiment with principles of organizational learning and systems dynamics. There was no manual or other organization to learn from. There wasn't another company to copy or ask how it should be done. This group was unique and the antics they used were in many ways unorthodox and curious to anyone who did not understand or appreciate what was being attempted, so it wasn't publicized outside the PDL²T.

My first exposure to the field of system dynamics and systems thinking had come as a graduate student at the Massachusetts Institute of Technology (MIT) a number of years earlier. System dynamics had been one of my favorite classes because it brought the interdependencies of complex business systems together in an understandable and compelling manner. Systems thinking seeks to explore complex problems by understanding the dynamic interdependencies and causal relationships associated with systems issues. When I had originally called Earl from Paris, he had told me how the Harley-Davidson leadership had been exposed to Peter Senge, John Sterman, and the System Dynamics department at MIT. Earl had told me how the principles in the book, *The Fifth Discipline*,[1] and Senge's organization, Society for Organizational Learning (SoL), had greatly influenced leadership thinking and had explained that the leadership at Harley-Davidson was experimenting with causal loops and systems thinking to better understand the complex systemic implications of decisions. The progressive thinking really intrigued me although it conflicted with the biker image I had conjured up in my mind.

John Shibley was an external consultant who helped to facilitate the PDL²T. He described the team as a group of people whose mission was to collaborate in learning "to expand the innovative capacity of the organization." All people have the capacity to learn, but the environment in which they function is often not conducive to reflection and the engaged learning necessary for systems learning. John had been facilitating the group for years and it was his role to teach systems thinking principles and help the team apply organizational learning principles to the product development process. In most organizations people lack the tools and guiding ideas to make sense of the situations they face and to learn from them. John was there to make sure the team had the tools and guidance to learn. Any organization that wants to control its own destiny in a changing environment needs to continually improve its capacity to create and innovate. This often requires a fundamental shift of mindset across the organization. It was John's role to provoke this mindset shift.

The team needed a protected environment sheltered by senior leadership that encouraged intellectual curiosity, an environment that would allow the team to make sense of the ideas and situations they faced. This experiment could not be conducted in a fishbowl with the organization looking on. The forum also required an impartial facilitator versed, committed, and passionate about systems thinking and organizational learning with the ability to provide the insight and tools necessary for reflective learning. John was that impartial facilitator, there to teach the tools and help the team wrestle through difficult and often confrontational issues. The goal was to help the team explore and develop new mental constructs through systems thinking.

The PDL²T Journey

Harley-Davidson's initial involvement with organizational learning had been through senior leadership. Peter Senge and some other people from MIT originally worked directly with the senior leadership. After about a year, the senior leadership spawned a number of learning teams focused on a variety of crucial aspects of the business. John Shibley became connected with the Product Development Leadership Learning Team to improve the product development process. Many of the other learning teams disbanded or abandoned the systems thinking approach due to the difficulty and because it was so foreign to their way of doing business. Organizational learning requires trust and willingness for deep personal exposure.

Applying systems thinking as a cornerstone of organizational learning is difficult, and the initial years of the PDL²T were tumultuous. Over the years, a chasm had evolved between engineering and manufacturing that needed healing. Cross-functional product development could not happen without first addressing these old rifts. But the rift between engineering and manufacturing was not the only problem. Adversarial relationships had developed between many of the functional areas involved in product development. Harley-Davidson is an emotional company—perhaps the emotion and the passion for the product elicits it. There were times in the initial years of the PDL^{2}T when it was necessary to call a "timeout" in order to let people cool down and regain their composure. It never came down to fists flying, but there were times it came close. Sometimes, individuals had to take their conversation out into the hall to work things out before the group as a whole could move on.

By the time I joined the PDL^{2}T, it was a tight-knit group that had been in existence for several years. The team had evolved during that time. People matured and developed trust, and organizational changes brought about changes in the makeup of the group. When I asked people what it was like to be a part of the team's evolution, they would always bring up the "deep meaningfulness" of the experience. They talked about being part of something larger than themselves, of being connected, of being generative. They talked about a journey of inquiry and discovery, and how at times they would just be captivated by the learning experience. When I spoke to people who had rotated off the PDL^{2}T due to job changes, they all described the experience as a singular period of their professional lives lived to the fullest, a spirit that they would perhaps spend the rest of their life trying to recapture. I realized just how fortunate I was.

Learning Organizations

Real learning gets to the heart of what it is to be human. This applies in the context of individuals and organizations alike. For learning organizations it is not enough to survive. *Adaptive* learning is important and necessary for survival but a learning organization strives to evolve beyond survival and beyond mere adaptive learning. Learning organizations supplant adaptive learning with *generative* learning, learning that enhances the ability to create. The mastery of five key disciplines distinguishes learning organizations from ordinary organizations.[2] The five disciplines of a learning organization are:

1. Systems thinking.
2. Personal mastery.
3. Mental models.
4. Building shared vision.
5. Collective team learning.

Through these five disciplines, people become aware that they are agents acting within an often unseen structure or system of which they are merely a part. Product development is one such system, which we work within but cannot see. Through mastery of these five disciplines the organization becomes concerned with a shift in mindset from seeing parts to seeing the whole. In turn, there is a shift from seeing people as helpless reactors of unseen forces to seeing people as active participants in shaping and controlling their own destiny. Rather than react to the present, learning organizations seek to create their future.

Systems Thinking

Systems thinking is the cornerstone for organizational learning and the discipline that integrates the other four. The basic tools of systems thinking are fairly elementary. Systems theory, however, can quickly develop into very sophisticated models. Much of what is done in the guise of management is done through the application of very simplistic frameworks to what are in reality complex systems. We tend to focus on the parts that are visible rather than seeing the whole, and in turn, we fail to see the organization as a dynamic organism. Systems thinking argues that a better appreciation of the system leads to more appropriate action.

The human brain is a very sophisticated computational device, yet humans are forced to simplify complex problems in order to comprehend them. Business executives deal with complex issues comprised of multiple variables changing simultaneously and independently on a daily basis. For complex problems, traditional decision making is akin to solving multi-order differential equations in your head, so we are forced to simplify issues to the minimum of elements we believe best represents the issue at hand. Classically, we look to actions that produce improvements over a relatively short time horizon. However, when considered from a systems perspective, short-term improvements often involve very significant long-term consequences. For example, reducing the research and development budget can bring immediate cost savings, but may significantly damage the long-term viability of the organization.

Humans learn best through experience, yet we rarely directly experience the consequences of our most significant organizational decisions due to the time delay in receiving feedback. For example, a policy change to shift development funds to advertising in reaction to sluggish sales usually results in increased sales in the short-term. It may also result in promotion of the executive who made the decision. Only much later, when there is a new person in charge, is it discovered that the increased advertising has indeed brought sales forward, but there are no new products available in the development pipeline to maintain the sales rate over the long term.

When we constrain complex issues to a minimal set of variables we also tend to link cause and effect relatively near each other. Thus, when faced with a problem, the solution set we tend to focus on is close by. However, the nature of systems feedback is that there may be unintended consequences to an action resulting in highly undesirable consequences at a much later time. Over time, small changes can amplify as they build upon themselves. A seemingly minor action can snowball over time and result in an entirely different outcome than initially intended.

The systems thinking perspective is generally orientated toward the long-term or holistic perspective, making the understanding of delays and feedback crucial. Short-term feedback loops have little delay between cause and effect, thus feedback delays are inconsequential and they can often be ignored. It is the *long* feedback loop that presents the problem, due to the significant time lag between the action and its consequences. Long feedback loops result in the true impact only being recognized months or years later. Therefore, systems maps, models, and diagrams are commonly used as mediums to exchange ideas and to invite input for collective thinking and group analysis, to explore and show key interdependencies, and to provide a mechanism to record ideas.

Understanding the effect of delays and interdependencies is a key aspect to systems thinking. Interruptions to flow that influence the consequence of an action to occur gradually, delay an outcome, or veil feedback are very important. Due to our traditional methods of problem solving, people are not trained to see systems and often have difficulty seeing consequences to their actions. We tend to think linearly with simplified cause and effect relationships. It takes work to acquire the basic building blocks of systems theory, and learn to apply them. However, failure to understand system dynamics can lead to cycles of blame and self-defense. When this occurs the enemy is always out there, and the problems are always caused by someone else. Someone else is always to blame because we do not see how we influence the outcome.

System maps are used to describe the interactions present in the system. These maps are diagrams that show the key elements of systems and how they connect. They attempt to make the unseen interdependencies visible.

In *The Fifth Discipline*, Peter Senge analyzes the cold war arms race between the Soviet Union and the United States, providing a prime example of systems thinking.[3] In this example, Americans observed the proliferation of Soviet weapons through the veil of espionage, which obscured the true information and confounded the already complex dynamics of the situation. Americans perceived the Soviet weapons as a threat to America and in response Americans built their own weapons. This is very logical linear thinking, depicted as:

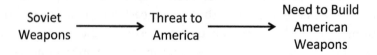

While the Americans saw the Soviets as a threat, the view from the Soviet leaders' perspective was very different. Similar linear thinking on the part of the Soviets can be depicted as:

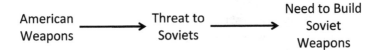

Both perspectives were correct. Both the American and Soviet leaderships could easily point to the other as the culprit of the arms race. However, a very simplified systems thinking perspective would identify that each nation directly impacted the outcome. The actions each nation took directly affected the problem they themselves faced. Depicted as a simple system dynamics model, the cold war arms race looks very different:

This is a vicious cycle in which a single action feeds on the previous action, reinforcing the effect as the series of actions build on each other, often causing them to spiral out of control. Whether it is nuclear arms proliferation or development problems at launch, there is a tendency to look outward and react to the problem from our unique vantage point. We become steadfast in our convictions and reinforce our position. We see our world through our own reality and filter out input that might contradict our resolute opinion; invariably we point to others as causing the problem.

For many companies, their product development organization has degraded into vicious cycles of blame and finger-pointing. In the early days of the PDL²T, finger-pointing caused by not seeing the larger system was very apparent. The "five whys" of problem solving had degraded to the "five whos" of blame. As the PDL²T learned to see the system in which they operated, they began to recognize their contribution to the system problem and began to realize that the issues they had blamed on others often originated from their own actions. Unraveling years of repeated cycles of blame is difficult and first requires building trust and respect—as well as opening up to those who had been accusatory. Rebuilding an organization is very difficult emotionally draining work.

Personal Mastery

Organizations are comprised of individuals. Organizations can only learn through individuals who learn, but individual learning does not ensure organizational learning. However, without individual learning, organizational learning cannot occur. Personal mastery is the discipline of continually clarifying and deepening our personal understanding of the world, exchanging openly our understanding of the unseen systems in which we operate through collaboration with others. Often the system appears different depending on the vantage point from which we observe it. Uncovering an unseen system is not unlike the fable of the blind men encountering an elephant for the first time. One man encounters the trunk, one the tusks, one the ears, one the legs, one the belly, and one the tail. Each man develops an opinion of the elephant based on what he observes. This observation becomes their reality. But it is not until all the blind men come together, relinquish their belief of reality and accept the perspective from each of the others that they can possibly comprehend the whole of the elephant.

Acquiring the discipline of personal mastery is difficult work, and learning to see true reality requires opening ourselves up to ridicule. Personal mastery necessitates opening our minds to learning, developing patience, and continuously striving to see reality objectively. It goes beyond competency and skill, although both are required. Personal mastery also goes beyond spiritual awakening, although it requires spiritual growth. Personal mastery is a special kind of proficiency and confidence in one's ability to the extent that one is able to question it openly and accept criticism from others. Personal mastery is not about dominance, but rather about balancing inquiry with advocacy, about acceptance of others' opinions even without fully understanding. It requires recognition that two divergent opinions can coexist and be correct—as it was for the blind men encountering an elephant.

Someone who achieves a high level of personal mastery lives in a continual learning mode with no end state. They never "arrive." Life becomes a journey of inquiry and intrigue. They are genuinely *interested* people. Personal mastery is not something to achieve, it is a process, and a lifelong discipline. People with a high level of personal mastery are acutely aware of their ignorance, their incompetence, and their growth areas, yet are fundamentally deeply self-confident.

Mental Models

Mental models are deeply ingrained beliefs we hold paramount. Mental models are assumptions, generalizations, or even pictures and images that influence how we understand the world around us. For example, mankind believed for thousands of years that the earth was the center of the universe. Their mental model was that the sun revolved around the earth. This mental model was created based on concrete events and patterns observed from earth's vantage point. Every morning the sun rose in the east and set in the west over an apparently immovable earth. When Galileo challenged the geocentric mental model suggesting that the earth revolved about the sun, he was ridiculed. The geocentric mental model was so ingrained that Galileo was prohibited from advocating his position by the Catholic Church. Galileo was eventually forced to recant his heliocentric ideas and spent the last years of his life under house arrest to protect the mental model of the people in power.

Mental models do not need to be so extreme as the example provided by Galileo. Mental models are simply deeply ingrained beliefs that control how we behave. They are the foundation of our belief system. We are generally unaware of the mental models we have constructed in our journey through life. We are often not cognizant of the way we have self-programmed our behaviors based on the mental models we build to simplify the complexities of our world.

Although we operate in a system that we are generally blind to, we experience events that occur as a result of the system. The events that occur as a result of the system are observable. Through astute observation, the patterns of events caused by the system can be recognized. However, the connection between specific events can be very difficult to observe. The underlying systemic structures that control the interdependencies of events and behaviors are unseen. The structures can not be directly observed, yet they exist and can be discussed, debated, and described in the context of systems maps. We unconsciously create our mental models of how the world around us works based on our observation of events, activities, and the various patterns that we surmise exist. Yet mental models are impossible to see.

A fundamental aspect of learning to understand involves developing the ability to reflect on the mental models that describe the essence of who we are; however, we hold these mental models veiled behind defensive layers. Organizational learning requires unveiling who we really are and lowering the protective barriers that hide our mental models so others can see how and why we think the way we do. Learning begins with reflection and it can only occur in moving between the domains of reflection and action. Learning to understand requires the discipline of uncovering the mental models we construct to describe the connection between cause and effect. Organizational learning starts by turning the mirror inward and learning to unearth our internal pictures of the world, to bring our mental images to the surface and expose them to scrutiny by others. Organizational learning requires the ability to carry on "learningful" conversations. These are conversations that balance inquiry and advocacy, where people expose their own thinking effectively and make that thinking open to the influence of others.

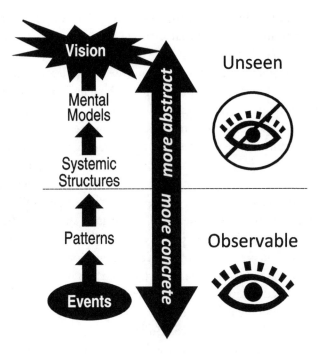

For any organization to develop the ability to work with mental models, people must first learn new skills and adopt an orientation of trust and openness to the thoughts and perspectives of other people. There must often be institutional change to foster and support the necessary evolution in personnel. Entrenched personal mental models protected behind invisible defensive layers thwart changes that could come from systems thinking. Moving an organization forward towards a learning organization requires transcending the internal politics and gamesmanship that dominate traditional organizations.

Building a Shared Vision

If there is any singular aspect of leadership that has inspired organizations throughout history, it has been the ability to establish a common picture of the future and a shared vision of what can be created collectively. Such a common vision has the power to inspire, to motivate, to encourage experimentation and innovation in achieving extraordinary results. Crucial for significant progress, a shared vision fosters a sense of the longer term, something that is fundamental to systems thinking. When a genuine shared vision (no to be confused with the all-to-familiar "vision statement") is built, people excel and learn, not because they are told to, but because they want to. A shared vision unifies the individual efforts across an organization toward achieving a common goal that all have become personally invested in creating.

Many potential leaders have grand personal visions that are never realized—because their personal vision isn't translated into a shared vision. They are unable to create a shared vision to galvanize and inspire an organization to action. The element that is generally missing is a discipline for translating personal vision into shared vision. They lack the principles and guiding practices that allow a group to build a shared vision. The art of building shared vision requires establishing a common perspective of the current situation, then involves the skill of unearthing shared "pictures of the future." Building shared vision requires constructing mental images that foster genuine commitment and devotion rather than compliance. Building a shared vision can take significant time and requires patience. However, in mastering the discipline of building shared vision, leaders recognize the counterproductiveness of trying to dictate a personal vision, no matter how heartfelt it may be. A good shared vision that the organization adopts as its own will take an organization much further than any personal vision dictated by a single leader—no matter how perfect the vision is.

A shared vision spreads through the organization due to the natural reinforcing process of human nature. Increased clarity, enthusiasm, and commitment rub off on others in the organization as people across the organization discuss the vision. Discussion of the vision forces people to learn more about the vision, allowing further refinement of the vision, and allowing the vision to grow even clearer. As the vision evolves and becomes more clear, enthusiasm for its benefits grow and coalition building ensues. There is a "zone of consideration" in adoption of the vision that emerges, which begins when the consequences of the vision become readily apparent. Champions of the vision then emerge as they adopt and accept the vision as their own. Eventually there is broad commitment across the organization. Individuals become invested in the shared vision and they won't let the vision die.

Developing common mental models of both the current reality and the desired envisioned state are vital in building a shared vision. Where organizations can transcend linear command-and-control dictatorship of a vision statement and grasp system thinking, there is the possibility of building shared vision and more importantly, in bringing a shared vision to fruition.

Team Learning

Team learning is the process of aligning and developing the capacities of a team to collectively create the results the members truly want. Team learning builds on both personal mastery of individuals and shared vision of defined objectives to establish an environment of sharing and creating knowledge. For team learning, individuals need to be able to act in concert. When teams learn together not only does the organization benefit, but individual members grow and develop more rapidly than they do individually, further facilitating maturation of personal mastery.

The discipline of team learning starts with dialogue, the capacity of team members to suspend assumptions and judgment to genuinely "think together." The choice of the word "dialogue" is significant in reference to team learning. To the ancient Greeks *dialogos* meant the free flow of ideas. It referred to concepts flowing through a group allowing the group to discover insights not attainable individually.

The ancient Greek notion of dialogue is critically important for team learning to occur. Dialogue occurs when there is a free flowing movement of ideas, when a group becomes open to the flow of a larger intelligence and thought is approached largely as a collective phenomenon. When dialogue is coupled with systems thinking it creates a language more suited for dealing with complex issues and there is a shift to focusing on deep-seated structural issues rather than short-term problems. Questions of personality and leadership style that often tend to divert attention are avoided.

To be successful it is also important to recognize the patterns of interaction in teams that undermine team learning. Intergroup dialogue work is a difficult process designed to involve individuals in a group setting to explore complex issues on which views differ, often to the extent that polarization and conflict occur. Initially, the Product Development Leadership Learning Team was a public arena designed to provide a safe yet communal space to express anger and indignation about past injustices. The role of the facilitator early on was to help group members avoid unproductive language, cultivate new listening skills, improve communication patterns, value the differences of others, and develop shared understanding through the use of systems maps to tease out hidden mental models.

Evolution to team learning through dialogue required fostering an environment that enabled participants to speak and listen in the present while understanding the contributions of the past in developing a shared vision for the future. The environment that enabled this shift in consciousness for the PDL^{2}T was important as well. It was created through attention to factors such as the choice of location for the dialogue, the establishment of communication protocol, building relationships based on trust, and premeditated design and facilitation of the dialogue. Each member of the team had to collaborate willingly, be vulnerable, respect the opinions of the others, and truly believe in the authenticity of all the participants.

As the PDL^{2}T matured, the team began to explore their most closely held mental models against the context of systems thinking. The intensity of emotions remained, but the nature and the manner in which they were expressed changed over time. The role of the facilitator evolved to become one of challenging the team to share their perceptions of the world in the context of systems maps as a medium without either forcing their perspective on the others or conforming to the perspective of others.

Over time, dialogue ensued and learning broke out. Dialogue affected the thinking of the PDL^{2}T because it challenged core assumptions and long-held mental models. Once the team members were able to suspend their own thoughts and assumptions long enough for others to share their opinions without hostilities, it resulted in "collective thinking." Learning together allowed the PDL²T to explore far more creatively, and opened entirely new directions of thought from the past. Team learning started when shared meaning and a collective consciousness was created which transcended the individuals searching for facts to advocate long-seated personal positions from the past. As dialogue ensued in the PDL²T people stopped beating down others in an attempt to win them over. People become cognizant of their own thinking as they reflected on their perception of reality and communicated it with each other. This established the foundation of learning and social transformation.

●　●　●

"Sure, John," I said, as I put away the papers I had been reviewing, "let's go through the PDL²T agenda once more to make sure that we've got it right." John and I would invest many hours on a PDL²T meeting during the weeks between meetings, not because the meeting agenda was complex, but because selecting the correct topic for discussion at the right time was very complex, and we could only tackle one or two topics in a day. We invested the time to choose the right topic and to carefully script our involvement in the dialogue of the meeting.

Due to the intensity of dialogue, the only way to transition between topics was a natural break, and the only natural breaks were lunch and the time until next meeting. There was a progression of running dialogue over the course of the months and years recorded through reflective notes as the team dealt with the complex issues of product development. I would review the past reflective notes to remind myself of the themes that ran through the dialogue and then work off these themes to steer the team in a particular direction. The challenge was always to identify the next logical topics in the progression of the group's learning, and then determine if a topic could be tackled in half a day or if it required a full day's discourse. There were times when lunch was pushed back for many hours because I miscalculated the depth of a topic's dialogue and passion it evoked. In the context of team learning, lunch occurred when a topic was closed, not by the clock on the wall or hunger, although admittedly, hunger on occasion helped to bring a dialogue to closure.

A very important aspect of team learning is to recognize that when there is disagreement, a group will talk for ten or fifteen minutes on a topic. But when there is agreement, a team will talk for hours on a topic as they build on each other's ideas and learn collectively. It is important to recognize that silence does not constitute agreement. Contrary to conventional thinking, silence generally means something is missing and there are unresolved differences in the group that need to be uncovered.

"I think the group was way too quiet in the last meeting when we touched on the role of the project leader and the clarity of the development process. There's an issue there that needs to be brought out into the open. It's important that they all understand the importance of a common process before we roll out version seven of the development methodology," I said to John. "I agree," John replied. "So I'll work on teasing that out of the group and see if we can't get them to build a systems model of the issue. I'll try to get the team to draw the diagram on the board. That should stimulate some good dialogue."

Our conversation went on for several hours as we debated scenarios of how the meeting might progress and each of our roles in moving the group forward under each scenario. We finally parted ways, agreeing to meet at 7:00 the next morning to set up the conference room.

CHAPTER 4

The PDL²T

A conversation is a dialogue, not a monologue. That's why there are so few good conversations: due to scarcity, two intelligent talkers seldom meet.

Truman Capote

The Harley-Davidson conference center is located on the sixth floor of an old warehouse across the street from the Juneau Avenue headquarters. At one time it housed parts and accessories when the headquarters was still a factory. The building was converted from warehouse space to office and meeting space in the late 1990s but kept the look and feel of the 1920s industrial-era warehouse it had once been. The original red brick and glass block were used to portion sections of the warehouse into conference rooms. Blackened steel tread plate and angle iron mounted to the bottom portion of the walls gave the look of an industrial wainscot in the conference rooms. Accent walls were finished with a warm tan or green. Cabinets were made of varnished pressed wood and angle iron. The ceiling of the room was the poured concrete of the floor above painted white with the heat ducting visible. When Harley did something, they did it right. The building evoked just the right balance between raw edge and functionality. The environment created a garage-like feel that was casual and relaxed, a place you felt like you could kick back and talk with friends—just the right atmosphere for reflection and learning.

The staff that ran the conference center was great to work with. They were there to make sure that everything was in order for meetings, and would arrange lunch and snacks. Salted popcorn was always a favorite. The staff also provided a service to set up the room in advance. There were a number of standard room layouts that you could pick from, and they were very good about making sure everything was in place by the time the meeting started. It was as simple as a phone call or filling out a form to let them know what you wanted for snacks and lunch, how many flipcharts or audio devices you wanted, and the room layout. You could request that the room be arranged in a "U" shape, or have the tables arranged in a classroom setting, or group the tables in sets of two, or just about any other arrangement that you could draw on their form, and they would have the room ready when the meeting began.

But when I requested to have all the tables removed from the room and the chairs arranged in a circle in the middle of the room, that was a problem. No tables and just chairs seemed to cause some sort of a short in their mental circuits. Meetings do not happen in a corporate environment without tables, even at Harley-Davidson. But a circle of chairs and no tables was the protocol for the PDL²T. Tables create an artificial but psychological barrier for protection, whereas a circle of chairs—where everyone in the group is exposed—fosters trust and openness to the thoughts and perspectives of others and creates an environment for dialogue where everyone is equal.

I learned from John that if we stacked the tables against the wall, arranged the chairs in a circle in the middle of the room, and were out of the room before the morning coffee was delivered, we could generally get away with rearranging the room ourselves provided we put everything back the way it was before we left for the day. I was in the conference room at 7:00 A.M., sliding tables toward the wall when John walked in and dropped his backpack on the floor in the corner of the room. Together, we made quick work of stacking the tables, and we were done well before the popcorn and coffee arrived. We headed up one floor to the cafeteria for breakfast and waited for the rest of the PDL²T to arrive.

Shortly before 8:00 we returned to the room and took a seat. We spread a stack of reflective notes from the previous meeting on the floor. As others came into the room and piled their jackets and helmets on the stacked tables, each person would quietly take a seat, pick up a copy of the reflective notes, and begin to read and reflect on the learning from the previous meeting. When everyone had arrived and it looked like most of the group had finished reading, John or I would suggest that we begin a "check-in" and the other would get up, close the conference room doors, and pull any unused chairs out of the circle to tighten up the ring.

Check-in was a very important aspect of our meetings. It was a mechanism to purge our minds of everything that was going on outside of the meeting and clear out all outside distractions. Check-in is a tool to transition from the normal daily activities and lower our personal shields, which protect us from others. It is a means to begin opening up by sharing with the rest of the group our particular state of mind at that moment. The process could easily take an hour or more. Planning for the day needed to take this into account. Check-in started by selecting a check-in object. People would generally volunteer an object. Sometimes someone would bring in a particular object that held some meaning or significance for them and they would explain the significance to the rest of the group as they stared. For a while we used a "straw-man" which someone's daughter had made for the group. It was a doll made from twisted straw and represented all the "straw-man" ideas we created as a group. Gold coins were also popular, but most often it seemed that we would use Kirk's Harley-Davidson ring. He always wore an enormous gold Harley-Davidson ring with the Harley bar and shield cast in the top and eagles cast in the side. It was convenient to use when nothing else was proposed.

Kirk is six foot four, an imposing man with a kind and genuine demeanor who had been with Harley-Davidson since before the buy-out of the 1980s, and had a wealth of knowledge and history to share. Although he fit the outward description of a typical biker, on the inside he was anything but the typical biker stereotype. As a well-read individual and opera fan, Kirk always brought a unique dimension to the group.

If there was no other check-in object offered up Kirk would slide off his gigantic gold ring and hand it to someone to begin check-in. The rules for checking in were simple: the person holding the object spoke and everyone else listened silently. Everyone had a chance to speak in turn as the check-in object made its way around the circle. As each person finished speaking, the rest of the group would welcome them to the meeting.

It was expected that members would open up and speak about what was on their mind whether it was good, bad, or indifferent. At times someone would say, "I had a fight with my wife last night and I'm a bit out of it today," then go on to share what was on their mind. During check-in, people would share that their child scored a game-winning goal that week and how excited they were for their child, that a child had been accepted to the college of their choice, that work was getting them down and they had not slept most of the night, or that they had just booked a cruise. Check-in generally also evoked at least one comment related to the reflective notes that they had just read as they connected back to the previous meeting.

Check-in was a means of purging the mind, leaving all distractions outside the conference room door, becoming vulnerable, and preparing for reflection and dialogue. During check-in, John or I would capture any pertinent thoughts on a flip chart, and when everyone had cleared their minds and been welcomed to the meeting, we would begin. We would reiterate the topic or topics for the day, then openly review the intended topics against the list generated during the check-in. If there was a burning desire to adjust the meeting based on a relevant topic from check-in, we would modify the meeting agenda. Generally we had spoken to enough people in advance and prepared well enough that the intended topics were accepted, and topics that came up during check-in were added to a list of potential future topics.

Systems Thinking

That particular day John opened the meeting and suggested that we delve into the role of standardized product development methodology and how it relates to success in execution of projects. I recalled how years earlier when Roaring Motors wanted to improve product development, they had dictated changes to the Common Corporate Product Development Process. But this time it was different. John suggested that we build a system dynamics model to help get all the perspectives out for discussion and visualize the interdependencies. He then reminded the group of the systems dynamics modeling protocol. A particular item or action is connected in the system with an arrow and either an "O" or an "S" is placed at the arrowhead to indicate whether the action drives the next activity in the "opposite" direction or in the "same" direction. He picked up a marker and went to the board to sketch his favorite example.

"There's this group of pioneers," he began. "These are early settlers that journey across the country in search of a place to build their homes. They come to a beautiful and tranquil river valley and decide to build a town along the banks of the river." He began to draw on the board as he told his story. "People build along a river," he writes on the board.

People build
along a river

"They build their town, and the town prospers for many years," he continued, "but eventually the river floods. The river goes well beyond the normal spring runoff and the flood destroys the town." He talked while he added to the picture on the board (see next page). He drew arrows from action to action and placed an "S" by the arrowheads, indicating that the actions move in the same direction. The more the pioneers build, the more the floods destroy. He also added two slashes across one of the arrows, indicating a significant delay in the system.

"The town has a strong pioneering spirit, and they are heavily vested in their little community," he continued. "Over time the town has become a small city and it becomes a battle of river versus humanity. The hearty pioneers are resolute and won't let the river destroy their city, so they rebuild and the city perseveres." John continued to draw on the board as he told his story. When John finished drawing

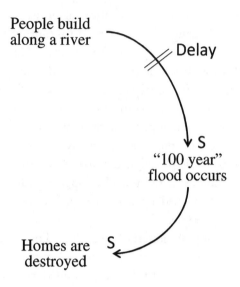

the causal loop he placed an "R" inside the loop and circled it, indicating that it is a "reinforcing" loop.

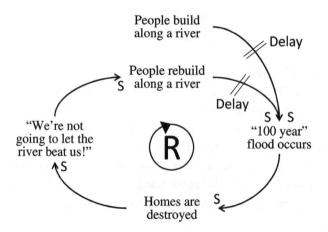

"The community has created a reinforcing loop," he explained, "a self-feeding vicious cycle that builds upon itself. The more vested the community becomes in their homes and the town, the more stubborn they become against the river and the forces of nature. The delays only serve to make the situation worse because the longer the delay, the more they are able to build. If the delay is long enough, many of the people that experienced the disaster are gone, and new people live in the town and build on the banks of the beautiful and tranquil river that runs through their town.

"The only way to change the system," he reminded the group, "is to break a link, add a loop, take away a loop, or eliminate a delay. In order to create a balancing loop—one that will eventually self-correct and find a balanced point of equilibrium to offset the vicious death spiral of a reinforcing loop—something has to change." John reminded the group that a stable system has balancing loops and reiterated his point by drawing a "B" on the board, circling it for emphasis.

The team had all heard John's story many times, but John's story provided a good reminder. They began to share their individual experiences and reveal their mental models about standardized methodology, phase gate methods, and issues related to developing products. At the time, Harley-Davidson was using a phase gate method, and everybody in the room was intimately familiar with the current process. Many had product development experience from other companies as well, so it wasn't long before there was a very vibrant and lively dialogue regarding phase gate and standard methodologies. The most intense conversation, however, dealt with what was wrong with the current process; everyone had an opinion based on their own mental model and experience.

Learning to See the Product Development System

As scribes for the process, John and I worked feverishly to keep up with the ever-changing direction the dialogue took as we attempted to capture the conversation in a systems model and record the group's input on the board, all the while interjecting comments or ideas to steer the group as we had rehearsed. The dialogue ebbed and flowed through the morning. At times the room was emotionally charged and by the time lunch arrived the team was in heated discourse. As lunch grew cold a basic diagram began to evolve. Finally, well into the afternoon, a diagram emerged that established a common perspective of the current situation.

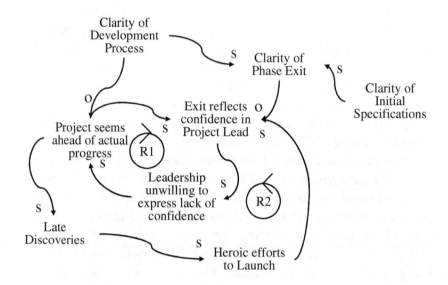

The system model that emerged after hours of dialogue was a vicious cycle based on the clarity of the phase exits in the phase gate process with two primary reinforcing loops. The model that the team drew represented how they believed the system worked; it depicted the phase exit reviews as the controlling mechanism for the development process. Although the phase and gate development process was instituted to control financial risk, a consequence of the system was that phase exits had become the pacing mechanism for the entire development system. To move from one phase of a project to the next, a project team was required to make a presentation to an executive committee and request an exit to begin work in the next phase of the development process. In order for the executive review board to make the decision to enter a new phase they compared the requirements against what the development team told them they had completed and used a phase exit check sheet to define the tasks that needed to be completed for a successful phase exit.

In order to evaluate a project's progress and decide if a phase exit is warranted, two aspects are required: clarity of the development process, and clarity of the initial specifications. The systems model depicted these aspects intersecting at the phase exits (Clarity of Phase Exit, at the top right of the model). The better the understanding of the phase exit criteria and the more clearly the project specifications are defined, the greater the clarity of the phase exit. In the systems model it follows that these actions move in the same direction. However, as the exit criteria of the development process become less clear, or the specifications are unclear, or if there are issues with the project, the phase exit decision becomes increasingly unclear and more dependent on the confidence in the project leader.

The intent of the phase gate process is for the exit reviews to serve as a means to inform the leadership of project status and build confidence in the project as spending and financial commitments escalate through the development cycle. In the phase gate process, the rationale for requiring executive sign-off for increased spending levels is that executives can then manage the financial exposure of the company by restricting spending or canceling risky projects. In reality it rarely works that way. Just like at Roaring Motors, once a project is started, it's essentially committed. The project is either required due to government regulation, or the sales revenue is needed to meet growth objectives—and canceling a project or delaying it are rarely pleasant alternatives. So even though the phase gate system was instituted to manage financial risk, the basic control mechanism—canceling the project—is rarely a feasible option.

There is tremendous pressure on the review committee to move a project forward. When clarity of the phase exit goes down, review committees become increasingly reliant on confidence in a project leader. If a project leader has successfully delivered projects in the past and the exit criteria or the project specifications are not clear, then the review becomes a vote of confidence in the project team's ability and reputation. The exit decision becomes a vote of confidence in the project leader. In the systems model, the clarity of the phase exit and the confidence in the project leader move in opposite directions.

When phase exits degrade to confidence in the project leader, review committees are increasingly reluctant to express lack of confidence, particularly if they appointed the project leader. It follows that if they lack confidence in the project leader, then they must replace the project leader. This creates a reinforcing loop. As the phase exit becomes more dependent on the confidence in the project leader and the review committee is unwilling to express lack of confidence, the project tends to appear further ahead in the development process than it actually is. At subsequent project reviews, this cycle is reinforced as the system perpetuates.

There is also a second reinforcing loop that further fuels this tendency. As a review committee places more confidence in the project leader and the project seems further ahead than it actually is, issues are generally uncovered in the project. Late discoveries and design loop-backs to fix them begin to occur. When there are late discoveries and redesign is required, heroic efforts are necessary to deliver the project. The greater the heroics, the greater the confidence the project leader builds in the minds of the review committee. This loop serves to further reinforce the tendency to make exit review decisions on the basis of confidence in the project leader based on reputation—until the project leader fails. But as the system map indicates, the failure of the project is rarely caused by the project leader; rather, it is caused by the system in which the project leader operates.

When a project fails, the failure is generally blamed on the project leader rather than recognizing that the system in which the project leader operates is a much greater determinant of success and failure than the project leader. By the same token, a project leader is rewarded when the project is successful. The reward for success is the opportunity to lead a project again—until he fails. When a project fails, the project leader is chastised. There is little recognition that the environment we create establishes an unseen system—and a bad system will beat good people every time.

Learningful Conversations

Most organizations unintentionally create systems that require extraordinary people to deliver ordinary results. These extraordinary people are rewarded for their ability to game the system. In a complex system, success in one area is often achieved at the expense of another area unless a holistic approach is applied to the overall system. When a development process is created with an understanding of the dynamics of the system, a development system can be created where ordinary people can collaborate to deliver extraordinary results consistently across the entire development portfolio.

After consuming the cold pizzas and a well-deserved break, the team came back together to figure out how to fix the system and create a shared vision of the future. It was time to figure out how to break a connection or create a balancing loop to offset the vicious reinforcing loops. It wasn't long before everyone was embroiled in heated debate. The product development process is one aspect of business that everyone has an opinion on, and everyone was eager to share their mental model of how to fix it. There was clearly much more advocating of position than listening going on, and it took a while before reason prevailed and the team actually entered into dialogue. Dialogue requires "learningful" conversations, which balance advocacy with inquiry.

Emotionally charged topics had a way of causing the PDL²T to revert back to traditional debate, with everyone advocating their own position. The balance between inquiry and advocacy necessary for dialogue and learning is often difficult to maintain. Advocacy merely states a point of view, then searches for ways to promote the position and discredit others, while disclosing as little of the rationale in the process as possible. Inquiry requires asking about someone else's point of view and encouraging others to ask about yours out of genuine curiosity. It requires sharing the rationale for your perspective through disclosing your mental models and opening yourself for criticism.

Figures 4–1 through 4–4 were developed by the PDL²T to define and describe expectations the members had of themselves in balancing advocacy and inquiry. They express a code of conduct established to enable dialogue and establishing learning conversations. At times a member of the group may refer to these concepts to keep the team in check.

Once a conversation has degraded into a debate, returning to dia-

Figure 4.1

Balancing Advocacy and Inquiry

Advocacy – Stating your point of view. Driven by <u>disclosure</u>.

Inquiry – Asking about another's point of view and encouraging others to ask about yours. Driven by <u>curiosity</u>.

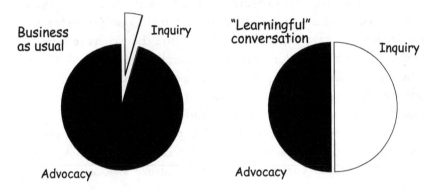

logue is difficult. As with any negotiation, finding common ground is the best medium to move a group locked in debate toward dialogue. The desire to improve Harley's product development process, along with the systems model the group created collectively in the morning, provided the common ground and distraction necessary to interrupt the debate. As we turned our attention to the model on the board, it became possible to challenge points of view through exposing where on the ladder of inference the position stemmed from—not challenging a position or opinion, but rather inferring how the point of view was achieved. If everyone has the same information and uses the same reasoning process, they will eventually arrive at the same conclusion. Open evaluation of facts and exposure to the reasoning process provides visibility to differences. Through exposure of facts and disclosure of the thinking process used to reach a conclusion, it is possible to return to constructive dialogue.

The systems model from the morning provided the backdrop to

Figure 4.2

Regular vs. "Learningful" Conversation

	Regular	**Learningful**
Goal	Win—Your point of view prevails.	Learn—Build shared understanding.
Sensibility	$\boxed{A} \longrightarrow \boxed{B} \longrightarrow \boxed{C}$	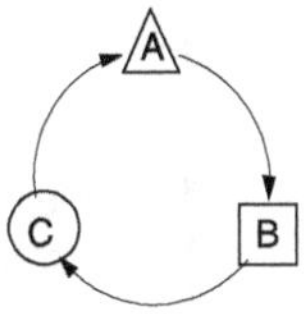
When advocating	Present opinions as data, but pretend you are not. Hide your reasoning.	Separate data from opinions Reveal your reasoning.
When challenged	Defend your view, but pretend you are not.	Invite inquiry into your position as a way of improving it.
When inquiring	"Pin"people—To prove them wrong.	Understand—How is this person right?

challenge how suggested changes would impact the outcome of the model. John and I sketched in additional loops reflected in the swirl of conversation, adding and removing loops as the conversation ebbed and flowed. Focus on the model helped the team return to constructive dialogue although points of view were still presented as facts and there remained the tendency to advocate a particular position.

The ladder of inference (Figure 4-3) describes the attribution process from facts to opinions. Understanding where a statement stems from on the ladder of inference helps to quantify the degree to which a statement is factual or degree to which the evaluation of the facts have been filtered. All opinions and positions result from directly observable facts. These concrete, directly observable facts pass through a variety of cultural and personal filters that refine the facts into information that we evaluate and use to attribute into our opinions. Facts are concrete, universal, and the same for everyone that observes them. However, everyone views facts through different filters that they have developed over time. Although positions and opinions are commonly

Figure 4.3

The Ladder of Inference

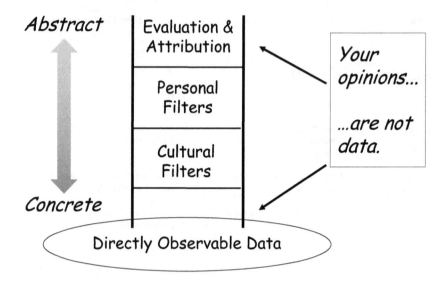

presented as facts, acknowledgement of the filters helps to establish a common perspective of the facts.

Two perspectives of the same facts can lead to entirely different abstract opinions. Recognition of the attribution of the facts due to filters we unconsciously place on concrete data allows us to trace how we arrive at our opinions as we move from concrete data and facts to abstract opinions and positions.

When a group is engaged in dialogue, it is important to know where you are on the ladder of inference. Attribution of facts through cultural and personal filters is normal, so it is important to recognize where on the ladder a positions stems from. Particularly when dialogue shifts to debate, it's important to ground the ladder on something solid; some concrete, directly observable fact. To facilitate dialogue it's important to disclose your reasoning process as you move from concrete facts toward abstract attribution of the facts. Sharing how you

Figure 4.4

The Ladder of Inference in Conversation

- Know where you are on the ladder.
- Ground your ladder in something solid—a directly observable fact.
- Disclose your reasoning process. (Advocacy)
- Ask about other's reasoning. (Inquiry)
- Go up and down ladder consciously and publicly.
- See attributions as theories to be tested. (Inquiry)

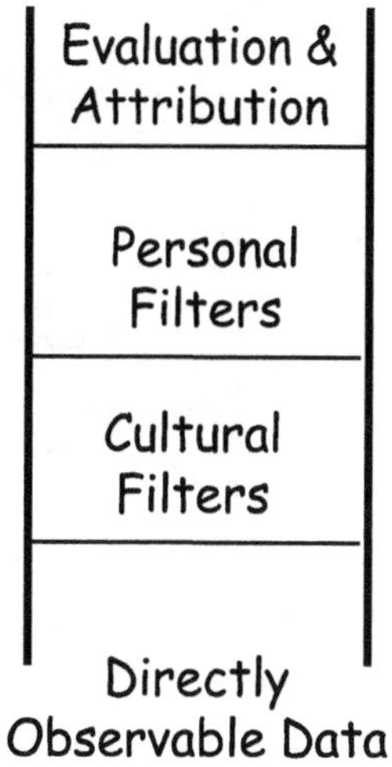

Evaluation & Attribution
Personal Filters
Cultural Filters

Directly
Observable Data

make your attribution helps to expose filters. Disclosing your reasoning process and asking others about their reasoning process without judgment is important. Moving up and down the ladder consciously and publicly is an important aspect of learning through dialogue. To learn collectively, we must recognize that our attributions are in reality theories to be tested.

Creating Shared Vision

It was late in the afternoon by the time a shared vision evolved and a systems model (shown below) emerged from the afternoon's dialogue. Many different perspectives and alternatives had been explored and evaluated. In the end, the most simplistic description that the team agreed reflected the issue we faced involved three balancing loops. All three balancing loops highlighted the criticality for creation and application of standardized work.

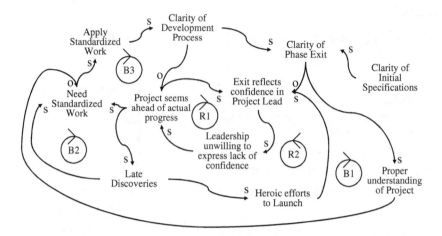

The first balancing loop (B1) was grounded in the clarity of the phase exits. Lack of clarity in phase exits results in not properly understanding the condition and objectives of the project. As standardized work is established and applied to the development process, over time it increasingly clarifies the development process itself, offsetting the vicious cycle of reliance on the reputation of the project manager.

The second balancing loop (B2) initiated from late discoveries, and also pointed to the need for standardized work to minimize those late discoveries.

The third balancing loop (B3) directly linked the need for standardized work with the project *seeming* to be ahead of its actual progress.

The shared vision created from the day's work clearly pointed to the need for clarity of the development process to offset the firefighting mentality the organization had adopted. Proactive product development had degraded to chasing problems. Every day was spent fighting the biggest fire that flared up that day. But instilling discipline and instituting standardized work is not a welcomed scenario in a creative development organization. Standardized work limits individual flexibility and is sometimes erroneously perceived as constraining creativity. The Harley-Davidson product development organization is made up of passionate, emotional people who take pride in their creativity. This "cowboy mentality" of fiercely independent individuals spent as much of their creative energy on the process they used as the products that emerged from the process. Each product was different and each time the process was applied, it was applied differently. There was no foundation for learning and improvement.

It was nice to see recognition by the group that standardization of the process was important. However, the Product Development Leadership Learning Team had built a reputation of being high on learning, but significantly lacking on application. Revision of the methodology to stress discipline and standardized work would be a challenge regardless of the insights of the day.

Protocol of the PDL²T required that meetings conclude with a "check-out." The check-out process is similar to the check-in used to begin the meeting, but at the end of the meeting each person reflects on the activities of the day and shares their perspective with the rest of the group. One by one, each member of the PDL²T summarized and relayed their learning from the day. Some shared a nugget of wisdom they had acquired but most were drained from the long day and just wanted to go home, so they kept their closing remarks short. After the last person had spoken and everyone had left the room, John and I put the tables and chairs back in their proper places, happy that we had achieved our objective—the recognition by this group that standardized work and a uniform methodology was critical as a basis for improving the product development process.

I thought back to my own experience at Roaring Motors. People tend to equate "standardized work" with "work standards" imposed on workers by so-called experts who define the work, then tell workers what and how to perform their job. This method of creating work standards undermines the value of workers, who generally know their job best, and alienates them from the improvement process. This mindset would need to be overcome if we were to instill standardization into the development process as a basis for continuous improvement. This creation of "standardization" would be based on a belief that workers closest to the work know the improvement potential best.

In contrast to work standards, standardized work is determined collectively by the group closest to the work. It is the agreed best method and sequence for accomplishing each work element. It defines the interaction of people and the flow of information. As the documented and agreed-upon best way of accomplishing work, standardized work becomes the foundation for continuous improvement. As each improvement is incorporated into the latest standardized work, all workers are engaged to collectively find and agree on the best way to accomplish work. For us to improve the development process, this mentality of continuous improvement would need to be created to engage the organization in the effort of creating standardized work.

Actual change never directly emanated from the PDL²T meetings. Change only happened when someone took what they had learned and had the courage and conviction to sponsor, promote, and drive change outside of the meeting. For change to happen, someone had to take an idea and apply it outside the safety net of the PDL²T learning environment. The activities of the day provided the necessary endorsement to begin moving learning from inside the confines of the PDL²T into the real world of product development.

PDL²T Meeting Process

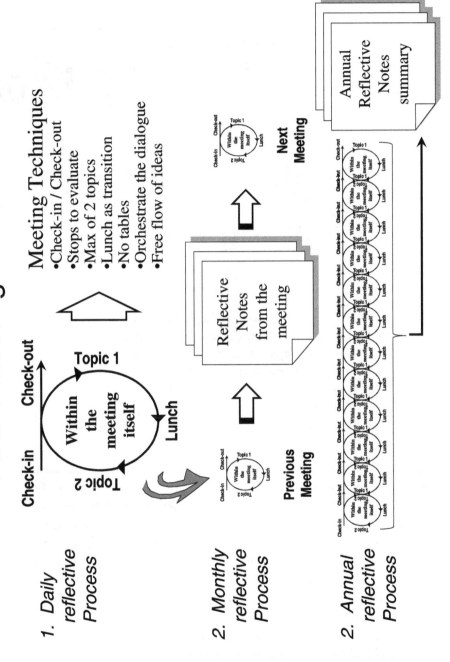

Meeting Techniques

- Check-in / Check-out
- Stops to evaluate
- Max of 2 topics
- Lunch as transition
- No tables
- Orchestrate the dialogue
- Free flow of ideas

Check-in **Check-out**

Topic 1

Within the meeting itself

Lunch

Topic 2

1. Daily reflective Process

Reflective Notes from the meeting

Check-in Check-out
Topic 1
Within the meeting itself
Lunch
Topic 2

Previous Meeting

2. Monthly reflective Process

Check-in Check-out
Topic 1
Within the meeting itself
Lunch
Topic 2

Next Meeting

Annual Reflective Notes summary

2. Annual reflective Process

CHAPTER 5

Firefighting and the Tipping Point

It must be remembered that there is nothing more difficult to plan, more uncertain of success, nor more dangerous to manage than the creation of a new order of things. For the initiator has the enmity of all who would profit by the preservation of the old institutions, and merely lukewarm defenders in those who would gain by the new ones.

Niccolo Machiavelli

I was at my desk reading the 2001 model year Launch Assessment report when Kerry interrupted me. She walked into my office carrying two bound booklets. "I found copies of the 1999 and 2000 launch assessments in my files," she said, placing the booklets on my desk. "I think you'll find them interesting." Kerry Luczak had been a part of the product development office since its inception. She managed the project review process and conducted the monthly mock-up reviews that had become an important part of the development process for Harley-Davidson.

Because Kerry scheduled and conducted mock-up and project reviews, she had been involved in every project for years. She had collected a wealth of knowledge and information over the years and shared it with me as she told me stories from the past. She let me know the things that had worked and the things that had not. Kerry suggested that I read the launch assessment reports that were written as a part of a collaborative study with MIT, so I took her advice and diligently plowed through the reports.

The MIT Connection

Organizational learning and the use of causal loops to understand complex system dynamics issues was introduced to Harley-Davidson through MIT. The product development office leveraged that relationship through participation in a multi-year study to better understand the product development process. In conjunction with the organizational learning efforts of the PDL²T, the product development office worked directly with the Sloan School of Management and the MIT Center for Innovation in Product Development to better understand the underlying systemic issues present in product development.[1] The study was undertaken in cooperation with the National Science Foundation and involved a handful of companies representing the automotive, telecommunications, semiconductor, and recreational products industries. The objective of the research was to better understand the underlying system dynamics of product development.

Nelson Repenning headed the study through the System Dynamics department at the Sloan School of Management. Every summer one of Nelson's graduate students came to Milwaukee to conduct "fieldwork." Fieldwork consisted of graduate students reviewing all the ongoing product development projects in the development center and conducting in-depth interviews across the organization. The analysis and interviews were used to determine what worked and did not work in the development process that particular year. The students compiled the information from their fieldwork into detailed reports called launch assessment reports. The launch assessment report documented each student's findings, and included their written evaluations as well as system dynamics models they created to describe the underlying systemic structures they perceived. When the students returned to school in September, they presented their findings and left behind the launch assessment report that documented their efforts. It was these reports that Kerry had recommended I read.

The fieldwork and the launch assessments conducted at Harley-Davidson were compiled with the information gleaned from the other companies as a basis for the larger study, which attempted to expose the underlying drivers for the effectiveness and the ineffectiveness of product development on a systemic basis. The research uncovered two important concepts persistent at each of the companies studied. These two systemic properties were subsequently determined to be universally present in product development regardless of company or industry. The study identified the phenomenon of *firefighting* as a key impediment to effective product development and determined that there is a *tipping point* where an organization enters unrecoverable cycles of firefighting. The recognition of firefighting and the revelation of a tipping point became the foundation for the initial improvement efforts to the product development process at Harley-Davidson.

Firefighting

Firefighting is the practice of reactively pursuing issues as they surface in the development process. Firefighting is distinguished by last-minute heroics to save a project. John Rock at Roaring Motors typified the antics of a firefighting hero. In a firefighting mode, the end of a project is characterized by the seemingly endless pursuit of one problem after another. Firefighting causes organizations to spend unplanned time and energy to solve urgent, unanticipated issues through reallocation of important resources. Firefighting is one of the most universally common and costly syndromes in product development, yet it is little known and understood.

Firefighting exists in a bimodal semi-stable state like a ball on the plateau of a hill. As issues surface in the development process, they cause disruptions. If the issues are relatively small compared to the resources and knowledge available to resolve them, the issue may gen-

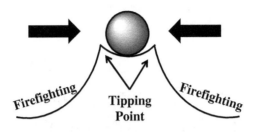

erate some panic, but the system can absorb the temporary disturbance and return to a normal state as the problems are addressed. However, if the issue is large or resolution of multiple issues becomes protracted, the system decays into a permanent state of ongoing firefighting. The point at which the system either returns to business as usual or descends into spiraling degradation is referred to as the tipping point. The less slack resource available in the business-as-usual mode, the less of a disturbance is required to "tip" the system as fires spread from project to project across the portfolio.

The Tipping Point

The notion of a tipping point refers to the phenomenon in which small changes will have little or no effect on a system until a critical point is reached. This critical point is often unseen and unrecognized until *after* it has been crossed. The tipping point refers to that point at which a minor change "tips" the system into a new and irreversible condition. The term is borrowed from the field of epidemiology to describe when an infectious disease reaches a point beyond which any local ability to control its spread is breached and it becomes an epidemic. Recent examples include Ebola and SARS.

Similarly, a tipping point occurs in product development when local firefighting can no longer contain the rework necessary to save the project. This condition becomes more prevalent as organizations become leaner and more efficient with limited resources. As slack resources are reduced in the effort to streamline the organization, a tipping point is more readily crossed due to the inability to absorb unexpected issues within a project.

Past the Tipping Point

Over time the development organization at Harley-Davidson had grown accustomed to firefighting. The unplanned reallocation of resources to fix problems late in the delivery of projects became a predictable part of the product development cycle. Fixing problems often required multiple unplanned and undesirable loop-backs through the design cycle, in which a design team returned to work that had been previously done, to correct a newly discovered problem. Typically this would involve the tweaking of the existing design, but on occasion, more drastic solutions were required.

While firefighting has been widely criticized in both popular and scholarly literature, it remains a common occurrence in most product development organizations. Firefighting occurs when it is realized that a particular issue, or the combination of multiple unresolved issues, can prevent the success of a project. Unfortunately, this realization tends to come late in the development cycle, often because the enthusiasm and optimism expected from project leaders and reinforced through the incentive system ingrained in most organizations creates a culture in which the discovery or escalation of problems is delayed.

Project leaders are usually selected based on their optimism and "can do" attitude. Typical project leaders like to fix things and don't readily ask for help. Leadership develops the expectation that project leaders handle problems. Project leaders are then in turn more reluctant to admit defeat, opting to fix things themselves or within the team. Many times the role of a project leader is like rowing a boat upstream of a waterfall. The project leader is the oarsman rowing with all his might. The current of the river constantly pushes the boat toward impending doom—the edge of the waterfall. Similarly, projects flow through the development process. The flood of late discoveries and new issues constantly pushes the project toward peril, disruping the project from flowing smoothly through the development process.

A good project leader never quits. The project leader is the last person to give up on the project, just like the oarsman is the last person to give up in the boat. From the vantage point in the boat, it is often difficult to recognize the rapids in time to break free from the current that sweeps everything over the waterfall. From within a project, it can be difficult to recognize there are too many issues to resolve in time for launch until a crisis is imminent. It often requires someone on the shore to recognize the peril to the boat, just as it often takes someone outside the project to recognize the threat to the project.

To better understand the phenomenon of firefighting, system maps are used to describe the causal loops and the dynamics of the system. Utilizing causal loops to describe project-related firefighting helps to uncover the underlying causal relationships and the organizational behaviors that results in firefighting.

Creating new products involves fundamentally uncertain tasks with unproven technologies and processes. As design problems emerge, redesign is often required to correct the issue. These rework cycles, or design loop-backs, result in unanticipated work for the development organization. The picture below depicts the typical design loop-back cycle.

As product development progresses through the development cycle, problems surface. The discovery of problems that require redesign results in unanticipated need for extra resources and a departure from the desired linear development process employed at most companies. As issues pile up, they begin to impact the critical path for the delivery of the project. Consciously or subconsciously, issues are evaluated against the time remaining to complete the project. Issues may apply to a single item on the critical path of the project, or to multiple aspects of the project across a wide variety of project attributes.

Design loop-backs are best described as development rework cycles necessary to fix unexpected problems found in the development process. Most organizations accept development loop-backs as a normal and unavoidable aspect of product development. However, due to the

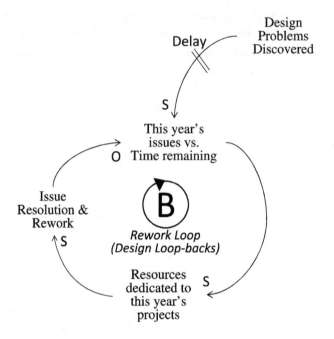

unexpected nature of design loop-backs they create more work for the project team. Although the need for redesign loops are expected in new product development, the magnitude of the work, the impact on the rest of the portfolio of projects, the timing, and the nature of the issues invariably come as a total surprise. As issues mount, the ratio of remaining issues to resolve, compared to the time remaining to complete the project, increases. The ratio of issues versus remaining time is only sometimes overtly evaluated, but it is always a hidden worry that keeps the project leader up at night.

As the issues mount and the remaining time grows shorter, pressure to resolve the issues increases. Additional effort is placed on resolving the problems. At this point the project leader may ask for help, recognizing that allocation of additional resources is unavoidable. But there are no slack resources. The project team is fully consumed and any possible additional resources are dedicated to other projects. The project team has no alternative but to work harder and redouble their efforts to resolve the issues. So the team members rededicate themselves to the project, committing longer hours and working harder in an attempt to resolve their list of issues. The Work Harder loop below depicts this activity.

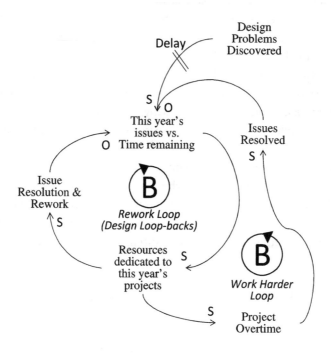

If the project team is able to quickly address the issues and reduce their overtime, the Work Harder loop subsides and the project returns to a more "normal" aspect of rework associated with product development. However, the longer the team spends in the Work Harder loop, the more fatigue sets in and the more likely that costly mistakes will be made. These mistakes result in additional design problems. A tipping point occurs when the team can no longer keep pace with the discovery of design problems.

A tipping point generally occurs well before the problem is recognized because of a system's inherent natural delays. A special condition exists for organizations that develop multiple projects simultaneously, particularly those that develop multiple model years or projects with staggered launch schedules simultaneously. These organizations can cross their tipping point and operate in a permanent state of ongoing firefighting as they "borrow" resources across the portfolio. Although the alternatives to firefighting, such as letting a defective product reach the market or canceling a project altogether, may appear less desirable than firefighting, shifting resources from later projects in the development portfolio to projects that are scheduled to launch earlier serves to perpetuate firefighting. Continually chasing unexpected problems results in an extremely inefficient and ineffective development system, yet this practice is very common. For organizations that develop multiple projects simultaneously, firefighting becomes epidemic when resources are pulled from future projects to rescue projects closer to production.

Many organizations permanently operate in a firefighting mode, exploiting the delays inherent in the system, and not recognizing the danger. The ability to fight fires is often viewed and rewarded as a necessary skill. Firefighting is often justified due to the messy reality of developing products in a complex system and competitive environment.

Like my manager at Roaring Motors, John Rock, some people become firefighting arsonists when they are rewarded for their heroics

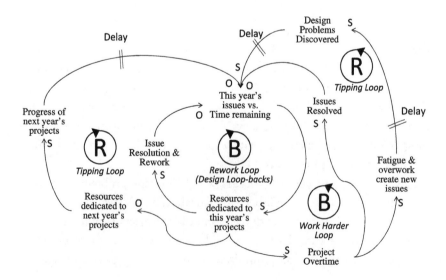

in fixing problems without recognizing that they are often the culprit in creating them. The destructive behaviors associated with firefighting are the result of organization's not being cognizant of the system dynamics associated with this condition and not recognizing that a tipping point has been crossed due to the delays inherent in the system. Firefighting is further perpetuated because there is a natural human tendency toward firefighting. Fixing problems under duress is exciting and brings an adrenaline rush. Solving problems brings recognition and accolades, so good creative problem solvers as well as product developers often become great firefighters.

The additional incentive of the reward system at most companies, and society as a whole, encourages fixing problems—but not the *prevention* of problems. There is little glory attached to projects that run smoothly. Focus, attention, and promotion follow the people who publicly save the organization. The recognition of firefighting and the underlying arson is seldom understood, yet understanding this is critical to improving the effectiveness and efficiency of product development.

The Beavertail project was intended to reestablish the prominence of a complete motorcycle platform. It had been one of Harley-Davidson's most profitable platforms. Motorcycle models from this platform had been the most copied by custom builders and competitors alike. The development efforts of Beavertail touched nearly 95 percent of all the parts from the previous model in an effort to address eroding profitability while also launching a completely new engine to give customers a reason to trade in and trade up. Because of the importance to the company, Beavertail was led by one of the company's most experienced project leaders.

Like most other major projects, as the project neared time to launch it became apparent that there were design flaws that needed to be addressed before production. One issue led to another as the design team ran from fire to fire in an attempt to save the project. The most serious issue was that the frame developed cracks on a severe-duty structural stress test. Before long, Beavertail had become the most important concern in the company. People worked day and night to resolve problems. Beavertail got head-of-the-line privileges as people set aside any other work to immediately address Beavertail. Even parts that were midway through a test were put to the side to allow Beavertail access to a test cell if they needed it. The intense focus by the entire development organization on fighting Beavertail fires idled many other projects as the redirected efforts of the organization eventually resolved the Beavertail problems. Beavertail launched and the project leader was proclaimed a hero for his leadership and valor in the crisis.

The damage that the Beavertail crisis inflicted on all the other projects in the portfolio, however, was largely overlooked. Only the people closest to the Beavertail project knew that every issue that came up in the crisis of launch was due to not properly having addressed it earlier in the development process. The development engineers have a saying: "At launch, all debts are forgiven." Beavertail reinforced to the organization that in the end, it does not matter how you get to launch, so long as you get to launch.

The MIT study exposed that design problems which drive the need for extra resources, although often attributed to outside forces such as changing requirements or supplier issues, are in fact most often the result of earlier firefighting efforts. Research showed that even the occasional use of firefighting quickly spreads to other projects, circumventing the disciplined execution of a product development process. Organizations that resort to firefighting in even a few isolated instances soon find that firefighting has completely replaced their more structured development process. Although firefighting is well intentioned initially, for many organizations firefighting *is* their development process.

Firefighting cannot complement an effective structured development process. Firefighting is an organizational pathology that severely degrades the effectiveness and efficiency of an organization's ability to develop new products. For nearly every organization, some degree of firefighting is the primary culprit for product development inefficiency. Unfortunately, reacting to the discovery of product design issues and the associated design loop-backs in the form of firefighting has largely become accepted practice in the development community. Product development at most organizations is crippled by the cancerous nature of firefighting and design loop-backs. Firefighting is rarely recognized, commonly misdiagnosed, and rarely understood.

Lessons from Beyond the Brink

There were many lessons that came from the MIT study.[2] The recognition of the phenomenon of firefighting was a big one. Even with our own data it was difficult acknowledging that as an organization we had crossed the brink. It took some time to accept that the development organization was operating in a permanent firefighting mode, beyond the tipping point. Discovering how to reverse the ingrained behaviors and tendencies would take many years. A firefighting organization requires extraordinary people to achieve ordinary results. In an exceptional organization, ordinary people achieve extraordinary results routinely. An exceptional development organization is built through reversal of the deeply ingrained tendencies and destructive mental models that draw organizations toward firefighting. Many of the actions and reversal of thought processes are counterintuitive to traditional thinking, making change extremely difficult.

There are three important realizations learned from operating beyond the brink:

1. Although firefighting is well intentioned and initially used only when a project gets into trouble, once initiated, firefighting quickly becomes the de facto development process. A reliance on firefighting serves to drive out proper, disciplined process execution.
2. An influx of workload can initiate firefighting and result in a permanent deterioration of overall system performance. While the cost of permanently overloading a development organization is tremendous, the implication of a tipping point is that the complexities of the development system make it extremely fragile with a propensity toward firefighting. Even a temporary overload can initiate a vicious cycle of costly firefighting.
3. The location of a tipping point, and the susceptibility of the development system to degrade into the firefighting phenomenon, is deter-

mined by the steady state of resource utilization. As competitive forces drive companies to be increasingly more efficient, they streamline their organization, with the result that smaller disruptions to the system draw the organization into a firefighting spiral.

Development managers today face an important trade-off between steady state of performance and the system's ability to accommodate unanticipated changes in resource requirements without descending into the firefighting cycle. Taken collectively, the insights from operating beyond the brink imply that the current methods deployed for aggregate resource planning used at most organizations are woefully insufficient in preventing firefighting. Development managers and company leadership with a desire to avoid firefighting must rethink their approach to managing multi-project development portfolios.

When a development organization is caught up in firefighting, people intrinsically recognize something is wrong but they rarely know exactly what or how to correct it. As performance persistently fails to achieve expectations, development managers and company leaders are most likely to blame the people who work within the system than question the structure of the system. As performance degrades through the vicious cycles of firefighting, managers are unlikely to learn to manage the system as they blame the designers, engineers, and project managers within the system. Unfortunately, the system itself provides little evidence to discredit the underlying hypothesis engrained in the managers' and leaders' way of thinking. Once an organization tips into firefighting, the performance of the system continues to decline even if the workload returns to a more normal level. Firefighting can tear an organization apart as leadership of the organization becomes increasingly frustrated with the perceived ineptitude of the development staff. Similarly, development staff become increasingly frustrated with managers who they perceive as lacking the understanding of the realities of launching new products and consequently set unachievable targets. As managers observe developers spending less time in the initial stages of development and more time chasing problems, it reinforces their mistaken belief that developers are to blame for the poor performance of the development organization.

People who operate within the development system are rarely directly to blame. Individual mistakes happen. However, consistent lack of performance must be attributed to systemic issues. To improve the development system, it must first be recognized that a bad system will always undermine even the best efforts of good people. Bad systems beat good people every time!

• • •

The diligent efforts of the MIT students to make the system visible, documented in the launch assessment reports that Kerry recommended I read, identified the specific aspects of how the general principles of firefighting applied to the Harley-Davidson development system. Although each launch assessment was created by a different student, themes emerged. Specific evidence and intrinsic analysis compiled over several years of field studies created compelling arguments to evaluate how product development could be done differently.

The detailed analysis of the MIT study provided a new lens through which to observe the product development system. This lens offered a new perspective, one that was counterintuitive to what we had known. Observing the development system through this new lens exposed previously unseen leverage points by which to manage the system. "Seeing" the system enabled us to understand the system, and understanding the system created the ability to establish specific causal relationships between actions and outcomes. Understanding the causal relationships of the system enabled us to control it.

Lean manufacturing has long espoused the virtues of flow in the manufacturing arena. Establishing flow in non-manufacturing arenas such as product development is significantly more challenging because of the intangible nature of the system. Within a manufacturing environment the flow of goods is directly observable. In manufacturing, takt time, explained in Chapter 6 is established and pieces per hour can be directly calculated. Moving away from the factory floor makes flow of the value stream more nebulous and the rhythm of the business is more difficult to quantify. Through the lens of the assessment reports and creation of systems models, *cadence* and *flow* were identified as two critical elements necessary to establish effective and efficient multi-project product development.

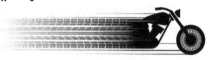

Cadence and Flow, Bins and Swirl

A process cannot be understood by stopping it. Understanding must move with the flow of the process, must join it and flow with it.

Frank Herbert

I t was late at night. Most of the lights in the Willie G. Davidson Product Development Center had been turned off by automatic timers hours before. On the main floor of the building, only the security lights and the lights in the conference room that Anthony Reese and I were camped out in were still on. The building was empty except for the security guards and a few third-shift technicians monitoring test cells in the basement. Anthony and I had taken over a conference room to prepare our slide presentation for the Product Development Management Association's international conference, for which we had agreed to deliver the keynote address. This was Harley-Davidson's 100th anniversary year. It seemed fitting that we presented 100 years of Harley-Davidson product development history together, as Anthony was responsible for engineering planning and I was responsible for the product development process.

Our title, "100 Years of Great Motorcycles," mirrored the company's milestone. We intended to share Harley-Davidson's development philosophy of designing motorcycles for the customer's experience. We would talk about the pride of the product developers, the rich heritage and tradition of Harley-Davidson. The fervent loyalty and devotion of Harley-Davidson's customers to the products was also an important part of any Harley-Davidson story. These are customers dedicated to the brand built upon the lifestyle created and supported by a 100-year lineage of great products. It is true that Harley-Davidson went astray for a time, producing inferior products that no one wanted. The blunders of a misguided leadership out of touch with their customers and their products nearly bankrupted the business. But the company found its way again, clawing its way back from the dead by fixing the quality problems and introducing a flow of new products customers cherished.

Although Vaughn Beals' and Rich Teerlink's leadership guided the business turnaround, it could not have been done without product development. During the dark times of the 1980s, when the company desperately needed new and exciting products, the product success of Harley-Davidson can largely be attributed to Willie G. Davidson's leadership. The small team of designers in the styling studio and the dedication of the development teams that executed their brash and innovative designs started a trickle of new products. At first new products were created by mixing and matching parts to refresh existing designs, while major projects such as the four-cylinder water-cooled Nova project were canceled. But the new products created necessary breathing room for the business as the FXR debuted in 1982 and the Softail in 1984. Ultimately, the brazen and stylish products powered not just the company's rebirth, but the incredible growth the company enjoyed for nearly a quarter century as the small trickle grew to a steady flow of new products.

Willie G. Davidson is the chief styling officer for Harley-Davidson and the man for whom the development center is named. He is a man of few words. I quickly learned that when he speaks, it's a good idea to shut up and listen. He is an icon in the world of styling, yet genuine, humble, and generous as a teacher. Every designer at Harley-Davidson is ingrained with his fundamental principles of design: "Look, sound, and feel is the essence of the motorcycle." Harley-Davidson produces an emotional product and the success of each motorcycle developed is dependent on how it stimulates the senses. It is the experience with the product that establishes loyalty. In the eternal debate between form and function, Willie lets no one forget that "form follows function, but both succumb to emotion." The emotional connection between product and consumer can never be overemphasized. It is the emotional ties that create the binding relationship with a company and a brand.

As one of the founder's grandsons, Willie clearly holds a vested interested in the company's success. But when it was most needed, it was the creativity, determination, and sheer passion for motorcycles that drove development success. Ordinary people accomplished extraordinary results. They found ways to refresh old designs and create new motorcycle models when there was no money for either. In the process they forged important elements of the Harley-Davidson development culture that remain to this day. There may be those who were there at the time and those who came after, but the impact that 100 years of legacy brings is etched in the bricks and mortar of the company. Progress comes through first acknowledging the past, then building upon it.

Anthony and I were working to create a meaningful story that showed the interrelationship of product design and company success, one that paid homage to the rich lineage of Harley-Davidson. It was a challenge to compress this rich history into an hour-long story and still be meaningful to the audience.

Much of Harley-Davidson's colorful history is carefully preserved in company archives. We spent many hours sifting through information that had been meticulously chronicled to make sure that we got the story right. In the process I learned a great deal about the development challenges of those who had come before me, and I gained a renewed appreciation for their efforts. Willie would often ponder the incredible success of the company and shake his head as he remarked in amazement, "All this from motorcycles." The meaning and impact of those few words grew on me as I studied Harley-Davidson's past.

While we prepared to tell the story of a 100-year legacy developing product designs for the customer experience we learned that Harley-Davidson had won the Outstanding Corporate Innovator award (OCI). Winning the OCI award is an honor given to companies with a record of exceptional product development. It was a fitting tribute on the 100th anniversary of the company, but the OCI award created an additional obligation to share the current evolution of the development process responsible for the current flow of new products that powered Harley-Davidson's success.

The Outstanding Corporate Innovator

Each year the Product Development Management Association (PDMA) selects one or two companies that exhibit an exemplary product development process. They look for companies that are truly outstanding and in addition are willing to share the process that makes them successful. These exceptional companies are acknowledged through the Outstanding Corporate Innovator award. The intent of this award is to acknowledge extraordinary companies as a model for others to emulate.

The road to the OCI award is arduous. First, PDMA members nominate potential recipients of the OCI award. Then the selection committee evaluates the development record of the company as well as their product development process documentation, which must be submitted by the companies. The selection committee narrows the field based on preestablished criteria, then a team of judges representing both academia and industry visit each of the finalists to assess their product development process firsthand. The assessment team reviews the company's development documents and conducts interviews to evaluate each of the finalist's development system. The award is then given to those companies that exhibit a consistent record for successful product development and utilize a development process the selection committee considers to provide a sustainable competitive advantage for the company.

We had been informed that Harley-Davidson was nominated for

the OCI award, so while we prepared our keynote address we also collected and submitted process documentation to the selection committee. One criterion for the award was consistent performance over time. Since Harley-Davidson went public in 1986 it had grown steadily, powered by a constant flow of new products, achieving a compound annual growth rate of 17 percent. Earnings grew even faster at a compound annual growth rate of 36 percent. Although it was easy to demonstrate consistent performance, it was a challenge to describe the development process that powered it.

The current evolution of the Harley-Davidson development process was based on the learning of the PDL^{2}T, through causal loops and systems thinking. The research with MIT on firefighting and recognition of the importance of disciplined standardized work was evident in the process, but there was no document to explain the connection. The standardized work in the product development system was built upon a foundation of cadence and flow. Cadence and flow are unfamiliar concepts to those mired in a phase and gate mindset. We had learned the importance of cadence and flow through intense introspection, hours of dialogue, and years of launch assessment reviews.

Phase and gate development methodology is a philosophy for product development oversight used to maintain financial control on development spending. It has brought much needed discipline to the development process and improvement for many companies, including Harley-Davidson. However, it has largely become a risk management protocol for distant and disengaged leadership. Toll gates throttle development and the process tends to instill bureaucracy. Our process sought to produce a flow of new products via a carefully architected development cadence. We were in the early stages of discovering and learning how to apply these concepts in our phase gate world. These concepts were new to us, but totally foreign to the selection committee. In spite of the strange language we used and the unusual antics we employed, the consistent business success intrigued the selection committee enough to take a closer look.

When we learned that we were a finalist for the OCI award, it created a whole host of challenges. We had to figure out how to explain the underlying philosophy of cadence and flow to the team of judges.

It meant explaining the importance of "hard dates" and "bins" and "swirl." We would have to demonstrate to the judges how our development process functioned by first explaining the concepts and then connecting them in a coherent manner to the development system. These concepts had become familiar to us as we used them every day, but for outsiders they were bizarre.

The judges spent a full day with us, which allowed us to immerse them in our process and convey the underlying principles of our product development philosophy. Although the selection committee could not comprehend the underlying philosophy or the intricacies of how we developed the principles, the judges understood enough to convince the selection committee that Harley-Davidson employed a progressive and unique development system that consistently delivered results.

Winning the OCI award meant we would share our process. We struggled to describe a development system based on philosophies few had heard of and concepts most people did not comprehend. But we believed we had an important message, so we labored in the conference room trying to pare our message to the bare essentials while making it understandable. We wanted to tell the story of our learning journey in the PDL^{2}T and systems thinking in a meaningful way. We grappled to describe how this experience established the creation of our development process. Unable to cover everything, we decided to focus on two of the more fundamental concepts we had employed: cadence and flow.

Product Development Flow

The backbone of business is new product development. Business success is derived through the repeated execution and the continuous improvement of key business processes. Achieving sustainable earnings growth requires a product development process that provides a continuous flow of new products for the business to exploit. The flow of new products fuels growth and prosperity by refreshing existing products and introducing new products to the market as innovation stimulates sales. Continuous improvement of the product development process to improve the flow of new products is essential for growth. Stagnant or inconsistent new product development is directly reflected in sluggish or unpredictable business performance.

As low-cost manufacturing has become universally available on a global basis, the ability to innovate and introduce new products has become the strategic differentiator for success. Companies become "one-hit wonders" when they introduce a phenomenal product or service, only to subsequently flounder and fail because they lack a process methodology to establish a flow of products.

Even more common than the one-hit wonders are companies with erratic development performance. These businesses may have a development process, but a hit-and-miss record for product introduction. While they produce enough new innovation to sustain the business, product development is unpredictable and inconsistent for generating the desired growth. Only a few companies have recognized that their success is dependent on the consistent and continual flow of new products and have succeeded in creating a system to achieve it. It is the persistent and relentless introduction cadence of new products connected to the business objectives for the company that establishes product development success and sustainable, predictable business growth. Harley-Davidson had become one of these companies.

Product Development Cadence

In the manufacturing environment, "takt time" refers to producing goods or services according to the pace of customer demand. Although the term has been in existence for a long time, lean manufacturing seems to have brought it back into vogue. Takt time is the most basic time element necessary to meet production requirements. It is the metronome that balances all aspects of production. Takt time (T_T) is defined as the available work time (T_A) divided by demand (D) for the products over the same period.

$$T_T = T_A / D$$

Through this definition, takt time can be broken down and defined for ever smaller elements of the production environment. It can be used to establish the production rate for a plant or for an individual machine or an assembly step. In a physical environment such as a manufacturing plant, takt time can be calculated by dividing the available time for production by the sales demand for the products (that is, the number of units needed). It can be measured through direct observation and paced by machines and assembly lines. Takt time determines the pace of production flow. The optimal flow is achieved when takt time is balanced across all steps in the operation.

The corollary to takt time for the product development environment is "cadence." In the product development environment cadence is the basic time element that supports flow. Cadence is the rhythm and the heartbeat that drives effective product development. When cadence is applied throughout the development system, it serves to synchronize the development activities according to demand. Takt time is a very critical concept as applied to the production environment, where product flow is visible. Cadence is even more critical in the product development environment, where flow is not inherently observable.

Takt time is crucial in balancing production with customer demand. Takt time provides immediate feedback to the lowest operational level in the process and identifies whether demand is being met or not. But how should takt time be calculated in a product development environment? What is the demand for new products? Sales may deem the demand for new products infinite if left up to them. What is the available time for development when engineers spread their time over multiple projects?

Cadence is the metronome to pace work in all areas of business outside standard, routine production. Just like air traffic controllers establish the landing patterns and cadence of airplanes to synchronize arrivals regardless of size, distance traveled, experience of the crew, or any other attribute, so that the planes follow an identical, predictable pattern when landing, a pattern and cadence that encompasses all aspects and varieties of projects in the development portfolio must be established in product development.

For product development, it is important to first establish a new product introduction rate to define the delivery cadence and synchronize the flow of work throughout the development system. The product introduction rate must be a planned pace negotiated across the business, in balance with achieving business objectives. Similar to takt time, this planned product development cadence provides the organization with the critical planning elements needed to organize work. The product introduction cadence may be one project per year or five products per month. It is critical that the cadence to drive product flow is clearly defined and tied to business objectives. Cadence can then establish a steady rhythm for the organization.

The idea of a product development cadence is not new. The alignment of cadence to product development is borrowed from Thomas Edison. In Edison's time it was generally believed that the act of invention was pure happenstance or isolated genius. Edison rebuffed this notion, stating, "Genius is 1 percent inspiration, 99 percent perspiration." Edison went on to demonstrate his conviction by bringing together the right people, in the right environment, with a disciplined process to create world-changing inventions on a regular basis. He drove his development staff hard to produce results. Working in an iterative and incremental manner, Edison set an objective of producing one minor invention every ten days and one major invention every six months.[1] The unique environment Edison pioneered in Menlo Park and West Orange, New Jersey, has been widely adopted in research and development organizations, but the notion of output cadence from Edison's "invention factory" has largely been lost.

The application of project management techniques to facilitate product development has become standard. Many businesses have established cross-functional, co-located teams to improve their product development process. Even chief engineers or heavyweight project managers have been put in place to drive project execution. Although each of these actions is put in place to aid project delivery, they often unintentionally pervert the fundamental need of multi-project product development, which is the need to establish consistent predictable flow through an organization-wide cadence.

When an organization focuses on driving optimization of each individual project, many seemingly logical efforts to improve product development unintentionally undermine the very goal they intend to accomplish. Actions that optimize individual projects generally serve to suboptimize the portfolio of projects as a whole. In the extreme case of the Beavertail project, for example, head-of-the-line privileges optimized the resolution of Beavertail issues while bringing many other development projects to a halt. Although much more subtle than the case of Beavertail, without first orchestrating a steady cadence in conjunction with the organization's business objectives and capability, work eventually conflicts and impacts the effectiveness of the development organization. In the case of significant shared resources it is worth noting that the impact is even more acute. When work bunches up, it causes project delays that in turn require shuffling priorities, which further exacerbates the problem. When projects are individually optimized, the bunching and delay of work creates a domino effect across the development portfolio. The whipsaw of work results in unpredictability in the development system, eventually forcing projects to be modified, delayed, or canceled altogether. This phenomenon is a primary contributor to ineffectiveness and unpredictability in product development

To unilaterally optimize the overall flow of projects across the entire development portfolio, a product development cadence must be established. To optimize the whole requires suboptimization of individual projects. However, establishment of product flow through a uniform cadence creates substantial improvement to the overall efficiency of the development system. Operating to the appropriate cadence provides for the most efficient and effective use of resources and facilitates planning across the entire organization.

When product development cadence is established it is possible to describe the relationship between the product introduction rate, the size of the project portfolio, and the project completion time mathematically. Borrowing from the discipline of queuing theory, Little's Law states that the long-term average number of customers in a stable system (N) is equal to the long-term average arrival rate multiplied by the long-term average time a customer spends in the system (T), depicted as:

$$N = \lambda T, \text{ or } \lambda = N/T \text{ }^2$$

By manipulating Little's Law to fit product development, the new product introduction rate—development throughput (TH)—is found by dividing the work in process in the development portfolio (WIP) by the time to complete a project (CT), which can be shown as:

$$TH = WIP/CT$$

The cadence of new products can be determined from this relationship. Why is this important? Leadership must determine the rate of new product introduction (TH) that supports their long-term business objectives. This can only be the role of senior leadership because it often involves deselecting highly desirable projects from the portfolio (WIP) to balance the capability of the development organization. Leadership must then proactively manage the development system to ensure that projects start, progress, and launch according to a steady cadence (CT).

Projects within a portfolio vary in scope, scale, and complexity. It is important to be cognizant of the factors that drive the ability to deliver projects when development cadence is established. The characteristics that make a large, complex, new technology project succeed are different from those required for routine changes to existing products. Yet in order to establish cadence, all types of projects must mesh cohesively.

When priorities are shifted or projects are canceled and replaced with other projects it disrupts cadence and reintroduces the waste and inefficiency that cadence is intended to eliminate. Although there is tremendous pressure to gyrate among projects or to vary the output of the development organization due to the constant influx of new customer information, both must be carefully managed. Just as in the manufacturing organization where production leveling (*heijunka*) is critical, the product development organization works most effectively and efficiently when it adheres to a smooth synchronous cadence. Over the long term, both the company and its customers are best served by establishing and maintaining a predictable robust cadence.

The Application of Cadence and Flow

The PDL²T learned about the systems dynamics aspects of flows and the impact of delays over many sessions. Working through systems models highlighted the tremendous inefficiencies created by the lags and delays inherent in complex systems. The study with MIT further applied the principles of flows and delays directly to the Harley-Davidson product development environment. Yet true learning and ultimately comprehension only happens by moving between the domains of thinking and doing. The PDL²T turned into a "thinking committee" over time. "Doing" remained the obligation of individual members who had enough conviction and belief to take action.

The initial application of cadence and flow to the Harley-Davidson product development process began with Anthony Reese's frustration in the organization's inability to budget. Anthony was responsible for engineering planning and took the initiative to apply what was learned to his area. As a strategic thinker and insightful individual, he took action to drive the application of cadence and flow principles to planning the engineering budgets. Through astute observation of historical engineering spending data, he recognized that there were certain types of projects that repeatedly occurred.

To simplify engineering planning, Anthony forced project leaders to designate their projects according to specific criteria, and defined as small, medium, or large projects. The three project classifications were based on an evaluation of historical engineering budget data in an attempt to move the organization toward a smoother workload. This segmentation of projects was intended to simplify engineering planning by establishing standard project types. Within the engineering environment, projects varied in scope, scale, and complexity. Large, complex, new technology projects had significantly different characteristics for success than routine changes to existing products. These budget planning designations helped to quantify project objectives to move from chaotic workloads to standard categories of engineering efforts.

Another factor which supported the establishment of cadence and flow in the product development process was that Harley-Davidson introduced new products on an annual cycle. New models were introduced at the dealer show every July. The annual dealer show is a huge week-long party for dealers and principals held at a different location around the country. The event is always the biggest event of the year for sales and marketing, and is intended to energize the dealer network

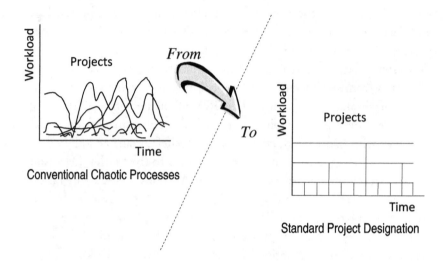

into placing orders. All aspects of The Motor Company are involved in the annual event to some degree. Although sales and marketing lead the show, even service and dealer training play a role. It is the single most significant selling event for The Motor Company.

The high point of the show is always the unveiling of the new models. When it comes time to unveil the new models, the crowd gathers in the exhibit hall with bated breath. People arrive well in advance to stake out their spot to see the show. The new models are introduced with pomp and flair. They are unveiled on stage with a fanfare of smoke, lights, and music to the eagerly awaiting audience. The excitement electrifies through the crowd. The new products draw a chorus of oohs and aahs as people get a glimpse of the products. Enthusiasm builds as people cheer and clap. No project leader wants to miss this event when their project is unveiled. This annual introduction event, which signals the start of production, drives the completion timing of projects.

The combination of standardization of project types with the convergence of projects in July established the foundational elements of cadence and flow. From a project management perspective, there are three variables to manage: scope, schedule, and resources. Historical data indicated that successful projects used approximately the same amount of resources within each project classification. This allowed fixing the project resource allocation for each project type. The completion deadline of July fixed the end point of the schedule. Fixing the starting point of projects bound the allowable scope of projects. Having these three fixed project management variables allowed standard elements for capacity planning and budgeting.

Bins

The result of standardizing the three elements of project management (scope, schedule, and resource) established elements of work that became known as "bin" classifications. The use of bins established a cadence of projects and set the foundation for aggregate resource planning. Aligning this cadence to customer demand allowed coordinating the sales and marketing needs with the resource constraints of the development organization.

The obligation to align the business and market needs with the product development capacity fell on the Product Planning Committee (PPC). The PPC was the organizational body charged with keeping the portfolio of products relevant and was responsible for long-term strategic product planning. It was the job of the PPC to make sure that Harley-Davidson had a steady flow of cool products to sell. The committee included the president of Harley-Davidson Motor Company and key vice presidents from each of the functional areas responsible for creating or selling new products. The PPC had the knowledge and power to balance the business needs with the business capabilities. The PPC was the intersection of creating demand (manufacturing customers) and producing product (manufacturing products). The PPC had the responsibility to align the development cadence with the business growth needs. Bins became the standard product development building blocks used by the PPC for product planning.

Bins were important because they allowed the organization to plan and align resources for projects by rightsizing project scope to strike a balance between business needs and development capabilities. Sales, marketing, styling, and engineering identified opportunities in the market and presented them to the Product Planning Committee. In turn, the PPC created the product life cycle plan and the project portfolio to deliver it. No individual project was necessarily optimal because it was constrained to fit within the preset parameters of bins. However, the overall portfolio greatly benefited by the ability to manage the overall life cycle of all the projects through standard building blocks. The PPC was able to create a cadence of projects that flowed through the development organization to fill the combined needs of the business. Bins became program management shorthand in segmenting development projects into risk/complexity/resource families.

Bin designations segmented projects into six categories based on the risk associated with delivering the project, and the magnitude of the project. The specific bin designation was based on the project hours (small, medium, or large), the timing (standard timing or off timing), and the degree to which the project team intended to follow the standard methodology (follow standard methodology or only complete statements of work).

Major breakthrough development efforts were classified as bin 6 projects. They were intended to create revolutionary new platforms of products to reach new customers or major redesign of existing product platforms. These projects were strategic in nature, intended to significantly grow the business and energize customers over a long time horizon. Bin 6 projects were often used as the mechanism to reach out to

	Bin 1	Bin 2	Bin 3	Bin 4	Bin 5	Bin 6
Follows Process	Yes	Yes	No	Yes	Yes	Yes
Follows Timing	Yes	No	No	Yes	No	Yes

Bin Designations

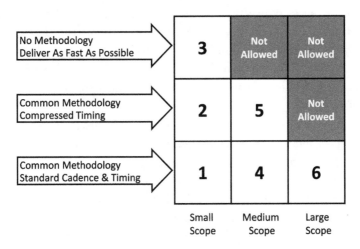

new customers not served by the existing products or stimulate the existing customers to "trade in and trade up." Due to the risk and complexity associated with these projects they were always required to complete all statements of work, follow standard methodology, and adhere to standard timing.

The intent of medium-sized bin 4 and 5 projects was to develop major derivative products. Bin 4 and 5 products were evolutionary extensions of existing product lines and tactical in nature. These projects were intended to support the business primarily through meeting the needs of customers already in the Harley-Davidson family. Medium-sized projects were always expected to adhere to the development methodology, but in order to address an unforeseen market opportunity, medium-size projects could be executed under compressed timing. Due to the disruption to the cadence and subsequent decreased product flow caused by their compressed timing, bin 5 projects were highly discouraged and rarely done

Small projects were primarily operational in nature, although they could entail an evolutionary new model for an existing platform. They were primarily intended to support the business through serving existing customers. Bin 1 projects delivered changes ranging from small product enhancements to new models. Bin 2 projects were similar to bin 1 projects except executed under compressed timing. Bin 3 projects were small changes that needed to be done immediately. These were generally introduced as a running change to products in production to address a safety, quality, manufacturing, or legal concern. Bin 3 projects only needed to complete the appropriate statements of work to introduce the change.

New product development risks fall into two broad classifications: project risks and market risks. Project risk increases with increased size and complexity of a project while market risk increases with decreased reach and distinctiveness. The standardization of projects into bin classifications was intended to minimize both of these risk categories by aligning bin designations at the minimum total combined market and project risk level. Anthony Reese was instrumental in developing this concept and would often draw the diagram below to help explain the concept to others.

Standardization of bin designations attempted to find an equilibrium between these opposing risk factors. Market risk for new products increases when the project does not provide enough significant differentiation from previous or competitive products to have the desired impact in the market. Market risk is the risk that after a product

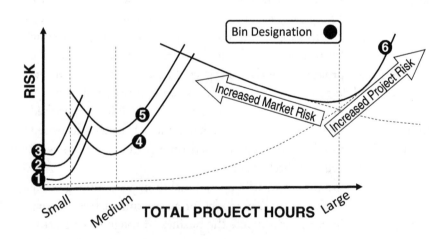

has launched and the development investment has been made, sales do not materialize to recoup the investment. Market risks go up as project scope decreases for any given category of project type.

Project risks are those risks associated with the management complexities and technical reach of delivering a project. The greater the technical challenges and the larger the development team required to deliver a project, the greater the project risks. Large bin 6 projects inherently have the greatest overall risks. To reduce the project risks, bin 6 projects were executed through dedicated, co-located teams. They had seasoned, full-time project managers and received the greatest oversight, support, and attention. Medium-sized projects were significantly less complex, so although they generally had dedicated project leaders, the rest of the project team was part time and the team was not located together. Small projects have the lowest overall risk and as a result generally did not have a dedicated project leader. All the team members for small projects tended to be part-time participants in an ad hoc team environment.

Heuristic Rules of Thumb

The cadence and flow of bins dictated how the entire development organization was planned, organized, and managed. Bin designations allowed the organization to operate at peak efficiency by rightsizing projects as a part of the life cycle plan. Bin designation also facilitated portfolio and life cycle management by aligning a cadence of projects to flow through the product development system.

Cadence is critical to the innovation process. Although depicted in the figure on the next page as a uniform pattern across all business areas or platforms, bins could shift in sequence within a business area/platform or across business areas/platforms. The primary determinant for bin placement was for market demand to pull new products through the system. The prioritization of projects and scheduling of bins was managed by the PPC. The established formula required that total aggregate resource load across all business areas should equal the planned available capacity of the development organization. Since bins

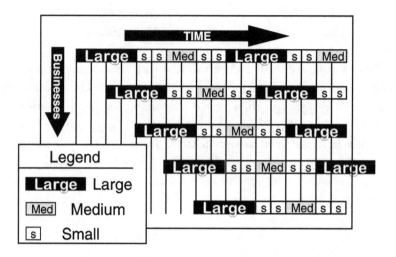

had standard designations of scope, schedule, and resources, the resource burn rate was understood. The aggregate burn rate of all the bins at any given point in time needed to be less than or equal to the development system's capacity.

This system not only established a flow of product, it also allowed the design of the organization. The number of business areas/platforms that could be supported could be determined and planned. The resource needs of the organization could be established well in advance. Even the development space, laboratory equipment, and type of research and development environment could be deliberately planned.

As the leadership worked with the system and learned from direct application, heuristic rules of thumb evolved. Due to the disruption to flow and the added complexity to the system, only three types of projects were encouraged, bin 1, 4, and 6. Bin 2, 3, and 5 projects were highly discouraged in favor of streamlining projects to fit within a standard classification. Due to the strain on the team, no back-to-back bin 6 projects were allowed for the same project team or business area. Double bin 6 projects (simultaneous development of a complete new chassis platform and new engine family, for example) required two years off until the next bin 6 project to let the system recover. Based on the capacity designed in the development system at the time and the balance between bin 6 platforms feeding bin 1 models, a maximum of three bin 6 projects could be accommodated in the pipeline at a time. To create the product life cycle plan, bin 6 projects were placed first, followed by bin 4s, then filled to capacity with bin 1 projects.

To ensure proper cadence, the flow of projects was managed and throttled by the product life cycle plan. The PPC determined the appropriate alignment of bins in accordance to their perceived market demand for product. At times the PPC expanded proposed projects or scaled them back to "rightsize" projects to fit a particular bin size and desired cadence. The constant cadence of projects in the form of bins created a flow of new products through the Product Development System. Projects in the form of bins fell into a rigorous development execution cycle. Once a project was selected in the product life cycle plan by the PPC and determined to be feasible, it was expected to launch according to a set schedule

To maintain development progress within the set schedule across the entire portfolio of projects, the schedule component of project management was standardized. Hard dates were set for exiting phase gates. Hard dates are annual fixed dates on the calendar for each phase exit in the development process. These hard dates were consistent from year to year based on the launch date and bin size of the project. Hard dates also maintained flow because they allowed the entire organization to align plans and converge based on key project criteria. Due to the synchronized cadence created through this alignment, everyone in the organization knew when their service would be needed for every project.

The Innovation Swirl

The flow of new products was fed by the "swirl." The swirl is named for the conceptual depiction of a constant and continual "swirl" of ideas ever present and under consideration. These concepts, ideas, and business opportunities came into the system throughout the year, and swirled and churned behind a firewall that prevented the barrage of enthusiasm and creativity from overwhelming the development organization. Moving ideas through the firewall and assigning them to a bin to carry them through the development system was the role of the Product Planning Committee. As business concepts passed through the firewall they exited in the form of a bin. Ideally all projects would fit neatly within the bin format of 1, 4, or 6, although 2, 3, and 5 were also possible.

In the swirl, ideas circulated in a "swirl" of conversation competing for attention, time, and legitimacy. Within the swirl coalition building began as key individuals learned about the ideas. Concepts and ideas were assessed based on financial cost and organizational effort. They were evaluated based on the "common good" of the company versus one fraction of the business, and they were assessed against other ideas in the swirl and the ever changing market forces. Affection for the idea would grow and a high-level champion would emerge, or the concept would remain in the swirl ever churning and evolving.[3]

The role of the PPC was to constantly evaluate the market needs and feed the product life cycle plan to meet the business objectives. Although there was no formal process for consideration of a particular concept, the "zone of consideration" began as market forces, business

The Swirl Model

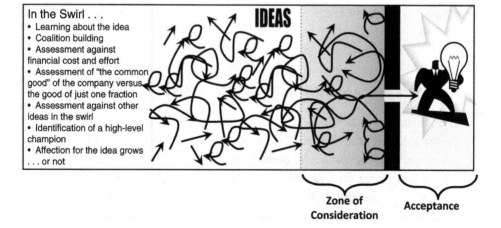

In the Swirl . . .
- Learning about the idea
- Coalition building
- Assessment against financial cost and effort
- Assessment of "the common good" of the company versus the good of just one fraction
- Assessment against other ideas in the swirl
- Identification of a high-level champion
- Affection for the idea grows
. . . or not

IDEAS

Zone of Consideration

Acceptance

needs, and ideas aligned. Ideas came into legitimate contention when the consequences of the change became apparent in the context of business and market drivers.

Before an idea passed through the firewall, the political will and fortitude of the ideas and supporters was tested and vetted. Although formal acceptance of an idea was documented in meeting minutes, the actual decision rarely occurred in the meeting. Acceptance of an idea occurred over a period of time through multiple conversations and dialogue. Some ideas exist in the swirl for many years before they evolve or morph into a concept with enough support and legitimacy to fill a market need. Official "acceptance" of an idea only occurs when there has been sufficient support created and the idea has withstood sufficient challenge; subsequently, the PPC assigns a project team to evaluate the concept in the context of a bin. Formal acceptance takes place when the concept passes through the rigor of the firewall, is approved through vote, and scheduled on the product life cycle plan.

Concepts and ideas stay in the swirl until they evolve, expand, contract, and have a passionate champion that can sell the concept up, down, and across the organization. Concepts are rarely killed once they have been accepted because of the rigor of the swirl and the firewall that identifies successful projects and prevents the wrong concepts from emerging. Once an idea exits the swirl and is approved, the project team drives the project to launch through the phase gate methodology. Cadence and flow, bins and swirl all work in harmony to ensure a continual stream of new products to drive profitable sales growth for the company.

Harmonious execution across the enterprise is crucial to maximize the effectiveness and efficiency of the product development system. Although ideas are encouraged to constantly enter the swirl, it is important that they pass through the firewall at the proper cadence, matched with the organization's capacity and in accordance to the business objectives of the company. In addition, appropriate vetting of ideas ensures organizational commitment and minimizes the likelihood that the project will be killed prior to launch or fail in the market.

CHAPTER 7

Supply and Demand

Don't judge each day by the harvest you reap but by the seeds that you plant.

Robert Louis Stevenson

"**Y**ou're an idiot! Why the hell would we want to change the development process?" "It's going great! We're growing every quarter." "Every motorcycle we make is sold. There's a waiting list of people wanting to buy our motorcycles!" "We're the best. Stop trying to fix something that isn't broken." It seemed that almost everyone had the same sentiment. From every direction, the message was the same.

The worrying and sleepless nights had started months before any involvement with the PDMA or any outside evaluation of our process. The reason to compete for the OCI award had been to see how good we really were and to learn how to get better. Great companies are paranoid. They are afraid of falling behind, afraid of losing their edge, and afraid they might falter. I had seen it when I first joined Harley-Davidson. The people who had survived the darkest days never wanted to see them return, and they were paranoid. You could see it in their eyes and hear it in their voices. Over time the organization grew and changed. New people joined the company, diluting the memories of the past. Confidence and arrogance has a way of creeping in with success. In the eyes of some, complacency had begun to set in.

There was no rational reason for concern. Life was good. The development process was humming along. In fact, it was at redline, running flat out as it churned out exciting new products. The cadence of new products flowed predictably for the most part. There were plenty of issues to deal with, but that was to be expected from any complex system. But I was uneasy. I worried about what lay in wait below the surface. I was concerned that product development could not develop new products fast enough to support the aggressive business growth objectives.

Every business has two primary functions, manufacturing customers and manufacturing products. For many years Harley-Davidson had manufactured customers at a rate much faster than they could manufacture products. Beginning in 1986 when Harley-Davidson went public, there was a surge of new products introduced that powered the rebirth of the company. From 1986 through 1999 Harley-Davidson more than doubled the number of motorcycle models available through its dealerships from eleven to twenty-one, as depicted in Figure 7–1 below. The introduction of new products without the capacity to produce them created a backlog of hungry and eager customers.

The introduction of high-quality new products fueled the desire for Harley-Davidson motorcycles. The rapid escalation of new product offerings had created the resurgence of the company. But in so doing, the desire for the new products manufactured more customers than the production plants could produce motorcycles to support. The backlog of customers created waiting lists, with some customers having to wait as much as two years for their new motorcycle. Customers often took any motorcycle that was available rather than wait for the specific color and model they might have wanted.

For a company still reeling from a close call with bankruptcy, the response to the backlog was appropriately conservative. Initially, the response was slow and deliberate as the supply-demand imbalance grew. For a company that had so recently struggled to survive it must have felt good to have a backlog of customers. At the same time, there was also a nagging concern that the backlog of customers was not real

Figure 7.1

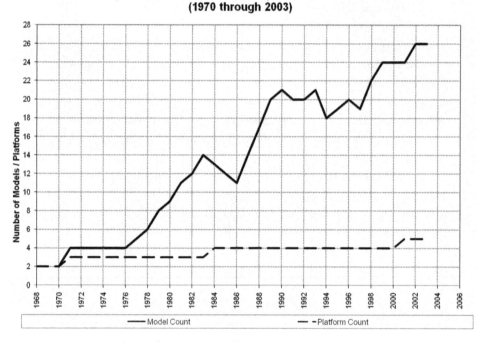

**Harley-Davidson Available Motorcycle Models & Platforms
(1970 through 2003)**

and that the demand for Harleys would evaporate. Perhaps the high demand for motorcycles was a fad and the customer backlog was a temporary fluke. Investing too much money too quickly to create a product manufacture rate that was too high would not be prudent.

In the past, demand for motorcycles had fluctuated, but this time the imbalance and the backlog of customers continued to grow. Dealers no longer sold motorcycles but rather managed a waiting list of customers. As the list of waiting customers continued to grow, some dealers saw an opportunity and took advantage of the imbalance of supply and demand as they increased their prices in excess of The Motor Company's manufacturer's suggested retail price. Many customers became discouraged and bought from the competition, allowing other brands to enter the American heavyweight custom and cruiser motorcycle markets dominated by Harley-Davidson.

For a long time, Harley-Davidson's growth was throttled by its limited ability to produce products. When demand far exceeds supply, there is little direct pressure on product development to fuel growth. From 1990 through 1997 the introduction of additional new models slowed as the introduction of new products prior to 1990 drove demand well beyond what the factories could supply. Leadership attention was squarely placed on manufacturing operations to increase production. Getting quality products out the door became the singular strategic focus for the company. The growth of the company became purely a function of how much product could be manufactured and shipped each quarter.

Harley-Davidson was forced to address the customer backlog as demand continued to outstrip supply. Although initial response to the issue was conservative, it grew more aggressive over time. By 1997 Harley-Davidson's response went beyond refurbishing plants to building entirely new production facilities. Between 1997 and 1998 Harley-Davidson opened the Pilgrim Road engine factory in Menomonee Falls, Wisconsin, and the vehicle assembly plant in Kansas City, Missouri. These two facilities doubled the number of vehicle assembly and engine manufacturing facilities in the company, which was reflected in the revenue and profit numbers, shown in Figure 7–2.

Revenue and profits grew handsomely as the ability to produce products grew. Production operations did their part to manufacture products as the product manufacturing rate climbed from below 50,000 units in 1986 to over 250,000 units in 2002. The company became accustomed to the dramatic growth as every quarter resulted in a new record for units shipped to customers, sales revenue, and profit. After a near-death experience, life was good as Harley-Davidson eclipsed more than eighty consecutive quarters of growth and prosperity. The true American icon was alive and well. Over the twenty-year period since the initial public offering (IPO) in 1986, revenue grew at an astonishing 17 percent compound annual growth rate (CAGR). Profits grew at an even more amazing CAGR, between 25 and 36 percent.

New products created desire and drove sales as customers traded in and traded up. An ever broadening array of new models, styles, and

Figure 7.2

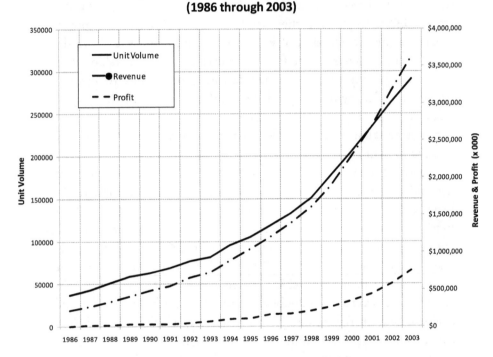

**Harley-Davidson Unit Volume, Revenue, & Profit
(1986 through 2003)**

features brought new people to the sport of motorcycling and to the Harley-Davidson brand. Harley-Davidson's market share grew to well over half in the classifications in which they produced products. As Harley-Davidson began commanding a significant majority of market share, the only way to continue to grow was to grow the motorcycle market as a whole. And grow the market they did, as they proactively set out to create and execute a product life cycle plan to manufacture new customers: the U.S. motorcycle market grew at rates unseen since the return of the GIs after World War II.

The swirl of ideas and the cadence of bins that delivered the flow of new products were controlled by the Product Life Cycle Plan. Although bins identified the type of project and vehicle platforms defined the commonly shared design attributes, customers don't care about bins and platform architecture. Ultimately, customers purchase a specific motorcycle model. Sales are dependent on the right model being available and exciting the emotions of a prospective customer so they will buy it. Buying a motorcycle is not a rational decision. It is an emotional decision. Thus the role of product development is to refresh and introduce an ever widening array of exciting products.

The sale of products is dependent on having the right model available for sale when a customer comes into the dealership. It is the responsibility of the development organization to refresh existing models to make sure they remain relevant and to introduce new models to drive excitement. Between 1970 and 2003 Harley-Davidson averaged the ability to simultaneously refresh existing products while introducing new products at a rate of 0.74 additional models per year. In other words, Harley-Davidson could maintain the existing models and introduce an additional new model in three out of four consecutive years.

As the capacity to manufacture products increased and more products were shipped to customers, the backlog of customers decreased.

Figure 7.3

Harley-Davidson OE Available Motorcycle Model Count, Revenue & Profit (1970 through 2003)

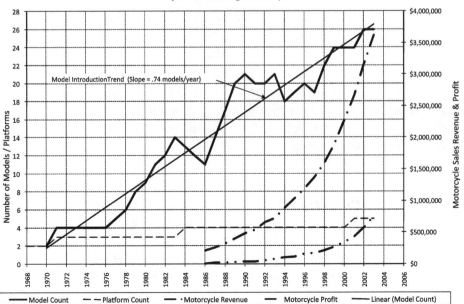

Harley-Davidson began preparing the business for an eventual reduction in growth rate and began to talk about a "soft landing." A soft landing was intended to gradually align supply and demand as growth slowed over time. Many in the investment community had already anticipated that the growth rate could not be sustained.

Concern grew in small pockets that growth could not be sustained at the incredible rate seen in the past. Sales revenue had grown at an exponential rate while new product introductions had expanded linearly on average. If new product introduction truly influenced revenue growth then at some point as the customer backlog eroded, the growth rate would converge to the introduction and refresh rate of new products. Based on the investments in production capacity, the limits to growth were shifting from our ability to manufacture products to our ability to manufacture customers. Growth would become dependent on our ability to attract new customers.

The concern over reduced growth rates was not universally held, and an appropriate course of action for the business was debated. System dynamics modeling provides insight into the behavior of complex systems and can be used as a means to extract mental models so people can express what they are thinking. System dynamics models can also be created via computer programs to predict the behavior of complex systems. A computer-based systems model is created by expressing the interdependencies of interactions within the system in terms of numerical equations. The systems model can then be tested and validated by feeding it past data so that it in turn can predict future behaviors of the system. Although system dynamics models may not always be explicitly accurate (they don't provide the exact number), they are very effective in providing insight for strategic decisions (they accurately identify trends and compare alternatives well).

The System Dynamics Model
of the Motorcycle Business

Through our work with MIT, a system dynamics model of the motorcycle business had been created and was used to provide insight into policy decisions for the company. The existing model was updated and validated to provide insight into the appropriate course of action related to supply and demand. The model was intended to provide deeper understanding of the business condition by learning from history how the system behaved in the past, then evaluate and test decision options to predict what would happen in the future under each scenario. Some of the directly observable historical data that fed the model included factors such as the average waiting time for a new bike, the average actual price paid for new bikes compared to the manufacturer's suggested retail price (MSRP), and the average price paid for used bikes, as shown in Figure 7–4. Based on a wide variety of input data, the model projected the aggregate demand for new Harley-Davidson motorcycles. With knowledge of the production rate and planned shipments, the model could calculate the demand-supply ratio and show how it changed over time.

Company revenue is a function of the conversion rate in filling orders based on customer demand through the shipment of products. If the rate at which products are manufactured exceeds the rate at which customers are manufactured, then the backlog of customers re-

Figure 7.4

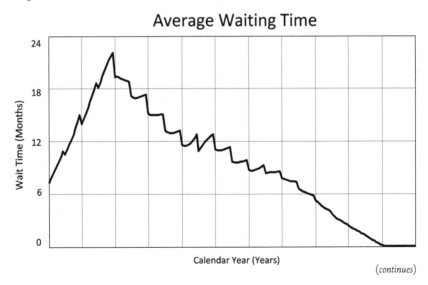

Average Waiting Time

(continues)

Figure 7.4 (continued)

Average New Bike Street Price vs. MSRP

Average Used Bike Street Price vs. Original MSRP

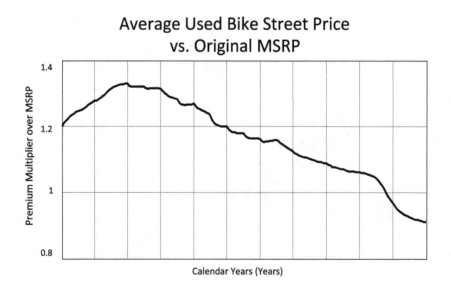

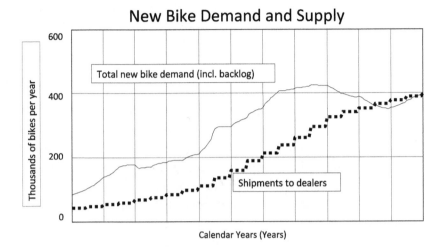

duces. Once the backlog of customers is exhausted, any excess ship-ment of product beyond the customer demand results in increased dealer inventory. An excessive increase in dealer inventory beyond a temporary adjustment carries with it the potential of a tipping point in price if the demand–supply ratio flips below 1.

Sustainable, long-term revenue growth is limited to the aggregate manufacture rate of customers. Revenue can grow faster than the cus-tomer manufacture rate if there is a backlog of demand because some customers will pay extra for a limited supply. Long-term company growth is sustained when the demand–supply ratio remains equal to or greater than 1. As indicated in the New Bike Demand and Supply graph above, the demand-to-supply gap was narrowing. It also pre-dicted that without intervention the gap would close completely and flip below 1. Although the model was not accurate enough to pinpoint the exact date this condition would occur, the time was clearly near.

Building the business model provided a useful means for testing the consequences of a variety of potential policy decisions. The model was used to learn if the condition could be averted or how best to address the impending condition. Improving the demand-supply ratio either meant increasing demand or reducing supply. The three most plausible options explored were to reduce shipments (reduce the manufacture rate of products), increase marketing (increase manufacture rate of customers), and invest in new products (increase manufacture rate of customers).

A Soft Landing by Reducing Shipments

The idea of a soft landing to gradually bring supply in line with demand was an ideal scenario. For many years Harley-Davidson had been reaping the benefits of pent-up demand. Customers had been manufactured much faster than production capacity could be installed. Bringing the growth of the company in line with the rate of manufacturing customers would allow long-term alignment of supply and demand. However, this meant a reduction of the incredible growth the company had enjoyed and to which the investment community had grown accustomed. The business model indicated that this was a very viable and plausible strategic option (see Figure 7–5). Reducing the planned growth of the company by 20 percent would result in a leveling off of supply and demand in about five years. Reducing the planned growth rate by 40 percent reduced the trend faster, but neither option was extremely attractive since it required scaling back the growth rate of the company.

Generating Product Demand

Sales and marketing departments are traditionally tasked with manufacturing customers; that is, generating product demand. Advertising and promotions are the common tools used to create customer interest and product awareness and drive sales. Depending on the industry, many companies invest large sums of money through their marketing and sales departments to generate customer interest and drive demand. The study of advertising and promotions effectiveness has become an important science in identifying the type and the degree to which marketing efforts companies invest and to ensure appropriate returns. In

Figure 7.5

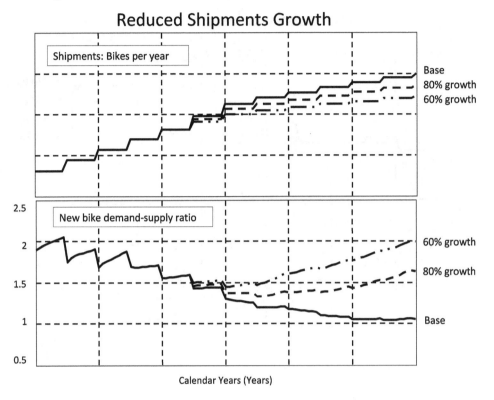

Reduced Shipments Growth

determining the best course of action to improve the demand-supply ratio, increasing the marketing budget was an important element to evaluate as an alternative.

As expected, the business model reflected the hypothesis that increased marketing spurs customer demand. The model predicted that advertising and promotional efforts would have an immediate effect on increased customer demand. Through a sensitivity analysis, increased spending levels of 25, 50, and 75 percent were evaluated. In every case the model predicted that increasing the marketing budget increased customer demand and improves the demand-supply ratio without the need to reduce shipments. The overall impact and the time required to recover from the drop in the demand-supply ratio varied from three

Figure 7.6

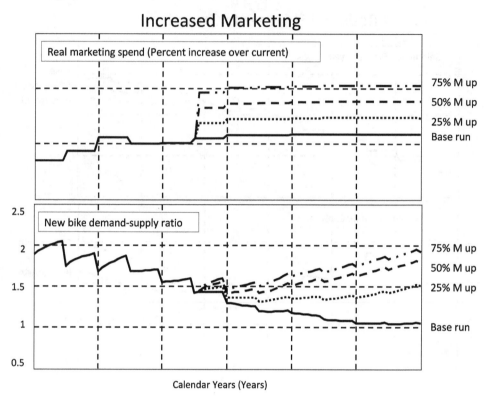

to seven years depending on the amount spending increased. The business model verified that increasing marketing is a viable means to increase customer demand, supporting the action many companies take.

Developing New Products

Introduction of new products was the final business strategy evaluated. The model predicted that introduction of new products has the greatest and longest lasting impact on the demand–supply ratio (see Figure 7–7). The degree of impact is dependent on the significance of the product introduced. A bin 6 project, for example, provides an immedi-

Figure 7.7

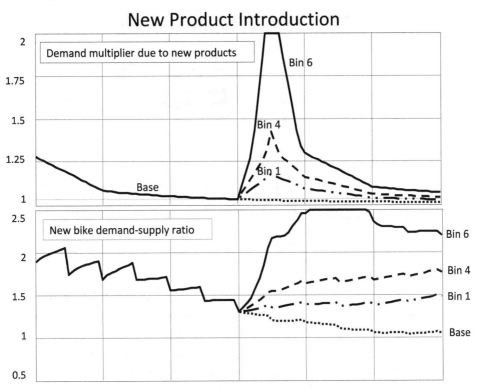

New Product Introduction

Calendar Years (Years)

ate surge in customer demand with the residual impact lasting more than six years (see Figure 7–8). Even a bin 1 project has as much effect on the demand-supply ratio as a 50 percent increase in marketing. So from a strategic investment perspective, investing in new products has the greatest impact on customer demand and the best return on investment. Introducing new products has an immediate and profound effect on the demand–supply ratio and is significantly better for driving growth than other alternatives.

The significance of the study is that it clearly pointed to improved product development as the strategic direction for maintaining long-term growth. The model explicitly linked growth with the introduction of

Figure 7.8

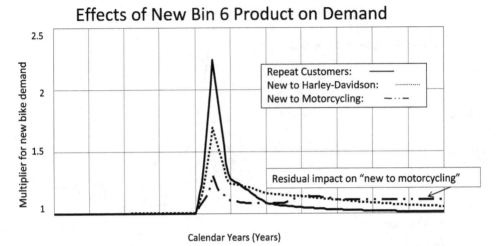

Effects of New Bin 6 Product on Demand

Repeat Customers: ——
New to Harley-Davidson: ....
New to Motorcycling: — ·· —

Residual impact on "new to motorcycling"

Multiplier for new bike demand

Calendar Years (Years)

new products. Although the specific impact on demand varied depending on specific customer segments, product development was clearly defined as the key to successful long-term growth. Understanding the role that new product introduction played for growth and quantifying the impact by bin and customer segment reinforced the importance of a clearly articulated product life cycle plan to facilitate cadence and flow.

Not everyone was convinced that the output of the study was accurate. There wasn't much argument about the strategic direction the model suggested, but rather that a problem existed at all. Many didn't see the current situation as a problem. Business was booming and sales were projected to keep going up.

In spite of mixed opinions, for a few, the situation needed to be addressed. There was no proof or concrete evidence, but improvement of the product development system became a priority for a small group that believed the predictions of the model. To increase customer demand meant the product development organization would have to improve the throughput of new products, and we set out to achieve it.

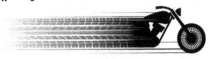

CHAPTER 8

A Left Turn: Implementing Lean Principles in Product Development

It's what you learn after you know it all that counts.

John Wooden

"Don't bring lean manufacturing upstream to product development! The application of lean in product development and manufacturing are different. Some aspects may look similar, but they are not! Be very leery of an expert with experience in lean manufacturing that claims to know product development." Jim Womack's words stung as I hung up the phone. I thought I had landed on the perfect solution to improve product development and drive growth. The application of lean tools and techniques worked so well in manufacturing, why couldn't I apply them to product development?

The most important aspect of fixing a problem is to be clear about

131

the problem you are trying to solve. I called Jim to figure out how to apply lean manufacturing to product development, but I had jumped to a solution. In reality, there wasn't even agreement there was a problem, let alone what it was. Business was booming and Harley-Davidson's sales continued to climb. The company boldly announced that we intended to continue our double-digit growth indefinitely. Yet in spite of all the optimism, for some of us, a crisis loomed.

The system model identified the need to improve new product throughput even though there was not yet proof or any outward appearance of a problem. We were manufacturing products faster than we manufactured new customers. We had crossed the tipping point but the backlog of customers protected the business as pent up demand delayed the consequences. With growth planned in the double digits and budgets capped at 2 percent there was at least an 8 percent gap if supply and demand were in line, so we seized closing the 8 percent gap as the incentive to improve product development. Closing the 8 percent gap became the motivation for improving product development effectiveness and efficiency even though some feared that the problem was much worse.

The application of a phase gate approach to product development has brought improvement to many companies due to the structure and discipline of the process. Harley-Davidson is one of those companies that benefited from introduction of a phase gate methodology. The OCI award even recognized Harley-Davidson as an exemplar and progressive company in traditional methods, a company for others to emulate. Executing the current system better might provide marginal benefit, but we needed much more than marginal improvement. We needed a paradigm shift and it had become obvious that the phase gate process that once provided us a benefit had become a millstone around our neck. The principles of phases and gates originally introduced to create discipline and structure in an amorphous environment was holding us back. The use of gates intended to reduce financial risk did not facilitate flow.

Harley-Davidson's average new product introduction rate of one additional model in three out of four years had served us well, but the system dynamics model predicted it would no longer be enough. We needed more output, not by spending more or working harder, but by working smarter. Increasing output by adding more people and more equipment was not the answer. We needed to fundamentally change our working habits and culture. We had to find a way to improve the effectiveness and efficiency of the product development system, rather than working harder, adding more people, or adding more equipment. I had returned to my old dilemma—there had to be a way to work smarter rather than harder. We needed a left turn.

Harley-Davidson's product planning committee refers to revolutionary new products as "left turns." Left turns are radical departures form the identified trajectory. A left turn cuts against the grain. Riding in a straight line is simple and right turns take little thought or expertise. Left turns are daring. A left turn takes thought, timing, and planning in order to cross the flow of oncoming traffic. Left turns are unexpected and difficult to follow. "Left turn" products establish market separation and create leadership positions. Left turns are the cool new products no one expects but that have tremendous impact on the business. We had introduced plenty of "left-turn" products, but now we needed a left turn in the way we developed our products.

The introduction of lean techniques to manufacturing has transformed the landscape of the traditional manufacturing environment. Implementing lean techniques in manufacturing has allowed organizations to work smarter with quantum improvements in effectiveness and efficiency. This was the result we needed. Perhaps bringing the lean techniques employed in manufacturing upstream into product development could provide similar results.

Don't Bring Lean Manufacturing Upstream

My learning journey to adapt lean manufacturing principles to product development began with a call to Jim Womack, head of the Lean Enterprise Institute. I had met Jim briefly while I was studying at the Massachusetts Institute of Technology. He had been involved in the seminal study in association with MIT that uncovered the notion of "lean." The term had been coined in the book *The Machine that Changed the World* to refer to the lack of waste in the Toyota production system.[1]

Jim was the researcher and author who brought "lean" to the world's attention, so I enthusiastically called him for his advice. His advice: "Don't try to bring lean manufacturing upstream to product development!" burst my bubble. It was not what I wanted to hear as I started my journey on wobbly legs. "We're focused on manufacturing," Jim had told me when I asked him for help. "Try calling Allen Ward; he studied the Toyota product development system." My hopes were rekindled when Jim suggested I contact Dr. Ward at the University of Michigan.

It took a while to track Allen down. When I finally did, the reception I got was not much warmer than what I had received from Jim. I began to wonder why no one wanted to talk about lean product development. Perhaps no one wanted to share their secrets, or maybe they didn't really understand it, I mused. "Buy my book and call me when you've read it," Allen told me over the phone. I ordered the book from Dollar Bill books. I remembered Dollar Bill as a little hole-in-the-wall photocopy shop at the University of Michigan from my college days. I did not expect much from a copy shop, perhaps a syllabus or class notes. When the book arrived, it consisted of eighty-four spiral-bound 3-inch by 5-inch photocopied pages filled with unintelligible gibberish between two laminated card stock covers. It would have been generous to call it a book. My initial instinct was to drop this crazy notion of lean product development, or just go against Jim's advice and implement lean manufacturing techniques on my own. I had already talked to a number of the big consulting companies. Most were still promoting implementation of phase gate methods. Others had lean manufacturing people applying the manufacturing tools in the non-manufacturing space. I wanted more and expected more, so I slogged on, determined to get someone's attention.

"Allen, I read your book," I said after I was finally able to reach him again. The book only took minutes to read, but reaching Allen had taken days again. "I have to admit, that I don't really understand it. Would it be possible to get together and talk about it?" I continued.

"I'm really busy and I don't have much time," he responded. "I don't care to waste what time I do have dealing with someone who is not really serious about implementing it," he continued. I had no clue what "it" to implement, but somehow I managed to convince Allen that it was worth investing a day with me. Perhaps it was just the intrigue of Harley-Davidson, but Allen agreed to come to Milwaukee for a day.

Allen was a former Army Ranger and the influence of his military career was clearly evident when we met. He was fit and trim. Everything about him was concise, blunt, and direct. Although flamboyant in his own way, he was very opinionated and freely shared what was on his mind. He was confident and brilliant. In our initial conversations I quickly realized that Allen had unique insights to product development. He clearly had something to offer, but getting it out in a usable fashion would be a challenge. Over time our relationship grew and Allen began to open up as we debated the virtues of applying lean techniques to product development.

Allen received his Ph.D. from MIT. His doctoral research dealt with the hypothesis of a design compiler. He theorized that if design attributes were constructed based on algorithms and fed to a computer, the computer would be able to optimize the various design alternatives much better than a human and in turn create a better design with less time and effort. After receiving his Ph.D., Allen moved to the University of Michigan to begin his teaching career and he continued to explore the notion of a design compiler. He began to investigate whether any company even quantified design attributes in the form of algorithms. He was intrigued to uncover the possibility of applying the principles of a design compiler to industry.

As Allen sought to uncover the principles of a design compiler in industry, over time a rumor emerged that Toyota may have been utilizing practices similar to the notion Allen had proposed. Toyota was developing new products at an astonishing rate. Although Allen had originally pitched his ideas to the auto companies in Detroit, his theories had fallen on deaf ears. The U.S. auto industry was beginning to cry foul as it struggled to compete against the onslaught of well-designed and well-built off-shore competition. Armed with a government research grant and the good will of Toyota, Allen and a graduate student named Durward Sobek began a research project to compare and contrast the product design principles of Toyota and Chrysler. This study became the foundational understanding in the application of lean principles to product development. As I worked with Allen and we applied these principles at Harley-Davidson, the system became known as "Knowledge-Based Product Development" because we felt it better represented the intent of the development system.

The Roots of Knowledge-Based Product Development

As I learned more about the application of lean principles to product development from Allen, and he began to decipher the gibberish I had tried to read in his "book," I became increasingly more convinced of the merits. Lean principles applied to product development worked harmoniously in creating cadence and flow. We had already identified the importance of cadence and flow and had adapted them to our process. Allen described methods to actually leverage them in the product development system that we had been unable to do. But the introduction of lean principles also created a dilemma. Harley-Davidson is a proud, iconic American company with a rich heritage and strong traditions. No one had any desire to be like Toyota. But we did need to improve product development throughput and it couldn't hurt to learn from others.

In the 1980s when Harley-Davidson had to fix their quality, Japanese management practices were a part of the turnaround. But that was a long time ago and the company had clearly been in trouble. And those principles were, after all, based on American ideas and practices taught by Deming, Shainin, Crosby, and Juran by way of Japan. It's just that American industry would not listen to them, so they went to Japan. Even the changes that had been made in desperation in the 1980s had eroded over time. Toyota practices could not possibly be transplanted into the product development process, the heart and soul of Harley-Davidson, and be expected to survive. The autoimmune system of the organization would reject them.

When I shared this fear with Allen, he grinned and said, "The foundation of these principles is not Japanese, it is American." Then he proceeded to tell me his version of the history of lean product development. "Just like Tiachi Ohno based Toyota's lean manufacturing on Henry Ford's work," he began, "knowledge-based product development is rooted in the work of the Wright brothers."

For eons man dreamed of flying, but until the early 1900s flight had simply been just that—a dream. Human flight was mostly relegated to the dominion of myths and legends. Perhaps in a sense of foreshadowing, the legend of Icarus tells of his flight from Crete, only to end in failure and death. Through the ages, man has continued to dream and fail. The development of a flying machine has been paid for with countless lives. That is perhaps why it is so amazing that the first successful controlled heavier-than-air flight came from the most unlikely of sources. The prize that had eluded so many did not come from an established company, a government, or university, but rather two uneducated brothers of little means who in the process of inventing the airplane created a different way of developing products. Orville and Wilbur Wright's dream and stubborn persistence brought them immortality for their development of heavier-than-air flight. Yet their greatest contribution may well have been the development process that yielded the airplane.

Strangely, it was the death of Otto Lilienthal in 1896 that inspired the Wright brothers to take up their study of powered flight.[2] The Wright brothers fully recognized the severe consequences of their development endeavor. Failure surely meant death. Initially they did not set out to invent the airplane because they deemed the problems to be too difficult. Instead they resolved to undertake a study to contribute and help advance the knowledge of flight. This mindset of creating reusable knowledge rather than designing an airplane laid the foundation of their development process—a process that cost them roughly $1,000 over five years and resulted in powered flight on the third attempt. Allen argued persuasively that their process merited investigation and was the foundation of knowledge-based product development.

The Systems Approach to Flight

The Wright brothers took a systems approach to their study of flight and recognized that there were three primary obstacles preventing successful flight: 1) construction of the wings, 2) the generation and application of power, and 3) the dynamics of the craft in the air. So they broke the problem into its constituents and took a deliberate and premeditated approach to the study of each. They felt that the issue of wing construction had largely been solved by Lilienthal's work with gliders. They began their development with understanding what had already been learned. So they wrote to the Smithsonian, which was the keeper of all information at that time, and requested all information pertaining to the design and construction of wings. Armed with this information, they set about designing various kites and gliders to better understand the construction and behavior of wings.

The lowest point of their development effort came relatively early, when their gliders did not behave as predicted. The Wrights nearly gave up on their project, but with resolute determination to learn and contribute to the advancement of knowledge, they discovered that it was the aerodynamic tables and not their hypotheses that were in error. Since they could only test gliders for a short period in the late fall when their bicycle business was slow and before winter set in, they had to figure out a different way of rewriting the aerodynamic tables. To create the tables, they invented a wind tunnel to test airfoils. They meticulously varied the parameters to establish lift and drag graphs. With new aerodynamic data they built new gliders. These redesigned gliders were transported by train from Dayton, Ohio, to Kitty Hawk, North Carolina, for testing.

With the verification that these new wings performed according to their theories, they set about addressing the issues of power and control. Their systems approach to attacking the larger problem of flight by breaking the problem into its constituents allowed them to define the weight allotment and power requirements for the engine. Creation of a lightweight power source fell on their technician, Charles Taylor. Taylor built the engine while Orville and Wilbur tackled conversion of power to thrust. Their earlier "hands-on" development of the aerodynamic tables resulted in the insight that a propeller is simply a spinning wing. They reused their knowledge of airfoils to develop highly efficient propellers necessary for thrust.

The final element of successful flight was control of the craft in the air. They were perhaps the first to recognize the problem with flight is not just building an airplane, but also learning to fly it. The ability to control the craft came in the breakthrough of wing-warping used to modify lift of the wings. Through wing-warping they created primitive ailerons, completing the final piece of their flight puzzle. With the ability to simultaneously control pitch, yaw, and roll of the machine, they acquired reasonable knowledge of all three constituent elements of powered flight. Then it became necessary to put the elements back together to address the larger overall system problem of flight.

The Wrights set about purposefully and meticulously creating the knowledge necessary to design a flying machine rather than just designing a flying machine. Rather than creating a design they thought might work and trying to refine it until it did, as others had done, the Wright brothers set out a planned course of study and discovery in order to create knowledge. In the process they created the knowledge they needed to solve the problems first, then they went about designing within those limits. They went through cycles of learning that explored possibilities while narrowing the set of possible solutions. Through deliberate learning cycles they safely discovered the limits of what worked and more importantly what did not work. They tested the limits and evaluated trade-offs in relative safety. They designed alternative solutions in sets as they tested the limits of their design. Because of their methods, the Wright brothers knew they had solved the problem of flight before they physically demonstrated it. When they finally had built the craft, they set about diligently learning to pilot a machine that could fly, recognizing that the pilot would be an integral element of any machine that would fly.

The roots of knowledge-based product development are firmly embedded in the sands of Kitty Hawk and the cow pastures of Ohio. The Wright brothers not only demonstrated human flight, but in the process invented a different way of product development. The Wright brothers achieved flight and survived through careful exploration and studying the limits of flight, then designing within their knowledge. The ramifications of this development process are astounding. Not only did they survive a very difficult and dangerous study, but they accomplished human flight in just five years. In the face of adversity, when the aerodynamic tables were wrong, they developed the wind tunnel and rewrote the tables. They flew successfully on just their third attempt.

The Wright brothers achieved the dream of flight through an organized, disciplined process of diligently orchestrated learning cycles. Each learning cycle was designed to create knowledge, which they captured on limit and trade-off curves. They had set out to undertake a study of flight and make a contribution in advancing the knowledge of powered flight. The process they employed was so successful that the result was the invention of the airplane. Clearly, there is much to be learned from their process.

Allen asserted that the method of product development the Wright brothers pioneered continued in aeronautical design until the computer age. Computers provided engineers so much computational power that limit and trade-off curves were largely done away with. The computer ushered out visual representation of knowledge in the form of physical limit and trade-off curves. Allen emphasized his point by telling of the development of the P-51 during World War II. As one of the last and arguably one of the most successful pre-computer-era airplanes, the P-51 was developed using the Wright brother's development methods. The first P-51 flew just six months after the War Department requested it. Certainly World War II provided incentive, but without the development methodology pioneered by the Wright brothers, this development pace could not have been achieved.

Allen contended that the Wright brothers' development method came to Toyota by way of the engineers who joined Toyota after World War II. After the war, Japanese industry was in ruins. The

Japanese aeronautical engineers who had so successfully developed planes using the Wright brothers' methods were now unemployed. Some of these engineers went to work for Toyota designing cars. They brought knowledge-based product development with them and adopted it to the Toyota way of business.

Allen continued his history lesson as he went on to explain the rationale behind how knowledge-based product development was integrated at Toyota by contrasting the early days of Toyota and Ford (see his chart below). The Toyoda family first made their fortune in the textile industry when Sakichi Toyoda founded Toyoda Spinning and Weaving, and Toyoda Automatic Loom. Sakichi Toyoda invented a loom that would automatically stop when the thread broke. Thread breakage was a major problem in textiles and this device allowed tremendous improvements to both quality and efficiency. The device automatically eliminated quality defects by stopping the loom when a thread broke and increased efficiency because it freed the worker to operate multiple looms because they would not need to watch each machine for broken threads. This led to the principle of *autonomation* (automation with a human touch) as quality became a hallmark of Toyoda and in turn of Toyota.[3]

Sakichi Toyoda was fascinated with automobiles and encouraged his son, Kiichiro, to study engineering with the purpose of founding an automobile company. As a result, the Toyota Motor Company was founded in 1937. From a simple beginning, the evolution of Toyota as a company, just as the evolution of Ford in contrast, was largely due to their environment. The founders of each, Kiichiro Toyoda and Henry Ford, were both visionaries and technical geniuses, but as each company matured, external influences placed them on divergent paths through history.

Henry Ford had direct personal experience as the chief engineer at the Edison Company, and as a craftsman. He lived in Detroit, which was the center of the furniture industry at the time, providing him access to skilled craftsmen, tools, equipment, and suppliers. Due to his location, he also had access to American universities and skilled engineers. Based on these environmental factors, Henry Ford could give orders and he could direct others. The Ford Motor Company evolved

Learning as a Company

Henry Ford	Kiichiro Toyoda
Visionary, technical genius	Visionary, technical genius

Skills available:	Skills not available:
• Personal experience	• Backward and rural nation
• Detroit furniture industry	• No adequate steel, castings
• Access to American universities for engineers	• First auto bodies hammered into pit to form
• Supply base in place	• Had to encourage universal learning
• Could give orders	

"Scientific Management": a system for command and control	Optimized system for learning

to a "scientific management structure." Ford used a system of command and control, with one person, Henry himself, directing the organization.

Kiichiro Toyoda, in contrast, was located in a rural part of what was a backward nation at the time. There no skilled craftsmen or suppliers to draw upon in the area. It was very difficult to get adequate steel and castings. In a farming community far from the cities and universities, technical knowledge was not readily available. The only formally trained engineer in the company was Kiichiro. Lore has it that the first car bodies were made by hammering steel sheet into a pit in the ground dug in the shape of an upside-down car. To survive and prosper, Kiichiro had to encourage universal learning. The Toyota Motor Company evolved into an organization optimized for learning.

Following World War II, Japan was a shambles and Toyota started acquiring engineers. The engineers primarily came from the defunct airplane industry, which had become accustomed to developing products by the Wright brothers' methods. This development system was adopted within an organization optimized and reliant on learning. According to Allen, lean product development practices grew out of the amalgamation of the Wright brothers' development principles in combination with Toyota management practices that encourage universal learning. For more than fifty years now, Toyota has been creating reusable knowledge.

It was this reusable knowledge in the form of check sheets, A-3 reports, limit curves, and trade-off curves that Allen and Durward discovered when they went to Japan looking for evidence of set-based development. [4, 5] This reusable knowledge powered the set-based practices that Allen had hoped to find when he and Durward first visited Toyota. In essence, they uncovered evidence of Allen's original hypothesis of a design compiler that simultaneously evaluates multiple alternatives and narrows sets of possible options to arrive at an optimal solution. They discovered it was not hidden in the neural networks of a computer, but rather embedded in the social structure of the organization and data sheets that each department meticulously built to visualize their knowledge. The Toyota development system was the design optimizer that allowed Toyota unprecedented ability to effectively and efficiently design and develop new products better and faster than their competition. It was a system that created reusable knowledge based on the pioneering efforts of Orville and Wilbur Wright, and which facilitated Toyota's extraordinary delivery cadence and flow of new products.

Work Smarter, Not Harder

Jim was correct: "Don't bring lean manufacturing upstream to product development! The application of lean in product development and manufacturing are different." I had jumped to a solution I thought solved my problem, but discovered I was not clear in my problem. The problem was not figuring out how to apply lean principles upstream to product development, but rather figuring out how to work smarter rather than harder in my own environment. There was no prepackaged solution, so the desire to learn drove my journey of discovery.

Allen impressed on me that applying lean practices to product development was not about finding clever ways to reclassify "waste" in the context of product development or to redefine Toyota's production system for engineers. Rather, the basis for knowledge-based product development is the creation of reusable knowledge through set-based design and the establishment of development cadence and flow.

CHAPTER 9

The Product Development Limit Curve

I hear and I forget. I see and I remember. I do and I understand.

Confucius

C hange begins with enlightenment. Changing the system starts with changing your vantage point so you can "see" the system differently. Development speed is often attributed to quick decisions. Early definition of the requirements and freezing specification quickly are often highlighted as keys to shortening the product development cycle. Yet the key steps required to bring a new product to market remain the creation and application of knowledge, regardless of how quickly the requirements are set. The challenge in creating an effective and efficient development system lies in shortening the entire process. Typical steps of a conventional development process are:

- Ideation—recognizing a need or opportunity; exposing an idea.
- Definition—establishing what the product will be; setting requirements and picking solutions.

- Design—establishing the parameters and documenting decisions.

- Development—verifying what works and fixing what doesn't.

- Production—determining how to make it, preparing to make it, and continuing to fix what doesn't work.

- Launch—beginning production, and continuing to fix what doesn't work.

Steps such as these are commonly reflected in the gates of a phase gate process. Each phase builds on the previous one and each phase has specific criteria that need to be met to move forward (see Figure 9–1).

There may even be a check sheet that needs to be signed by senior leaders to acknowledge completion of a development phase in order to pass through a gate. In this context emphasis is placed on the early phases so that the development teams can quickly progress to determining what aspects of the design meet the requirements and fixing those that don't. This process is a linear, "design then validate" process, which promotes "point-based" solutions. In point-based development a specific solution is selected that is deemed most feasible, then development teams validate the solution through testing. If problems are

Figure 9.1

Typical Phase and Gate Process

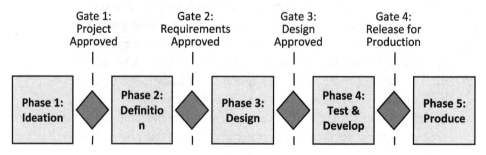

Phase (Stage): A set of logically grouped tasks and activities with defined deliverables
Gate: A "Go" / "No Go" project decision point

found with the design, then the development team loops back to redesign the product and fix problems they may uncover (see Figure 9–2).

Haste Makes Waste

Selecting a design quickly feels good because work begins and progress is made early. By selecting the solution, everyone can get to work and it feels efficient—until the design rework loops begin. The need for design reworks is often attributed to shoddy engineering in earlier phases rather than recognizing that they are inherent to the process itself. Under a linear, point-based scenario there is actually no way of knowing if all the requirements can be achieved by the design solution picked until the design is tested. Due to the organizational commitment to the design direction, these design–test–redesign loops often extend beyond just the development and test phases. Discovery of problems with the design often continues into initial manufacturing

Figure 9.2

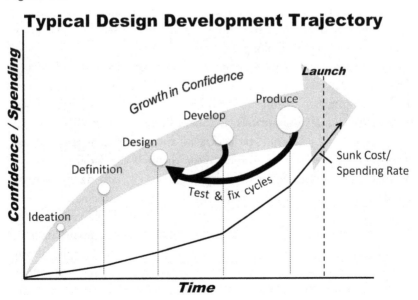

Typical Design Development Trajectory

and even past launch. Often the inability to pass tests forces launch dates to be pushed back until enough confidence in the design is created to allow the launch to proceed. This process is neither efficient nor effective. It is unpredictable and robs resources from future projects to fix today's problems. Unfortunately, this is the process used at almost every company in a variety of disguises, because it's what we've been taught and is often the only system we know. Allen called this process "point-based" development.

Although Harley-Davison recognized the importance of cadence and flow, the development methodology remained a phase gate point-based development process. Allen challenged the status quo. He emphatically decried phase gate methodology as evil, and introduced the concept of set-based concurrent development as an alternative that simultaneously evaluated multiple solution sets to address a business opportunity.

When Allen suggested set-based development as an alternative it sounded ludicrous. From my traditional frame of mind, set-based designed seemed like a lot of the same work we were already doing—but doing more of it simultaneously to reduce the odds of failure. But Allen's persistence stimulated a renewed look at the development process. Allen became my mentor, and through his guidance a process of enlightenment began that over time allowed me to see what had been hidden in plain sight all along.

The discovery began when existing data was revisited and viewed differently. Allen stressed the need to visualize information in pictures. There is a communication hierarchy in which written descriptions are better than verbal descriptions, numbers better than words, and pictures are best of all. The Harley-Davidson development process had already taken the step to establish flow through the cadence of bins. Because of the common methodology, the use of hard dates, and the standardization of bins, we could evaluate project information across the portfolio and compare data (numbers) over multiple years. However, when we evaluated five years of product development data in pictorial form (see Figure 9–3), it exposed the fact that in spite of our best efforts to standardize our methods and to create cadence and flow, there was in fact no correlation between exiting phase gates on time

Figure 9.3

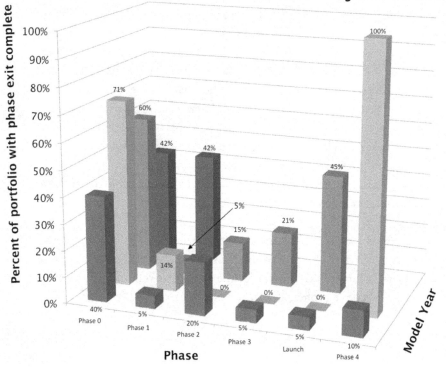

Phase Exits Do Not Predict Project Success

and the success of a project. In fact, exiting early phases of a point-based development process quickly has no positive impact on the success of the overall project. The data even suggested that the inverse may be true.

Why was it that the harder we worked to improve the system, the less predictable it became? The more we worked to ensure that requirements were set early, and the more effort we placed on freezing standards, the more likely we were to miss later phase exits. Each new cycle of new projects began with the enthusiastic objective to define standards early. But the more we pushed, the worse things became later in the process. The surface data of how the system performed begged for a deeper perspective of what was happening in the process.

Bad Systems Beat Good People

Further evaluation into the reasons that phase exits were missed established that there was definitely a systemic problem. We consistently missed the same gates for the same reasons across the portfolio year after year (see Figure 9–4). Early in the process, the reason for project delays was that written plans for the project that defined the scope and requirements were incomplete. Then gates were missed because feasibility had not been demonstrated. Even after demonstrating feasibility, projects could not exit subsequent gates because design problems were discovered. Unresolved high-priority test failures prevented exit of the final phases. The development pattern was predictable and it was consistent. In spite of the best efforts of good people, the system determined the outcome. Once again a bad system was beating good people.

There is a root cause analysis process called the "five why process." The name refers to the process of asking "why" until the root cause of a problem is uncovered. In place of the five why process, many companies have become proficient at the "five who process." The five who

Figure 9.4

Systemic Reasons for Missing Phase Exits

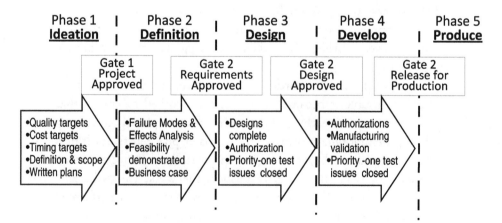

process asks "Who did it?" until an appropriate person to blame is identified. To be effective, it is critical that the learning and discovery process remains focused on why and not on who.

After reading countless After Action Reviews and constantly asking why, the singular root cause of project failures emerged. By far the majority of project failures occurred because project teams thought something was feasible, but learned later in the development process that it was not. This phenomenon is termed "false positive feasibility." False positive feasibility most often occurs when a point-based solution is selected in the development process, then tested to demonstrate its feasibility based on a pass/fail criterion. If the solution picked passes the test, it is deemed feasible.

However, the design evolves over the course of the development process to accommodate various changes from new learning. The design may be modified to adapt the product to accommodate more requirements or new needs. The feasibility tests are often only conducted on a portion of the solution. The feasibility test conditions themselves are often only a representation of the actual conditions the design may encounter later in the development process. On a pass/fail basis, when the feasibility test is passed, there is no indication of the margin by which the design passed. All of these conditions contribute to false positive feasibility.

In a point-based development process, commitment to a design is made early in the process. Then the solution is tested against a battery of evaluations to verify that it is good. As failures are uncovered, the point-based development process cycles through design loops to fix them. Successful projects are able to loop through the design iterations and fix all the problems that are uncovered in time for launch. Unsuccessful projects run out of time to resolve all the issues that are uncovered, or the point solution picked early in the process is determined to actually not be feasible under any conditions and the project is cancelled.

Allen continued to extol the virtues of set-based design, limit curves, and trade-off curves. He insisted they held the key to breaking the cycle of late discovery we experienced and would allow improved product development performance. But try as he might to explain it, and try as we might to understand him, there was a chasm between us we could not bridge. Set-based development seemed to be simultaneous development of backup solutions. Certainly the more simultaneous development we did, the better the odds of finding a feasible solution. Although more effective, it certainly didn't seem to be more efficient and we didn't have the personnel to attempt it. Allen could not show us an actual limit or trade-off curve, so the concept remained an academic exercise in our minds. Over time he continued to explain, and a few people continued to listen, but we still could not comprehend.

Design Rework Loops

The first revelation came after continuing to pore over the development data of previous launched projects. It bothered me that in spite of all our efforts to standardize the process, there was no correlation between successful projects and the metrics we used to evaluate progress. I continued to try to uncover what made good projects good and why projects failed. Allen was a catalyst to eventually see the existing data from a different vantage point, which finally brought enlightenment. The primary cause for project failure is false positive feasibility. It is the primary initiator of the unrecoverable spiral for doomed projects. From the principle of firefighting it is understood that an unchecked failing project could easily take down the entire portfolio of projects, or at least severely hamper the efficiency of the development system.

But what made "good" projects successful?

Our vantage point for observing performance data stemmed from a belief that our phase gate methodology controlled the development system. We scheduled projects based on what we determined to be appropriate exit gate timing. We managed our entire product development process through phases and gates. With the mindset that the phase and gate methodology actually controlled the development process, the development process appeared unpredictable.

Allen's persistent criticism highlighting the evils associated with phase gate methods caused a gradual shift in the vantage point in which data were observed. Allen talked about what he had observed at Toyota. He described their use of a development system that relied on disciplined development cycles, not unlike the system the Wright brothers used to uncover the secrets of flight. These development cycles began with a concept or hypothesis, followed by a rigorous study of the situation including modeling of some type, then concluded with a simulation and analysis before a project proceeded into the following cycle as the scope of the concept narrowed through each successive cycle.

Finally, it dawned that perhaps phases and gates did not control or manage the development process. Perhaps there was a totally different structure in play that controlled the cadence and paced product development. Perhaps we were ignorantly trying to control product development through the wrong means. Every system has an inherent natural frequency, a natural rhythm that can enhance it or destroy it, and natural leverage points from which to control it.

Enlightenment came in the revelation that product development is fundamentally based on learning and discovery. In point-based development, redesign loops are used to fix design problems uncovered in testing. With the enlightenment that product development may be more dependent on cycles of learning than the completion of gates changed the vantage point by which to "see" the system. Perhaps the design loops used in the point-based development process to fix issues discovered in testing were important. When the same unpredictable data was evaluated based on the test-and-fix design loops, there was complete correlation. Aligning multiple years of projects resulted in data that produced an R^2 value of 0.99 (see Figure 9–5), indicating nearly perfect correlation in predicting project success. Changing the vantage point by which data was seen brought the realization that our development process might actually be repeatable and predictable.

Product Development Is Predictable

As the aspects of successful and unsuccessful development projects became more apparent, there was a realization that the product devel-

Figure 9.5

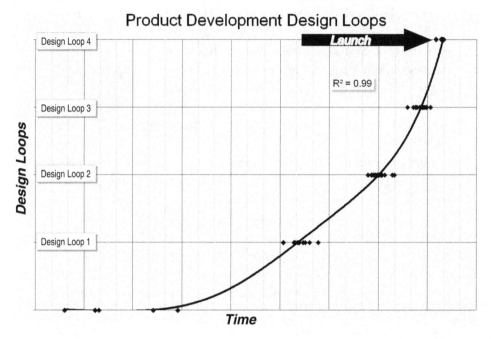

opment process was in fact completely consistent and totally predictable. Whether the pattern was driven by our efforts to create cadence and flow, or just happenstance, the revelation that test-and-fix loops predicted the development system was an important breakthrough. Why the system behaved in the manner it did was not known. Nor was it known how to alter the system. But the data visualized in the form of a curve provided insight to the behavior of the product development system and created a foundation on which to build knowledge.

Stripping away the facade of phases and gates allowed real learning to begin. The first revelation was how good projects and bad projects behaved in this context. Data showed that projects that fell to the right of the redesign loops curve had more difficulty than those on the left. This insight allowed labeling the area to the right of the curve as a risk zone, while the area to the left as a safe zone. Predictably, projects that operated to the left of the curve launched more smoothly than those to the right. The slope of the curve indicates project efficiency (not overall efficiency because it does not account for resource fluctuation). The slope indicates how much progress the project made in completing a test-and-fix cycle over a given time interval. The steeper the slope the more the project progressed in a given time period.

Early in the project the slope is very flat, while late in the project the slope is very steep. This is due to the company marshaling all resources to resolve problems when they are discovered late in the process and product launch is imminent. Late in a project, progress is made quickly, while early in the project the slope of the curve is flat. It takes a long time to move through the first test-and-fix loop. When launch is a long way off there is little urgency within the project. It is often difficult to get the proper attention and resources early in a project. Personnel may not yet be available because they are fighting fires on other projects. As a result, most of the project work is completed late in a project, when the company is willing to move heaven and earth to fix problems that threaten a scheduled launch. Nothing sharpens the senses like a sight of the gallows. Likewise, nothing provides greater incentive and focus for a project team than the recognition of impending peril, particularly with large financial implications.

Although the slope of the line indicates project efficiency (how much work gets done over a period of time), it does not mean that projects are actually more efficient when the slope is steep. Generally projects progress rapidly late in the development process, through inefficient means. Realizing the condition of the project, companies throw money and resources at fixing problems as the consequences of not resolving them become clear and imminent. The sunk costs are immense. Late in development, the additional cost to complete a project becomes marginal in comparison to the total amount already spent. Late problems even drive inefficiencies elsewhere in the portfolio as projects in peril get head-of-the-line privileges. Late problems become the highest priority for the organization; routine work is stopped and focus is shifted onto the imminent issues. I have had project leaders who've had their projects bumped shrug their shoulders and tell me, "Closest to launch wins," recognizing that the biggest, most important project closest to launch trumps all other projects and gets whatever resources it needs. Project leaders recognize that work gets done at the end of a project and count on getting whatever resource they need in a crisis.

The degree of curve in the redesign loop graphic suggests the degree to which a cadence and level flow is established in the development process. Level flow is achieved in uniform work cycles when the progression of work over time is linear. The closer the profile of the curve reflects a straight line, the greater the degree of cadence and level flow (see Figure 9–6). Deviation from linear flow drives inefficiency in the product development system because extra resources are essentially held in reserve or moved to accommodate the steepest slope.

The separation or spread of the timing in the cycling for each test-and-fix loop indicates the predictability and the variability of the process. Early in the process the predictability is lowest and variability the greatest. Early on there is the least known and the most to be discovered in the project, with no rigorous deadlines to drive progress in the way launch does late in the process. The design options available to

Figure 9.6

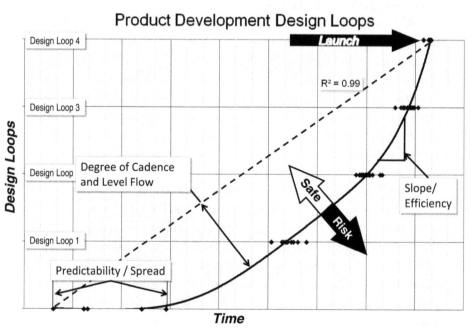

156

resolve issues are also the most diverse early. Few design decisions are frozen, restricting direction. This provides the development teams the widest freedoms and creates greater variation. As launch approaches development teams become more focused. Late in a project the design alternatives are greatly reduced. Often the optimal method to fix a problem can't be used; instead, the least expensive alternative that fits within the remaining timing is selected as schedule becomes king.

The first time the product development data was visualized in the form of test-and-redesign cycles, it happened almost by accident. Frustration with the lack of predictability in the phase and gate process data led to a search to find a better predictor of project success. Manipulating the data in various different ways caused the data to align in a picture that showed the redesign loop curve. It wasn't intentional nor was it initially understood. It was just interesting because the data aligned.

The first time I showed the picture to Allen, a slow crooked grin spread across his face as he studied the curve. He didn't say anything for a while and I watched his eyes dart back and forth across the page. Finally he looked up from the page and proclaimed, "You have a limit curve." It was nice to know that we had stumbled upon the seemingly rare and elusive limit curve, but what was it and how could it help us improve product development effectiveness and efficiency?

The bin process was mostly defined in terms of the phase gate methodology. Just as it was at Roaring Motors, our process was based on the amount of change in a project and the tasks that needed to be completed to exit phase gates. Product development, however, is more dependent on what needs to be learned than on what tasks must be completed to exit a gate. Steve Phillips, Harley-Davidson's Vice President for Quality, would often marvel about how it was possible for a project to get behind. He would tell me, "Two days before an exit review a project leader always tells me the team will be ready to exit a gate, but at the exit review all of a sudden they are more than a month behind. How the hell is it possible to get a month behind in two days?" Steve knew that they were always a month behind, but the project leader didn't know it. Perhaps it comes from seeing the system from the wrong vantage point.

Integration Points and False Positive Feasibility

When nothing seems to help, I go and look at a stonecutter hammering away at his rock perhaps a hundred times without as much as a crack showing in it. Yet at the hundred and first blow it will split in two, and I know it was not that blow that did it, but all that had gone before.

Jacob Riis

Tony Wilcox worked for me in the Product Development office, and was in charge of knowledge management. He walked into my office one morning beaming from ear to ear. "I've got something to show you," he said. "I've been doing some digging into how long it takes for projects to get through build-and-test cycles and I've come up with some interesting data."

"What did you find?" I asked, intrigued to learn what he had discovered.

"I pulled out a bunch of old purchase orders," he went on. "I was curious to see when orders were placed for parts compared to when they came in, and then when they were built into bikes and tested. Based on the purchase orders, each system seems to be pretty consistent in how long the cycle takes from program to program. But when you look at how long the systems take to get parts procured, there is a big difference between the systems."

"So what you are saying," I repeated back to him, "is that each vehicle system takes about the same amount of time to go through its build-and-test cycle from project to project, but each system has a different length cycle."

"Right. Take a look at this chart," he said as he put a chart (see Figure 10-1) on my desk. Along the bottom of the chart Tony had listed the various subsystems of the motorcycle. He had listed systems like frames, fuel tanks, fenders, seats, wire harnesses, etc. All the various parts of the motorcycle were grouped in subsystems by the way

Figure 10.1

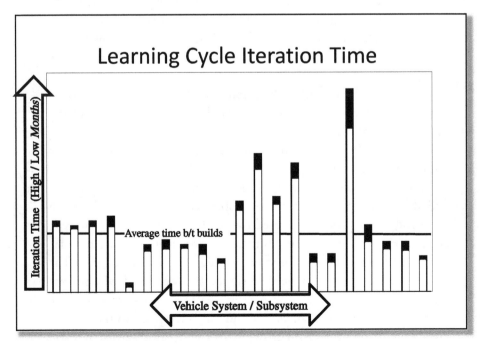

bikes were designed. Going up the left side of the chart he had graphed how long each system took for a typical part to go through a redesign loop. "Look," he said pointing to a line showing the average time between build cycles. "These systems always take longer than the average build cycle and these systems always take less than the average time."

"That's interesting," I said. "So the length of time it takes for a part to be redesigned is based on what kind of a part it is. It's amazing how consistent it is. But wouldn't you expect some parts to be above average and some to be below?" I asked.

"Yes, of course," he responded, "but the point is where the redesign loops happen on the development limit curve."

"What do you mean?" I asked.

"Look," he went on, "if you put the two charts next to each other, they map to each other pretty well. All the systems had purchase orders for parts early on, but as it got later in the development process, only some of the systems were still iterating designs even though there is no official design freeze at this point. According to the purchase orders, all the systems iterated designs early, but only the shorter cycle systems iterated later unless there was a major crisis," and he laid his iteration graphic next to a copy of the Product Development Design Loops chart that was lying on my desk for me to compare (see Figure 10–2).

"So, can we make the assumption that the shape of the product development limit curve is based on the design iteration cycles of the various systems?" I asked.

"It kind of looks like it from the data we have," Tony replied. "It sounds like a good hypothesis."

The discussion opened my mind to a different way of thinking. Did that mean that better projects operated toward the left of the curve and worse projects operated toward the right based on the type of problems they were dealing with in development? The product development limit curve was based on projects that had launched. What about failed or delayed projects? Perhaps this explained why project success didn't correlate to gate reviews. Gate reviews were somewhat arbitrary dates on the calendar and did not correspond to these iteration cycles. Were we focused on the wrong things in trying to improve

Figure 10.2

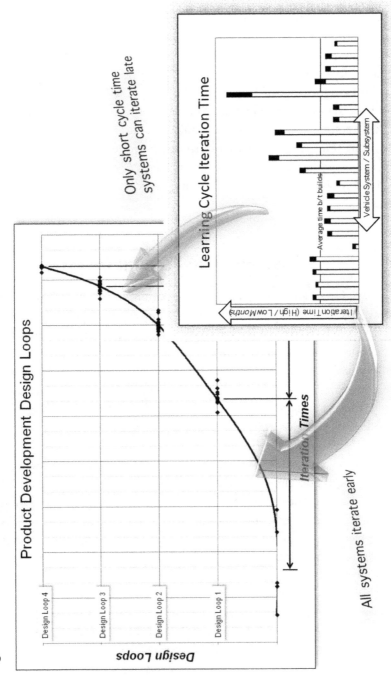

Only short cycle time systems can iterate late

Learning Cycle Iteration Time

Vehicle System / Subsystem

Average time b/t builds

Iteration Time (High / Low Months)

Product Development Design Loops

Design Loops

Design Loop 4

Design Loop 3

Design Loop 2

Design Loop 1

Iteration Times

All systems iterate early

product development? It dawned on me that value stream mapping phase gate activities to analyze the flow and timing of development tasks may have little to do with how to improve the actual flow of product development.

"Tony, I'm curious," I said. "I'd like to test out this hypothesis. I'd like to know if the product development process is really paced by design iteration loops or not. Let's take a look at the projects on the left of the limit curve compared to those on the right and see how the projects are different. I'd also like to dig into projects that didn't make launch and see why they were killed or delayed, based on this information."

False Positive Feasibility

It wasn't long before we had the information we needed to test the hypothesis. As the hypothesis predicted, projects that operated toward the left of the curve did indeed have fewer issues both through the development process as well as at launch than projects to the right of the curve. As long as projects only iterated systems that were within the timing indicated by the design limit curve, they launched relatively easily. But if a design iteration loop required modification to a system outside the timing of the curve, the project had problems. If a project slipped to the right of the curve late in the development process, it generally did not recover to the left. The high-visibility problems always occurred on projects to the right of the curve. For important projects to the right of the curve, the organization would move heaven and earth to make sure that they got launched. In a crisis even systems that typically took a long time to iterate could be done in much shorter time by cutting some corners and giving the project priority, with head-of-the-line privileges.

Projects that were delayed or canceled for technical reasons were always on the right of the curve. Many of the failed projects started on the left, but the projects spiraled out of control when design teams had to continue design iteration loops on systems that took longer to iterate than the curve allowed. These projects often started out as exemplar projects based on the phase gate metrics. These projects often exited the early phase gates on time, but they all failed tests at some point in the development process. Often, the test failures happened late in the process. Late test failures forced the design teams to keep iterating through design loops as they tried to develop their way out of their problems. Recognizing that these projects needed help, these projects often got priority in testing and design support. However, head-of-the-line privileges for late projects had the unintended consequence of delaying other projects in the portfolio and resulted in the spread of firefighting. When it became absolutely obvious that a project could not make launch, the project would be forced to reduce its scope, be delayed, or be canceled altogether.

Projects always failed on the right of the product development limit curve. In every case projects moved to the right of the curve due to false positive feasibility. Projects moved from the left of the curve to the right of the curve because a design solution the team committed to early in the phase gate process could not be proven to work in time for launch. Projects failed because designs selected in phases two and three could not go through enough test and redesign loops in time to exit phase four for launch. The metrics based on the phase and gate process rarely predicted the outcome of a project accurately. Many projects that exited the first few gates late launched fine, while projects that failed were often on time through the early gates. Monitoring projects according to the phase and gate metrics did not predict project success accurately, while the product development limit curve accurately predicted success of projects as well as which systems in a project were at risk.

The product development limit curve accurately predicted project risk based on which side of the curve the project was on and which system was being redesigned relative to the design iteration timing of the limit curve. The data indicated that product development was driven by the development redesign iteration loops and that false positive feasibility forced redesign. Project problems are predominantly caused by thinking that a solution picked early in the development process is feasible, only to discover later in the process that it is not. Overwhelmingly, projects fail because design teams can not iteratively develop their way out of a false positive feasibility scenario in time for launch.

Design Cycles and Integration Points

The revelation that different systems had design iteration cycles of different lengths was important. The recognition that certain systems were dominant at certain times in the development process helped explain the shape of the product development limit curve. The dominance of long cycles early and the lack of long cycles late explained the time interval of the curve. By the time we had figured this out, Allen Ward and I had become friends. He challenged me and stimulated ideas as we debated aspects of the product development system. Allen thought the product development limit curve was incredibly important and insightful and he insisted it should be published and shared. As we continued to debate what it all meant, it became a key to unlocking insights about the product development system. The limit curve visually represented product development in a way that forced us to think about product development differently. It was no longer phases and gates, but rather "design cycles and integration points."

Bins very effectively coordinated the overall development portfolio from a high-level strategic perspective. Now for the first time it was possible to see that integration points control product development. Regardless of the systems or functions involved, the issues with the project, or how many iteration loops occurred, everything has to converge at the integration points (see Figure 10–3). For example, if an integration point is a prototype vehicle build, the vehicle can only be built when all the systems are in place and the parts are available to build the vehicle. If there is a problem with a part, or one bolt is missing, the build can not be completed until the problem is resolved.

Integration points are significant events that bring together a meaningful cross section of the organization to accomplish some aspect of product development critical to the project. They are incredibly important to the coordination and pacing of the product development

Figure 10.3

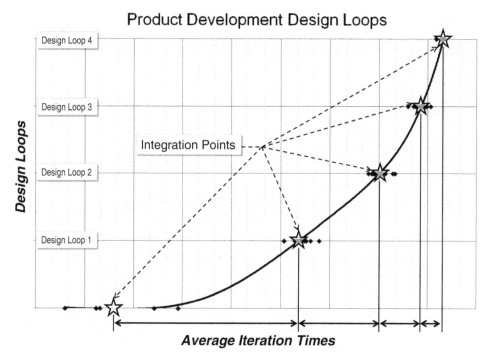

The realization that product development progresses by cycling through development loops separated by integration points was an important milestone in comprehending the system. Not only was the length of the design loop important in determining the shape of the development limit curve, but the loops also drove the efficiency of the system. Product development could progress no faster than the slowest

system because they create focus for the organization while coordinating and integrating development efforts towards convergence. They force communication, provide natural check points, and set the tempo for product development. They establish cadence, reduce process variation, and help maintain projects within the limit curve. The epiphany of integration points is that they control product development and are the leverage points to improve the system. When timing of integration points slips, it signals that the project is in trouble.

The realization that product development progresses by cycling through development loops separated by integration points was an important milestone in comprehending the system. Not only was the length of the design loop important in determining the shape of the development limit curve, but the loops also drove the efficiency of the system. Product development could progress no faster than the slowest system in that cycle. Integration of the systems could not proceed until all the systems were ready to converge. In some cases faster systems detracted. If one system could iterate designs in a month while another took six months, the faster system could refine their design six times through subsystem tests while the longer iterated once. Due to the mismatch of iteration times, it was not uncommon for a project to reach an integration point and have adjacent parts not fit together, because parts with faster iteration times were several design levels ahead of parts with slower development cycles.

It is not enough to just shorten the cycle time of the design loops. To work effectively, design cycles must also be synchronized. When some systems iterate much faster than others they create extra work. Even lengthening some of the shorter cycles to synchronize the design cycles provides improvement to the overall product development process. Significant improvement comes through a balanced synchronization of design loops in conjunction with reduction in cycle time.

It was becoming obvious that much of the work that had previously been done to improve the development process was in vain, if not actually counterproductive. Value stream mapping the phase gate process to streamline or eliminate activities was useless if the changes did not synchronize the design cycles or reduce the time of the longest cycle. The more we probed the system, the more secrets the system began to reveal. The keys to improving the system through leverage points were becoming apparent. But fundamental shifts in thinking were still needed for real progress to be made. The product development limit curve had been built based on successful projects. The causes of failed projects also needed to be understood. The issue of false positive feasibility still needed to be resolved.

CHAPTER 11

Learning Cycles

I have not failed. I have merely found ten thousand ways that won't work.

Thomas Edison

llen could not have been more insistent. "Phase gate is evil!" he shouted, pounding his fist on the table for emphasis. When I first met Allen Ward, he had made his position clear, "Phase gate methodology must be abolished," he had told me. This singular point remained a heavily debated topic between us. At first I could not comprehend Allen's meaning. But as I learned more, my views changed. As the product development system began to relinquish its secrets I developed a different perspective and saw product development from a different vantage point. Phases and gates gave way to development cycles and integration points. Phase gates were no longer the control points for the development process. The realization that integration points and design cycles drove product development allowed me to hear what Allen had been trying to say.

Traditional phase gate methodology promotes progression of product development linearly through distinct phases (stages) of development. Decision gates between the phases are intended to allow managers to control risk by stopping the flow of work from one phase

167

to the next. As a result, phase gate methodology encourages a linear, point-based development mindset. Gates spaced between phases results in batched information exchange. Typical phase gate development begins with an ideation phase that has as its objective official approval of the project. Once the project is approved, the definition phase begins, and project requirements are defined. After requirements are set the product is designed in the design phase culminating in design approval. When the design is approved the design is tested to verify that it meets the original requirements. (This is akin to "inspection" in lean manufacturing vernacular.) If the design does not meet the requirements, then the design is modified through redesign loops until it is ready for production. (This is akin to "rework" in lean manufacturing vernacular.) Sometimes this process results in the project team determining that a design solution can not be found to meet all the project requirements. In this case either the project is canceled or the project is compromised under duress so that it can still go into production.

Projects pass through each gate with the belief that there is a plausible solution. More specifically, a key criterion for passing through the design gate is this belief that the design is feasible or that a solution will be found. Yet in traditional development it is only learned in the last phase, just before production, whether the design is truly feasible. It is this point-based linear development mindset that results in false positive feasibility.

Allen Ward proposed set-based concurrent engineering as an alternative to phases and gates and linear development. This system is based on the process pioneered by the Wright brothers, coupled with Allen's notion of a design compiler, and further refined by what he observed at Toyota.

Knowledge-based product development incorporates set-based principles and encompasses all of product development, not just a single function like engineering or marketing. It builds on many principles, such as cadence (from Edison) and flow (from classical operations theory). Knowledge-based product development relies on planned learning cycles to narrow solution sets so the optimal design emerges in accordance to a set cadence and flow across the development portfolio tied to business needs. Knowledge-based product development relies on the creation of reusable knowledge by cycling through evaluation, definition, and design prior to design approval. As with the Wright brothers process, each learning cycle is designed with the intent of exploring various aspects of the project to find the limits and determine the trade-offs. Each learning cycle is intended to create specific pieces of knowledge. Each learning cycle is followed by a convergence point intended to eliminate concepts that do not work or will not be ready in time for production while validating the learning believed to have occurred. Reusable knowledge is created, captured, and used throughout each learning cycle, often in the form of limit or trade-off curves.

The revelation of a product development limit curve described in Chapter 9 demonstrated that redesign loops naturally occur between integration points in product development. But learning cycles are different from redesign loops. Redesign loops happened by accident, whereas learning cycles are planned, intentional cycles to create knowledge. In our phase gate process, our learning cycles were simply redesign loops. We had become an outstanding learning organization but unfortunately we seemed to learn the same lessons over and over under duress. We were blinded by the linear point-based development mind-

Knowledge-Based Product Development

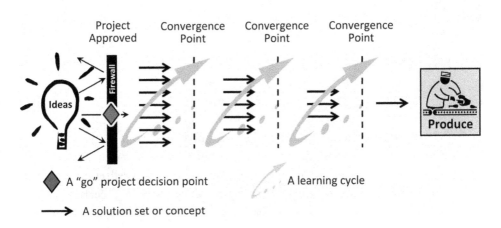

169

set of phases and gates, and in our rush to get to production we did not see the importance of planned learning cycles. We had accepted rework loops as a normal part of our product development process, used to fix project aspects that did not meet requirements. But rework loops drive waste in the development process. They waste time, effort, and knowledge because they are unplanned and unstructured.

The Learning Cycle

Learning is the foundation of improvement and the engine that powers product development. Specifically, experiential learning is the predominant form of learning in a product development environment. Thus, experiential learning cycles are the building blocks for experimentation and discovery necessary for effective product development.

The idea of product development learning cycles is based on the experiential learning principles and on the educational philosophy of John Dewey. In studying human development and, in particular, how humans learn, Dewey identified that learning occurs by moving between the domain of thinking and doing. Dewey described the process of experiential learning as iterative cycles.

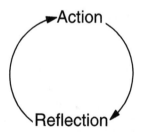

Although learning cycles can be described in various degrees of sophistication, the most rudimentary form of a learning cycle involves just two elements, action and reflection. Both action and reflection are required for learning to occur. With action alone there is no learning, and with no action there is no learning. Learning occurs by moving between the domains of action and reflection. We learn from the combination of thinking and doing. Clear and unambiguous feedback is necessary for learning to occur. As feedback becomes less clear, the ability to learn diminishes. The greater the separation in time and space between an action and feedback, the more difficult learning becomes.

The speed of the action–reflection loop is particularly important in product development. Reflection is the basis of product development as ideas are generated through careful consideration of a problem. This reflection is then tested against actions to determine the validity of the ideas. In most instances, product development requires multiple learning cycles. Thomas Edison demonstrated through his invention factory that innovation success is characterized by iterative learning cycles. He displayed tenacity for working through repeated cycles of reflection and reconsideration of actions, events, and decisions in creating the knowledge necessary to transform an innovation into a marketable product. The number of cycles is largely dependant on the complexity of the problem and the amount of learning necessary to close the knowledge gap. The importance of properly designed learning cycles for creating usable knowledge cannot be overstated.

W. Edwards Deming popularized a slightly more sophisticated model of the learning cycle which has become the backbone of continuous improvement.[1] He described continuous improvement as a continual cycle of learning through four steps, Plan, Do, Check, and Act (P-D-C-A). In an effort to continually learn to improve quality or any business processes, Deming's cycle provides a structured protocol for moving through various forms of action and reflection. The Deming cycle consists of repetitive steps in a logical sequence for learning and application of learning for continuous improvement. The P-D-C-A learning cycle, represented in the figure below, is the basis of lean thinking.

Learning cycles are the repetitive application of the scientific method to a specific problem. Whether described as action and reflection, P-D-C-A, or in any other form, learning cycles embrace the scientific method. The scientific method begins with a hypothesis and then evaluates that hypothesis against experimentation. As Edison es-

tablished, iteration is the basic tenent in applying the scientific method to cycles of learning. Every iteration—regardless of whether the cycle tends to confirm or disprove a hypothesis—extends knowledge. The purpose of engineering, or any other discipline associated with product development, is to create reusable knowledge that will be used in the development of new products.

For the specific application of learning cycles in product development, Allen proposed a particular version of learning cycle he called the LAMDA cycle. This model was based on what he observed in how the Toyota engineers approached problems. Similar to Deming's improvement cycle, P-D-C-A, Allen's LAMDA cycle refers to the actions necessary to identify, refine, and address a problem through acquisition and application of knowledge. LAMDA stands for Look, Ask, Model, Dialogue, and Act.

Knowledge-based development highlights that the effectiveness and efficiency of product development is entirely predicated on the ability to create and reuse knowledge. In order to commercialize innovation, product development has to close the gap between what is known and what is needed to solve development problems through creation of knowledge. Closing the knowledge gap can be done proactively or reactively, but the gap must be closed to institute change and develop new products. Thus the speed and effectiveness of learning cycles determines a company's ability to innovate. Repeated application of well-designed learning cycles will bring the organization continually closer to an optimal solution, while poorly executed learning cycles

can be divergent, or simply create confusion and produce irrelevant information.

Knowledge-based product development systematically creates reusable knowledge through effective learning cycles designed to provide ever increasing knowledge for solving relevant problems. Each cycle builds on previous knowledge with the objective of uncovering and documenting new knowledge. A learning cycle can either converge on specific knowledge or expand to encompass broader knowledge, but each learning cycle must be designed to increase the knowledge of the system under study and close the gap between what is known and what needs to be known so that product development can proceed effectively.

The learning cycle approach to product development is based on the premise that knowledge and understanding is constantly proliferating, but that at any point in time the knowledge available is finite and often incomplete. Knowledge-based product development establishes a structure to use learning cycles in concert with the scientific method to create a knowledge capture-and-reuse system for product development.

Product development inherently begins with incomplete knowledge. Critical information is often not available. The learning cycle approach provides an alternative to simply guessing and committing to a point solution or paralysis from the fear of not getting it right the first time due to lack of information. Learning cycle development does not require first time perfection and encourages the notion that it is better to be approximately correct and try something than to be precise but wrong. Knowledge-based product development recognizes the importance of learning cycles and establishes a structured methodology for creating reusable knowledge. The more the system is used, the more effective and efficient it becomes—because knowledge created is reused, that is, shared and built upon by subsequent projects. To stimulate maximum effectiveness, this knowledge is often captured visually in the form of pictures and graphs such as limit and trade-off curves, rather than in lengthy written reports.

Set–Based Product Development

We had stumbled upon the product development limit curve by accident. Once we realized what the curve was telling us, it became obvious that we had been focused on controlling the wrong things in our attempt to improve product development. The limit curve made the design loops clearly visible, but they were unplanned and unmanaged redesign loops rather than learning cycles. The product development process was managed through phases and gates that had no correlation with the iterative nature of product development. Gate reviews were disconnected from the learning cycles needed for product development. They were simply a mechanism for management oversight. The more we drove adherence to the system the more we unknowingly induced rework loops in the system.

False positive feasibility occurred frequently as projects were allowed to progress through the development phases only to discover problems later. The shape of the product development limit curve clearly showed that certain aspects of a design run out of iteration time before others. This forces the responsibility to fix the product from an area that may be the culprit to a different area that happens to have iteration time remaining, even if it is suboptimal for resolving the problem. Although the shift of the burden to resolve problems from long cycle systems to shorter ones may not be explicitly planned, the burden shift does becomes a part of the development system. When specifications are set early, and then followed by design and testing, there is no rationale to suggest that the design rework loops will ever allow the design to converge and bring the design within compliance. The more complex the project, the less likely it is that a design solution will emerge successfully.

This process is called "point-based" development. The name refers to picking a single (point) solution early in the design process, then committing to the development of that concept through test-and-fix loops. There may be alternate backup solutions identified, but these are typically variations on a theme and not intended to be used unless there is a problem with the primary path solution. Backup solutions are rarely effective because they do not receive the same attention as the primary development path. When backup alternatives are needed, they have rarely been developed to a stage where they are viable enough to keep the project on schedule. But if two alternative development efforts receive the same support and attention, then it would double the resource requirements for the project. It is precisely this mindset that initially kept me from understanding Allen's paradigm shift. Allen berated point-based development and the use of phase and gate methodology because it encouraged this linear development behavior.

Based on his concept of a design compiler, Allen argued that a better method of product development would follow the practices pioneered by the Wright brothers and explore knowledge first, followed by a design solution later. The Wright brothers had not set out to invent flight; they had set out to advance the knowledge of heavier-than-air powered flight. The Wright Flyer was simply the assimilation of the knowledge they collected. In the discovery of flight they demonstrated a superior development methodology. Based on this observation Allen proposed a set-based, knowledge creation approach to product development as superior to a point-based linear process. From our paradigm of phases and gates, Allen's proposal to develop set-based solutions sounded like a lot more work and much less efficient.

Allen cited his research at Toyota as evidence that set-based development was practical and far superior to other methods. He argued that Toyota's development prowess came from set-based principles. Although Toyota was very secretive about their knowledge capture process, he said that he had seen examples that supported set-based development. He described a specific example in the development of exhaust systems that he had uncovered in interviews during his research. He explained that Toyota may design and test fifty rudimentary muffler systems early in a new car design to build knowledge. Through the set-based development process, Toyota would give their suppliers loose requirements and ask them to build many different systems. These early rudimentary prototypes were used only to explore the limits of the possibilities for the system. The intent was to gain knowledge by defining the trade-off parameters and the failure limits. The data were expressed visually to capture knowledge. The knowledge was passed from project to project as each new project used previously developed knowledge and added to the knowledge and understanding.

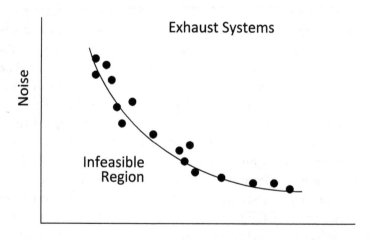

Allen proposed that the amount of prototyping and testing on a project should be inversely proportional to the knowledge gap that needed to be closed to resolve the design problem. The intent of the multiple sets was not to produce multiple alternatives for design solutions, but rather to create varied design parameters to explore specific attributes needed to close the knowledge gap. The method for picking the development parameters was a protocol similar to that for design of experiments. By developing limit curves that depicted feasible and infeasible design regions as well as trade-off curves that evaluated one design attribute against another, engineers were provided the knowledge necessary to design an optimal solution that was known to work.

This design philosophy of establishing feasible and infeasible regions had been the basis of Allen's research. Allen was convinced that Toyota's set-based design process of exploring the limits first and then picking a solution originated from the Wright brothers' methods. He firmly believed that Toyota used their knowledge in the same manner he had proposed as a design compiler, and that their business success in new product development is largely attributable to this design philosophy.

Whether Allen was accurate or not in his beliefs of Toyota's use of set-based design, and whether the process had a direct lineage to the Wright brothers became immaterial—Allen's arguments warranted consideration—Toyota has been very successful in an extremely competitive market for a very long time and I realized that anything I could learn and apply would be helpful, so I did my best to listen and comprehend. Perhaps Allen just told good stories or perhaps Allen's assessment of Toyota was completely accurate. Allen's enthusiasm often boiled over and his dynamic nature made it difficult to discern which was which. But Allen had many ideas and concepts of how things should be or could be. Yet in spite of his most earnest attempts, Allen's evangelizing efforts were rejected by most of the companies he visited. I was fortunate to work with Allen for several years until his untimely death in a plane crash during a thunderstorm en route to a company he hoped would listen. I learned a lot from Allen, but unfortunately only comprehended most of it after he was gone.

As in most major ideological shifts, comprehension requires changes in attitudes, values, and norms. Understanding only comes through a struggle of thought over time because so many of the ideas are counterintuitive to traditional points of view. Set-based ideas were difficult to conceptualize with point-based phase and gate thinking.

With more than three quarters of western companies using some type of phase and gate point-based development method, careers have been built with these principles ingrained. I was no exception. Comprehension required unlearning old principles and constructing fundamentally new frameworks of thought.

Experiential learning cycles are the essence of product development. In conventional linear point-based development, learning cycles occur as unplanned rework loops necessary to fix problems that stem from incomplete knowledge. Knowledge-based development recognizes that knowledge gaps exist in product development, and proactively bridges the knowledge gap through orchestrated, synchronized experiential learning cycles.

Set-Based Design

The important thing is not to stop questioning.

Albert Einstein

Tony Wilcox, who led knowledge management, walked into my office waving some documents in his hands as he took a seat in one of the visitors' chairs by my desk. "Look," he said, sliding two stapled packets of papers across the desk toward me.

"Test reports?" I asked, glancing at the cover sheets of the two documents.

He grinned. "Not just test reports," he said excitedly. "I think these reports help explain what limit and trade-off curves are and how we could apply them."

I glanced at the reports and could see that Tony had written one of the two reports years earlier when he worked in the test lab. Tony and I had been having an ongoing dialogue about the applicability of limit curves to our design process. The product development limit curve was interesting and it helped us separate design rework loops from phase and gate process phases, but the applicability, particularly to the design process still wasn't clear.

"I wrote that first report on a fuel-injected bike going to Brazil a couple of years ago when I was testing fuel systems in the lab," he said.

"I guess the other one just stuck in my head because it was so different. Something in our conversation the other day triggered my memory so I dug them out of the archives."

I picked up the test reports on my desk and took a closer look at them. Tony was an exceptional engineer and as I expected, his report was well written. The report was six pages long and meticulously followed the standard guidelines for test reports. On the first page was a good description of the test objective and the test conditions. As I scanned the first page I learned that fuel in Brazil has much higher ethanol content than fuel in the United States. I could see that the testing had been conducted at the request of someone on the Latin American sales team who had expressed a concern over the fuel economy and drivability of the bikes in Brazil. The guideline for Brazilian fuel allowed up to 23 percent ethanol, but the sales team had found samples with up to 30 percent ethanol and they wanted to make sure that our bikes would be okay with that amount of ethanol.

I could see that this particular test had been conducted on a motorcycle with a fuel-injected engine to address the question of whether the fuel economy and performance were within acceptable limits with Brazilian fuel. Further down the page I saw that all the pertinent test conditions were well documented. I turned the page. On the second page of the report was the test conclusion. The report stated that the motorcycle had passed the tests and that the fuel economy with Brazilian fuel was within acceptable limits. There were a few additional paragraphs that summarized the rationale for the increased fuel consumption.

I glanced through the next four pages and saw that Tony had included a well-written summary and discussion of the testing. It looked like a typical test report that could be found in any company or university laboratory. The report even described how special containers of fuel had been flown in from Brazil to make sure the test properly represented the local conditions. I laid the report back down on my desk and turned to Tony.

"Nice job," I said. "It looks very thorough."

"Thanks, but that's not the point," he responded. "Take a look at the other report and you'll see what I mean."

I picked up the second report for a closer look. The first page was similar to the other report, but the complete report was only three pages long. I quickly scanned the first page of the report and realized that this was the same test as the one Tony had conducted except it was a motorcycle with a carburetor instead of fuel injection. I flipped the page to read the conclusion. As I turned the page I could see Tony's eyes light up over the top of the paper as a grin spread across his face. To my surprise there was no specific pass or fail conclusion. Although the page contained a few descriptive paragraphs, it was mostly all graphs. I was puzzled and turned to the last page of the report, but it had no writing, just more graphs. I could see Tony holding back a laugh as I went back to the second page to read the short write-up.

The second test had been conducted by varying the ethanol content of the fuel from 0 to 100 percent ethanol. Both test reports answered the question from the Latin American sales team, but the approach was completely different. The second test did not use any special Brazilian fuel. Rather than testing to pass a specific condition, the second test *created knowledge about the effects of ethanol content in gasoline.* Without special fuel, the second test was easier to perform and it took less effort to write and read, even though it contained much more information.

The first test answered a specific question under specific conditions with a yes or no answer for the sales team. It effectively answered one very particular question but provided no useful information for future development. The second test also answered the question of the sales team but it created reusable knowledge that could be used to answer a lot of different questions under a variety of parameters (see Figure 12–1). Even though the effort was less on the second test, it created much more valuable knowledge. The first test was conducted with a linear "design, then test" mindset, the second supported a "learn, then design" mindset. The second report created reusable knowledge. If someone needed to know the effect of 15 percent ethanol, or 40 percent ethanol, the first test would need to be conducted again, but the second would not. If a design team needed to design to the new E85 fuel standard with 85 percent ethanol, the second test provides the information necessary but the first test is useless.

"I think I am beginning to understand," I said as I handed the reports back to Tony.

These tests were not intended to be set-based development but they provided the first breakthrough in understanding what Allen had tried to convey. Set-based development is not intended to be the simultaneous parallel development of multiple design options to reduce risk by increasing the odds. In fact, set-based development is a carefully

Figure 12.1

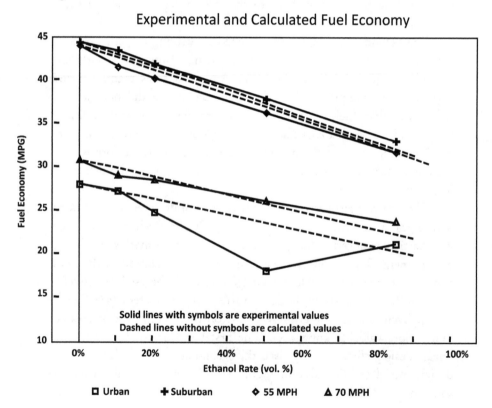

orchestrated development process that exploits the learning principles of experiential learning cycles to explore the limits of a design to understand the risks.

A New Framework for Product Development

At that moment I had been handed the keys to begin unlearning old principles and developing a new framework for conceptualizing product development. As Tony and I deliberated how this new perspective fit, we began to realize that set-based development is not about simultaneous design of multiple sets of alternatives and then testing to see what works. Instead, set-based development uses sets that intentionally vary parameters early in the development process to explore and understand the limits of what is feasible. Then the product is designed with the knowledge of those parameters.

Creating a new paradigm is a lot like building a jigsaw puzzle. The first pieces are the most difficult to connect. When the first pieces come together they feel like a breakthrough. Then each additional connection becomes easier to make as parts build on previous progress. Over time parts of the picture evolve and take shape. Sometimes one area may stall while another area makes progress. It takes persistence, but it seems that all of a sudden an entire picture emerges. That was the case for limit curves. The Brazilian fuel testing provided the breakthrough we needed as the first pieces of understanding limit curves came together. After months of Allen's failed attempts to explain the importance of limit curves and not understanding what he meant, all of a sudden limit curves were everywhere. It was not long after Tony had shown me the two test reports that the next piece of the limit curve puzzle fell into place. The test reports had shown how broad knowledge could be created and captured easily, but not how to apply it. No one had used the broader knowledge to develop anything. It had simply been used to answer a specific question for the Latin American sales team and filed in the engineering library.

The Second Piece of the Limit Curve Puzzle

It wasn't long before the second piece of the puzzle fell in place. It came in the form of a project intended to introduce a highly anticipated new model addition to a line of motorcycles, and it was the worst possible timing for false positive feasibility to happen. The project had exited the last gate review and manufacturing was in the process of ramping up for production. Marketing had launched their initial promotional campaign and the new bike had been announced to the press.

The early production bikes had been shipped to Daytona, Florida, for the annual Bike Week rally as demonstration bikes for customers to ride. Bike Week in Daytona is the annual gathering of motorcycle enthusiasts from around the country and around the world as they revel in frivolity and enjoy the sport of motorcycling. For two weeks in February, Daytona Beach is motorcycle Mecca. Bikers and biker wannabes alike converge there for this annual pilgrimage. Motorcycle manufacturers also converged there to cater to the hundreds of thousands of bikers. This venue would be the first public unveiling of the new bikes.

Meanwhile, back in cold and snowy Milwaukee, the project team waited with bated breath for news from the rally. At first it was good news, the new model was a hit. Customers waited anxiously for their chance to ride the new bikes. Then the news turned bad. The drive belts were breaking on the demonstration bikes when customers rode them. The drive belt simply transfers power from the transmission to the rear wheel of the motorcycle, but it is a critical part to making the motorcycle go. A broken drive belt means that the bike can't get power to the rear wheel and won't move.

The drive belt had been a concern early in the development process because there had been some unexpected failures on test bikes. This new model had originally not even been intended to use a new belt. The project had been approved with the intention of using the same belt as the previous model. Unfortunately early test failures forced the project team to expand the scope of the project and add the development of a new drive belt to the project. Because of the early test failures of the drive belt, the project had been under close scrutiny.

The project team had monitored the drive belt closely for problems during testing. Each failure had been addressed with a redesign loop resulting in a reworked design. Although there had been finger-pointing between the supplier and the design group early on, by the time the project reached the final gate review everyone thought that the issues had been fixed. There had not been any failures during the last design test cycle so the review board had approved the project for production. Now, with the first bikes ready to be shipped to dealers, belts were breaking on the demonstration bikes at the public launch event.

The development team was clearly out of time to rework the design. Delay of the bike was inevitable. It was just a question of how long the delay would be and how best to control the damage. There were alternate designs, but testing a new belt required thousands of miles of testing to build any confidence in the design and that would take months to complete. And even then, how would the team be sure? The last test had not resulted in any failures, but belts had broken at the rally. All the previous design loops had not produced a design that worked even though the last rework loop passed the tests. But there was no other option. The development team would need to redesign the belt again and then retest it. Product performance was paramount, and it would take months even if a solution were found on the first attempt. Management started scrambling to minimize the impact the delay would certainly have on other projects.

So the second piece of the set-based development puzzle fell into place—there was a clear need and an opportunity to apply what we had been learning to a real-world situation. Perhaps the urgency of the situation allowed us to look at the problem differently. Perhaps it was just time to try a different approach, albeit in parallel. Due to the difficulties and the amount of rework the team had gone through, a lot of information had been collected by the design team and the supplier during the development process. There was a lot known about the design parameters that affected the drive belt. But even though there was a lot of data, reusable and visible knowledge had not been created. Every problem with the test bikes had been documented in reports by the test riders. They had compiled notebooks full of documentation and test reports. The new bikes had been tested for thousands of miles and had eventually passed the tests, but the design had still failed. Allen often told me that most companies spend too much time testing and collect information and not enough time digesting it to create knowledge. In looking at our process, Allen had suggested that we stop testing for a while and compile our information into visible, reusable knowledge. We hadn't done it; we hadn't understood what he meant—but now Allen's words rung in my head, "It's not the test information you collect that's important, but how it's digested and made visible to create reusable knowledge that's important."

Could the test information we had already collect possibly contain a clue to the problem? It was certainly a place to start. The challenge was to digest the data and make the knowledge visible, so the test engineers began combing through the notebooks to find the data on belt failures. The data from all the different reports were compiled in the attempt to draw a picture. The picture began by plotting the mileage of each belt failure hoping that it would give a clue about the problem. But it didn't help. There was no particular mileage that caused the failures. In fact, it seemed that it was just a line with data points from 7,000 miles to 25,000 miles (see Figure 12–2).

Looking at the broken belts revealed nothing about the problem either. Each of the broken belts had the same failure characteristics. Finally someone asked the question of what load the belts actually broke at. This had never been an issue because the belt had been developed on the previous model with a larger displacement engine. The previous model with the larger engine had been in production for a year with no major issues. Since the belt had not been planned to be a part of the new model development project, the strength requirement for the drive belt had not been calculated.

Figure 12.2

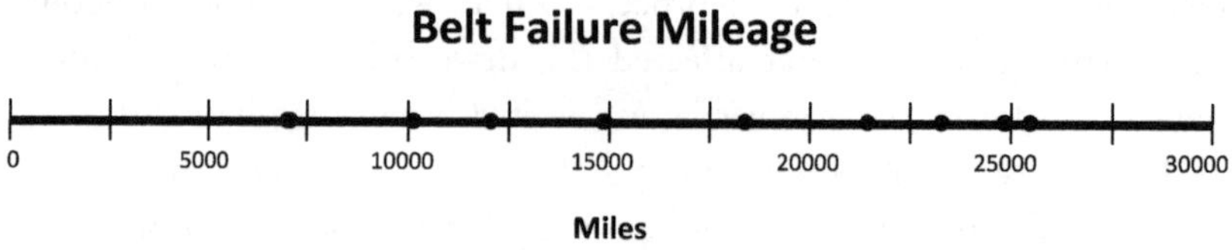

Belt Failure Mileage

Miles

Then the question turned to how much force actually caused the broken belts to fail. The actual strength of each belt could not be tested because they were already broken at the weakest point, like the weakest link in a chain. But by pulling the remaining belt apart on a tensile test machine it was possible to determine the next weakest "link." Plotting the mileage of the belt against the remaining tensile strength gave a bit more separation of the data (see Figure 12–3), but it didn't answer the question of why the belts broke, nor did it provide much general design knowledge.

When the tensile test results came back they showed that the broken belts had all failed below 10,000 pounds, although they were rated above that value by the supplier. Was it just a bad batch of belts that caused the problems? Now the finger-pointing started again between the supplier and the design team. There were plenty of choice words from both sides, but the development team still had to figure out if the problem was a manufacturing problem or a design problem. New belts were quickly expedited from the idled factory that should have been making bikes and put on the tensile test machine to be pulled apart. But when the testing was completed it showed that all

Figure 12.3

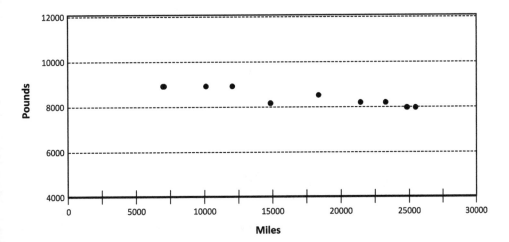

Remaining Tensile Strength after Testing

the belts in the test sample broke above the specification of 10,000 pounds (see Figure 12–4). The belts were good. This was also the same batch of parts that replacement belts had been taken from and sent to the rally to fix bikes at the show. Some of those belts had also already broken on demonstration bikes.

Unfortunately, the more data the team collected, the more questions it seemed to create. Why did the belts pass early, but fail late? Were there two sets of belts? What was the real impact of the test miles on the belts? With a bit of ingenuity, the team devised a way to run just the final drive belt and pulleys on a test machine to quickly replicate the test miles on a complete motorcycle. They broke the problem into its constituent elements. Within hours the team could run the equivalent of thousands of test miles. So they systematically began running belts on the machines to simulate test miles, then they pulled the belts apart to measure their strength. They quickly devel-

Figure 12.4

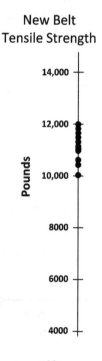

**New Belt
Tensile Strength**

oped a curve that demonstrated the degradation in strength of the belt as it accumulated mileage. Then, testing the motorcycles to determine what the ultimate impact load was, they discovered that due to the gearing and engine tuning, the smaller displacement engine could actually impart a higher load on the final drive than the larger engine in the previous model.

The design team digested the data to turn it into visible knowledge (see Figure 12–5). The previous model was designed without ever knowing the true characteristics of the belt. The previous belt was selected based on sales data from the supplier and it had passed the development testing. On the previous model there had been a few test failures, but nothing of significant statistical concern. The new model had a smaller engine and it had never really occurred to the develop-

Figure 12.5

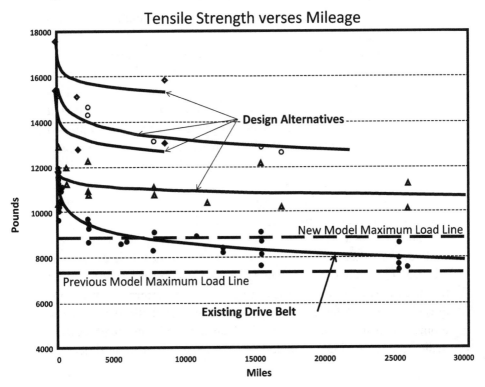

ment team that there might be an issue. Making the knowledge visible clarified the problem. The belt strength degraded as it accumulated mileage. With the old model, the belt didn't degrade to the point that it lost enough strength to break because the previous model had a lower maximum load limit. With the new model, the belts quickly degraded below the load threshold. When people at the rally rode the new bikes, they rode them very hard to test the limits. When we spoke to our professional test riders, we learned that they had known they needed to be careful in the way they rode the bikes. After all, they had also gone through multiple redesign loops and they had learned something in the process as well. They just made sure that they shifted smoothly and accelerated smoothly as they went through their test sequences to allow the belts to pass the test. But the real-world customers didn't know or care about belt failures, and did nothing smooth. They hammered the bikes mercilessly and used our product differently than our test riders had. They shifted hard and accelerated hard to see what the bike would do. They quickly found the problems with our design.

With the knowledge visible in the form of a limit curve, the problem was obvious. A set of alternative designs that varied the key parameters affecting the belt strength were quickly made and tested. This time the design team did not pick a solution, but rather constructed the set of alternatives in such a way that the design alternatives probed the envelope of possibilities. With test machines to simulate mileage, the team quickly had a picture that mapped their knowledge and the design space. With the knowledge visible, they simply needed to select the parameters to optimize cost and a variety of other attributes, knowing up front that the design was feasible.

The plant had not been idle for very long and the retest by the traditional method had not even started when a new belt design was selected. This time there was enough confidence in the knowledge that had been created that no road testing on actual motorcycles was conducted before the factory started production again. Rather than the months of lost production that had been feared, the plant quickly made up the lost time and bikes were shipped to dealers on time.

• • •

When Allen talked about set-based development it had been difficult to understand what he meant from a linear development perspective. "Set-based" sounded like simultaneously developing multiple sets of alternatives to reduce the odds of failure. It sounded like additional work and effort to reduce risk. But set-based development is not redundant development. Set-based development is a focused effort of using a set of varied design parameters to create knowledge. Set-based development relies on experiential learning cycles to build knowledge over time, defining what is known and what needs to be learned. By making the knowledge visible and defining the limits of the design space, set-based development exposes development risk. Set-based development is a focused approach of exploring the limits of the design envelope and then using the knowledge to design a workable solution by designing within the limits. Going through the exercise of creating a visual representation of what was known about belt failures and systematically filling in the missing information created the knowledge we needed for understanding the problem and then finding the best solution.

The use of set-based techniques to create knowledge and make the knowledge visible before picking a design solution resulted in a better solution with much less time and effort spent. From the exercise it was clear that the set-based development approach achieved a workable solution in less time and with greater certainty than a traditional linear design method that relied on quickly picking a seemingly plausible solution early, followed by testing to verify it.

The visual knowledge created by development teams through set-based development becomes immediately available for any other project team to reuse. Other projects can reuse the knowledge or add to the knowledge as needed for their project and expand what is known. Most importantly, set-based development makes it clear where the limits of the design are and what the margin to failure is. Limit and trade-off curves provide a convenient medium to collect, store, and share knowledge. The visualization of what is known and where knowledge gaps exist creates an effective technology roadmap that points the direction for future development efforts.

The pieces of the limit curve puzzle had come together and had exposed the virtues of set-based development in the process. Limit curves had been demonstrated in a critical design situation and had shown how set-based development was used to create reusable knowledge. Now it was time to build a knowledge-based development system by combining set-based development with cadence and flow through experiential learning cycles.

CHAPTER 13

Leadership Learning and Pull Events

A single hour a day, steadily given to the study of some interesting subject, brings unexpected accumulations of knowledge.

William Ellery Channing

Cadence and flow had been well-ingrained in the development process as a mechanism to drive the work stream of product development. It was great in theory but it lost a bit in the application. It was not that it wasn't practical, but rather that the cadence and flow of bins was only one of the pillars necessary to support effective product development. The issue was that false positive feasibility continually disrupted the cadence and flow of the system. The intent was correct, but not all the techniques were in place to make it effective. When I first met Allen Ward, what he described was intriguing because it provided the potential of eliminating the redesign loop-backs that disrupted flow of the process. The addition of set-based principles to create reusable knowledge became the second pillar in the creation of knowledge-based product development. The change process from the linear development mindset that had been ingrained in the organization for so many years to a knowledge-based development system was beginning.

The Product Development Leadership Learning Team had spent a lot of time, energy, and emotion on understanding how to change the development process. There had been both heated debates and open dialogue over the years in an attempt to understand how to change and what to change in product development. Unfortunately, there was more reflection than action, and the PDL²T was eventually disbanded. Yet the learning remained and enough people had gotten a glimpse of knowledge-based product development from Allen Ward and had read Michael Kennedy's book, *Product Development for the Lean Enterprise*, to ultimately form a core group of "true believers" with the conviction to take action and make a difference.[1] Now it was time to create a development system by combining set-based learning principles with the cadence principles of bins to truly get product development to flow through the development organization.

The Leadership Learning Change Model

Establishment of knowledge-based development enabling new products to flow began with the application of a change model developed through the dialogue and learning of the PDL²T. It was called the Leadership Learning Change Model. The Leadership Learning Change Model is based on experiential learning cycles and it applies the principles of Plan-Do-Check-Act to changing a complex system like a product development organization. The change model is based on the four P-D-C-A steps but modifies them to create the steps necessary to change mental models and create the shared vision that becomes the driver for change.

Changing a complex system such as product development necessitates building shared vision, one of the key disciplines of a learning organization. The first step of changing a complex system begins with astute observation of the existing condition. But physically observing a system in its generalized, abstract totality is not possible. A system can only be assessed through observation of specific *events* that occur as a

194

result of the system. Events are concrete, observable actions that happen in the course of developing products. Over time, individual observable events create observable patterns of behavior. These patterns of events are a bit more abstract than directly observable individual events, but the patterns provide additional information and implications regarding the unseen system. Although patterns can often not be directly observed, they can be seen through pictures and graphs. The importance of patterns is that they provide evidence to begin understanding the underlying systemic structures of a hidden system. The lack of a pattern between phase gate exits and successful projects, for example, as well as the pattern of rework loops depicted in the product development limit curve created an important picture that allowed understanding of the invisible product development system.

Assessment is the second step in the Leadership Learning Change process. Assessment considers the systemic structure that underlies the existing system that drives the events and patterns we can see. Open dialogue to assess what drives the observed patterns exposes the mental models that determine both individual and group behavior. This is the beginning of learning because dialogue over mental models leads to people being able to express their visions and ideas. First it is the mental models and visions of the existing system assessed against the actual performance of the system. It is the assessment of what was intended from the system compared with the observable patterns of events and output that the system produces. When it is recognized that the observable pattern of events does not correspond to the vision for the system, the third step of change begins.

The third step of the leadership learning change process is the collaborative development of new visions and mental models. Creating different patterns that produce different results requires changing the systemic structure of the underlying system. Changing the system requires developing new visions of the system based on new mental models of how and why the system behaves the way it does. New mental models may be validated through experimentation, but leaders must eventually define and implement the changes necessary to alter the systemic structure.

The fourth phase of the change model is implementation. Implementation requires changing the working habits and culture of the organization. As changes to the system are put in place they alter the events and patterns of the system. New patterns emerge as a result and the system produces a different output. The new events can once again be observed and the new patterns documented. At this point the leadership learning change process begins a new cycle of continuous improvement.[2] Figure 13-1 offers a visual representation of this process.

Driving change to the product development process via the leadership learning model exposed that not everyone chooses to participate in the change process. Many were uncomfortable with exposing their mental models. Some had grown accustomed to dictating a vision or having one dictated to them. Collaborative learning is difficult and often individuals are too invested in an existing system to be able to adapt. They are comfortable in the status quo and creating a new order is too uncomfortable for them. Unfortunately, some of these people

Figure 13.1

The Leadership Learning Change Process

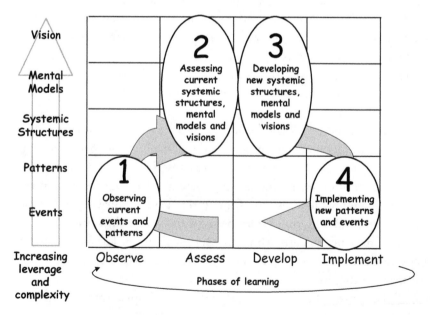

196

opted not to participate. Some even sought to undermine the process in order to maintain a system they had grown comfortable operating within. Nevertheless, a core group with the conviction that change was both necessary and possible began to create shared visions and mental models for the new system.

Armed with a new ideology and encouraged by pockets of success, the small group that chose to participate began to develop new mental models to describe the way the new system should behave. Understanding came through dialogue and the struggle of thought over time because so many of the ideas were counterintuitive to traditional thinking. It required unlearning old principles and constructing fundamentally new frameworks of thought. The overall improvement effort was guided by the primary focus to create flow across the development portfolio. The shift in thinking began with a shift from the design-and-rework loops to the creation of intentional learning cycles. With the recognition that improving the output of the development process would require changing the underlying system, we chose to focus on the integration points of the system as the lever for change. The product development limit curve had highlighted the correlation between integration points and successful projects. Now the focus of our change efforts intended to leverage those points.

Our new mental model was constructed on the notion that if we could control the integration points, we could control the system. The intent was to use the integration points to create a new systemic structure to drive the development process with evenly paced integration points as "pull events" for the process.[3] Evenly paced integration points meant that each learning cycle would eventually occur over the same period of time. Evenly paced integration points could be used to synchronize the entire system through the learning cycles of all the subsystems. Equal length learning cycles could also be used to establish standardized work for the learning process and systematically reduce the time of learning cycles.

Success in creating evenly paced integration points would be observable through the product development limit curve becoming linear, represented by the longer dotted line in Figure 13–2. The new mental model also identified that once the development process was synchronized and the development teams created reusable knowledge, then the learning cycles could be systemically shortened to reduce the overall development time. The shorter learning cycles and reduced development time should be observed by a shift in the slope of the product development curve as it became steeper (the shorter dotted line in Figure 13–2).

Now with a new mindset developed and a hypothesis in place of how to observe the changes, it was time to implement the changes to the system.

Testing the new mental model and changing the systemic structure began by creating pull events out of the integration points that had been highlighted by the product development limit curve.

The early phases of the development process had historically been the most difficult to control. Early events had the greatest variation in

Figure 13.2

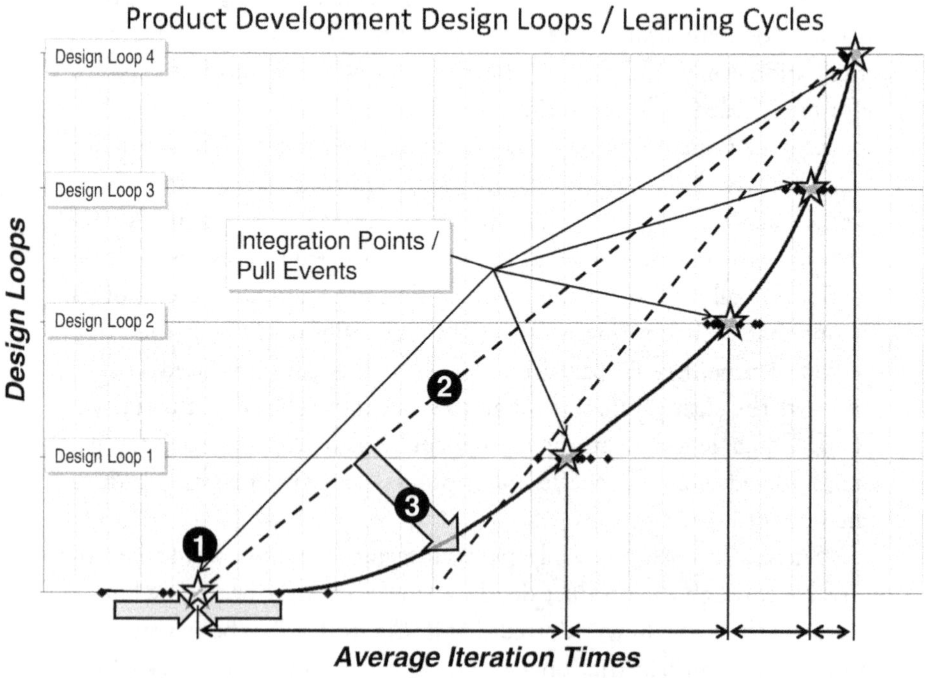

Product Development Design Loops / Learning Cycles

timing and involved the longest redesign loops. The early integration points were the least structured and thus were ideal for testing the new mindset. The first pull event was constructed with the intent of testing the hypothesis that the product development system could be managed through integration points. If the system could be controlled through pull events then it would provide the leverage needed to improve the system. Certainly there would be much more to be learned, but the fundamental mechanism of the new mental model would at least be validated.

Early Pull Events

It was early February and it was nice to be in sunny 90-degree Phoenix, Arizona rather than Milwaukee, Wisconsin, where it was cold and a steady mix of snow and rain had been falling for days. The first week of February had been picked months earlier as the first pull event date to test the new mindset of how product development worked. The date was selected because it roughly aligned with the average timing of a traditional integration point early in the development process.

It was the first of three steps planned in sequence to implement knowledge-based product development. The first step was to reduce the variability and improve the consistency of the integration points. Knowledge-based development required a shift from redesign loops to planned learning cycles and the integration points were identified as an important component to make it work. This first event was an initial experiment to test the validity of the new mindset. "Regardless of the outcome of the experiment," I thought to myself, "It sure is nice to be in Phoenix to ride motorcycles for a couple of days while my own bike is still mothballed in the garage."

The objective of the pull event was simple. It was designed to focus the development organization on a tangible event to force completion of a learning cycle with the objective to physically demonstrate it. The pull event had been orchestrated by having all the key executives responsible for planning and managing the product portfolio scheduled to be at the proving grounds for two days in February. The project teams were expected to demonstrate their projects with early prototype motorcycles for the executives to ride and evaluate at the proving grounds. Over the two days, a series of hands-on events were organized to review every project and for the Product Planning Committee to make a decision to approve the project, to modify its scope, schedule, or resources, or to cancel it.

The expected outcome was to leave Phoenix with a clearly defined product development portfolio that the organization was committed to deliver and to have that product development portfolio synchronized so the next learning cycle could be planned and coordinated through the next pull event. There was a strong incentive for the development teams to be ready because projects that were ready could get support. Projects that were not would be canceled.

Preparation and planning for this inaugural event began months before anything was announced to the project teams. Once the pull event was announced, monthly reviews and sometimes weekly reviews took place to make sure that the project teams understood the expectations and that progress was being made toward the objectives of the event. But changing the culture and ingrained work habits is difficult. Initial attempts at learning cycles more often resembled design rework loops than true set-based design cycles intended to create knowledge. Nevertheless, the change process had begun and that was good.

The focus and attention that the event generated through the organization was a surprise. The traditional phase and gate reviews continued unchanged, but the organization seemed to relate much more to the tangibility of a physical event. Gate reviews were paper-based and happened in a conference room. At gate reviews project teams made presentations and reported their status against various metrics such as the percent of drawings complete and the percent of suppliers identified. Pull events did not rely on paper presentations but rather physical demonstration. There was no question about the number of drawings that were complete or if suppliers could make the part. Either the parts were on the bike and they functioned, or they did not.

The week of the pull event arrived and it was time for final preparations and last-minute schedule adjustments. The motorcycles needed to be on the correct test tracks at the right time so the members of the

Product Planning Committee could rotate through the various areas to evaluate the projects. By the time I was in Phoenix, almost all the project teams had arrived with their prototype motorcycles ready to be reviewed. The Dillon team was there with their big 250-series back tire crammed under the seat of a Softail Custom. It looked cool—low and mean, with attitude to spare. There was a custom chopper to evaluate in comparison. It had a 300-series tire in back with long raked-out front forks and high drag bars. The JED team brought a couple of bikes with larger displacement engines that needed to be on the high speed oval. The Othello team needed to be on the sport track to evaluate their bikes against a number of competitors' sport bikes. And the Ulysses team needed a special test loop into the desert to evaluate how it performed off-road. Altogether there were nearly fifty projects to coordinate for reviews. It was late in the afternoon on the day before the event as we worked outside in the hot sun making sure that the shade tents, water stations, and motorcycles were all in place. Only one team was visibly absent.

The Viper project was missing and I knew they had run into a last-minute problem getting ready for the event. Someone had made a late decision to change something on the bike and the team had used the traditional "pick a solution and make it work" method of development in their haste. Unfortunately, the solution they picked did not work, and the team had been scrambling over the past couple of weeks to get new parts designed and procured. The Viper team room back in Milwaukee had looked like a project just ahead of launch rather than so early in the development process. The level of activity in the room had been like a beehive with people buzzing around. There were "rush order" tags and parts stacked on desks and in corners of the room. There was a sense of urgency in the air you could feel as soon as you walked into the room.

When the semi with the bikes left Milwaukee, Viper had not been on it. The latest report of its whereabouts placed it in a back room of the Kansas City factory, partially built and waiting for parts. Sadly, I crossed Viper off the rotation schedule and made the necessary adjustments as we headed to the hotel for a well-deserved shower before the kickoff meeting that night. It was great that nearly all the project teams had made the pull event. It proved that we could control integration event timing, but as we all piled into the vans to go to the hotel, I could not help being a little disappointed they had not all made it. Viper played an important role in the product plan, and without Viper other projects would need to make up the revenue loss. Adjustments to the product plan would be addressed on the last day of the event after all the projects had been evaluated and discussed. The concerns over Viper were left at the test track as the vans pulled away and carried us to the hotel.

The first night of the inaugural pull event went well as project teams and executives were briefed on the schedule of events and the various activities for the upcoming days. With formalities held short, the night quickly transitioned into a social hour. Part of the objective planned into the pull event was to create open dialogue between executives and the project teams in a way that cannot happen in the confines of a conference room. An important element of a successful pull event is team building, and nothing helps build relationships like food, drinks, and a common passion for cool products. I had an early-morning wake-up call to make sure I was at the track before the main group arrived, so the party was still going on when I headed for bed.

The next morning was another bright sunny day, but then again, I've never been in Phoenix when it wasn't. It was nice to be out in the desert early in the morning as the sun rose over the Superstition Mountains, and before the heat made the asphalt sticky. The desert was still quiet as roadrunners darted between the scrub bushes and a small group of us made the rounds to put the keys in the bikes and make sure everything was in order. When we got to the track where Viper was supposed to be we were shocked to find the Viper team setting up their bike for the day.

Flabbergasted, but happy to readjust the day's schedule I asked the team what had happened. "Well," the team leader started, "we figured you guys were serious about this pull event business and we didn't want our project canceled so we figured we should be here."

"Yeah!" Mark, the test engineer, interrupted. Pointing to the team leader, he said, "Chris made us rent a Ryder truck in Milwaukee and load up the last-minute parts. We drove that damn truck all the way to Kansas City to pick up the half-built bike and all the pieces they still had. Then we finished building the bike on the way down here in the back of the truck. Do you know what it's like driving a rental truck like this across the Rocky Mountains in February?" he said, poking at my chest with his finger. Then he grabbed my arm and led me to the front of the truck. "Look," he said, pointing to the front bumper. "We slid off the road in a snow storm in the mountains. It took us forever to get this thing out of the ditch. Because of the snow, we didn't get here till really early this morning." I looked up from the bumper at the Viper team that had also gathered around the front of the truck. Every one of them was grinning from ear to ear. I had never seen so much pride in an accomplishment. The look of determination in their eyes and the swagger in their step confirmed that pull events were the key to transforming product development.

Later that day, the Viper project team leader pulled me aside and apologized. "Hey, I'm sorry to mess up the schedule," he said. "I would have told you the bike was going to be here, but I really didn't know if they were going to make it. Those guys called me yesterday when they were digging the truck out of the snow bank." I just beamed, I could not have been happier. The story of how Viper got to the pull event quickly circulated to everyone in Phoenix. By the end of the day the Viper team was being talked about back in Milwaukee as well. The dedication and commitment to success, and the willingness to take risks to achieve a goal was normally only reserved for the last few weeks before "job one" when launch was at stake. The Viper team had proven the effectiveness of clear tangible integration points and the power of pull events.

Creating Leverage Through Pull Events

The Leadership Learning Change Model identifies the need to establish new visions and new mental models and then instill change through creating new systemic structures. Pull events validated that the new mindset and the new systemic structure we were attempting to create was directionally correct. But not all efforts to instill new

systemic structures were successful. Some of the efforts were intentionally undermined by individuals reluctant to change and some were just
plain wrong in concept or execution. Each new cycle offered a new
opportunity for learning and discovery. The lessons of what worked
and what did not work evolved over time. In establishing new events
and patterns in support of our new vision, important lessons emerged
from conducting pull events.

It was learned that:

- Pull events work effectively to leverage systemic change in product development. However, to be effective, pull events need to
be orchestrated integration activities that are scheduled according to a set cadence intended to drive interaction across the
product development system and pace the project portfolio.
They are most effective when they incorporate meaningful elements of the work. Pull events should evolve out of activities
that naturally occur in the development process.

- Pull events are most effective when they are binary and data
driven. Since pull events have a decision component to them,
the more closely the pull event results in a clear and unambiguous yes or no outcome, the better. The more closely cause and
effect are coupled, the greater the value in the activity both in
terms of learning for the next cycle, and in development speed.
Immediacy of feedback is also important. Efficiency of decision
making greatly influences the overall development speed and this
is particularly relevant for pull events.

- Effective pull events directly integrate leadership in the event.
Visible leadership engagement is important for pull events to be
effective in creating changes to the systemic structures of product development. Once systemic structural change occurs, leadership needs to continue to be coupled with pull events as these
events become the control points for the process.

- Pull events should be casual yet structured. They need to be
casual enough to facilitate frank and open dialogue, as a casual
environment helps create the setting to allow the necessary dis-

course. However, pull events need to be structured so that all parties involved know what is expected from whom and when. The associated consequences and desired outcomes also need to be clearly defined.

- Pull events work best when they are tangible and integrate across the organization. The more visual or physical the medium used in the pull event the more effective the event. Pull events should engage as many senses as possible and involve as many organizational disciplines as practical.

- Timing of pull events should also be carefully considered. Pull events need to align with the systemic structure of product development and should be scheduled uniformly across the project portfolio to maintain a constant rhythm. Since pull events define the convergence points for projects and the portfolio, they must also be scheduled in accordance with the practical capability or improvement limitations of the organization. Nevertheless, improvement reach should be encouraged. Pull events are not intended to create a crisis or become a whip, but rather are intended to create focus for the organization to converge on key planning events. Working to pull events forces the development community to keep the flow moving and serves to maintain projects within the bounds of the limit curve while reducing process variation

A key outcome of pull events as they become the end points for learning cycles is that they drive narrowing of set-based development solution sets. With each learning cycle new information is uncovered and visually displayed, allowing culling of the solution sets based on knowledge. Allen would refer to this as "killing the weak." Killing off the weak ideas should be done as an informed decision with knowledge that it does not work rather than killing a solution because the knowledge that it will work is lacking. When pull events align with learning cycles, one of the most important purposes of the event is to narrow the solution set through knowledge uncovered in the learning cycle. Each pull event narrows the field, to ultimately converge on the optimal solution based on knowledge.

CHAPTER 14

Quickening Product Development

One man with courage makes a majority.

Andrew Jackson

The initial pull event was successful because it proved that the new vision and mindset of using pull events to drive product development could work. The systemic structure we hoped to create for product development was directionally correct. There was, however, still a lot to be learned. There were many course corrections along the way in the struggle to implement improvement in an organization that didn't feel that it necessarily needed to change. We had learned that pull events are a valid mechanism for controlling and aligning product development; unfortunately it was also quickly discovered that it takes more than desire and determination to achieve pull events. The Viper team had demonstrated that with focus, commitment, and grit, a motivated team can overcome significant obstacles. But just like lowering the water level in a stream uncovers rocks and reducing inventory in manufacturing uncovers problems, the regimented cadence of pull events uncovers the obstacles as well as soundness of product development practices.

Creating a successful pull event is a microcosm of the product development process as a whole. But rather than years of development that ends in product launch, pull events segment the longer development process into multiple learning cycles, each with its own mini-launch, the pull event. These learning cycles are much shorter in duration and more intense than a traditional development process. As a fundamental principle of lean processes, pull events intentionally identify and remove slack time. Without slack time available within a learning cycle, it is difficult to catch up when a project falls behind. Knowledge-based development highlights issues at pull events rather than at launch, allowing them to be addressed earlier. Pull events shift project management from *railroad planning* to *combat planning*.

Railroad Planning versus Combat Planning

Planning is a crucial element in successful project management. Effective planning and control often mark the difference between a successful project and an unsuccessful one. However, traditional project planning typically follows the format of "railroad planning." Railroad planning works well for things that are very structured, like train schedules. In railroad planning, one person plans and schedules the work and duties for many others. Railroad planning is effective for tasks that are predictable and consistent but does not accommodate change well.

In projects that use railroad planning a "scheduler" creates the plan and determines the schedule for the project team to follow. Projects that use railroad planning are characterized by lengthy Gantt charts and schedules that identify exactly what each person is expected to accomplish by when, much like the 863-step CCPDP process at Roaring Motors. These plans tend to be task based, and for large or complex projects, scheduling can require a dedicated team because delays or problems mean that the plan must be constantly adjusted; otherwise it becomes obsolete. Modification to plans can be extremely cumbersome to recalculate. In railroad planning, minor schedule disruptions can have major implications on the project as a whole, because tasks and activities are so tightly interrelated. Minor delays in one project can quickly escalate to have major implications on the entire portfolio due to complex interdependencies. To compensate, slack time is commonly scheduled into the planning process.

Railroad planning assumes that throughput of a system is fixed due to the structured nature and interdependency of tasks and activities. Increased throughput is only achieved with additional resources. Railroad planning assumes that the master schedule will be followed and that progress will be maintained. It relies on point solutions as the most efficient means of completing projects. Railroad planning follows the adage of "do it right the first time."

In contrast, "combat planning" follows the mantra that "plans are good until the first bullet flies." Combat planning is suited to turbulent and ever-changing conditions. It relies on sound aggregate objectives, with each unit adjusting its plans to achieve its objectives based on the local conditions. Combat planning favors the prepared and is based on planning and committing to key objectives as a group. Everyone must develop alternatives in order to ensure achieving shared goals.

When a combat planning mentality is applied to product development through the use of pull events, product development becomes a sequence of objectives to conquer. Creating a sequence of objectives that build on each other until the project is ready for launch fundamentally changes the organization's approach to product development. Project length becomes a factor of the number of learning cycles and pull events necessary to create the appropriate knowledge. Everyone becomes focused on learning in order to achieve the next objective. Project management skills become important so everyone can adjust their work to achieve the objectives in a constantly changing and fluid environment. Combat planning relies on set-based thinking to ensure objectives are achieved.

The idea of converting naturally occurring integration events into planned pull events was spawned out of the dialogue over many conversations with Allen Ward. As we debated the difficulties of maintaining cadence and flow in product development, Allen described how Toyota used milestone events to create cadence and flow in their process. We had recognized the importance of cadence and flow and instilled it into our product development process, but we had lacked the mechanism to drive it. Allen described Toyota's development process as subservient to preset milestone events. When the product development limit curve identified the presence of integration events as the driver for product development we began to ponder how they could be leveraged.

Allen claimed that Toyota never ever missed a milestone event. He referred to the actions and attitudes that he observed at Toyota to achieve the milestones as combat planning. What he observed at Toyota was an attitude similar to what he had witnessed as an Army Ranger, so he coined the term "combat planning" to describe it. As an Army Ranger, the objective for the team was clearly defined, but the approach to achieve it changed constantly based on actual conditions.

Our dialogue turned to planning as we conceptualized how the idea of milestone events might "pull" the development process along and a combat planning attitude could be created. Pull events became our milestone events and we schemed how integration points could be converted to pull events. Together a plan was laid out to translate Toyota's milestones into Western thinking and adapt them to the Harley-Davidson process. By the time we were ready to begin the shift to pull events Allen was gone and we were on our own, but he had often emphasized the importance that Toyota placed on never ever missing a milestone event. Now that same conviction needed to be instilled into our team, never to miss a pull event.

The actions by the Viper team at the inaugural pull event were very encouraging and reinforced that we were headed in the right direction. But it was not long before it became clear that Harley-Davidson was not ready to adopt a combat planning approach to achieving pull events. Lean principles are simple and common sense in isolation, but when you attempt to apply lean principles to a traditional system, it quickly becomes extremely evident that they function in a very complex and intricate system. In fact, lean principles tend to lose much of their impact outside a larger system. The interdependencies are not immediately obvious until you try to apply them. A lean transformation is much more than just copying tools. It is understanding the thinking that is pivotal to success. And understanding only comes from thinking and doing.

Establishing and Using Help Chains

The first experiment with pull events was fairly tightly controlled. There were only a few projects involved and they were monitored very closely. Any issue that surfaced was quickly addressed. Unknowingly, we introduced combat planning into the experiment. We intended to create a controlled environment for the experiment but very close oversight of the projects unintentionally established "help chains." A help chain is simply the standard way for people to identify they need help with a problem, and for the appropriate people to respond. Help chains are the predefined protocol of who and how someone steps in to help when an issue is identified. In preparation for our first pull event, due to the intense direct oversight, project issues were immediately escalated (moved up the organization) for resolution and project plans were adjusted with a combat approach.

However, when we attempted to use pull events more broadly and encompass the entire portfolio, there were too many projects to monitor closely. Without a combat planning mentality and an oversight mechanism to address issues quickly, the new systemic structure was called into question. The complexity of projects and the sheer number of them threatened to undermine the system we were attempting to build. For the system to work, everyone in the organization had to focus on delivering their project to the cadence of the next pull event. Issues needed to be resolved quickly and effectively to maintain cadence and flow.

Lean systems inherently have little margin for error. In order to combat the lack of slack time, lean systems establish help chains to keep the system operating when issues arise. In manufacturing, the help chain is often initiated by an "andon" signal. When an operator needs help he turns on the andon light to signal that he needs assistance which initiates the help chain. When a team leader sees that an andon light is on they know exactly what to do. They immediately rush to the aid of the worker to assist them. Their objective is to resolve the problem within the cycle time in order to keep production flowing. If they are not able to resolve the issue together, then there is a preestablished protocol to effectively continue escalation of the issue until it is appropriately resolved. Preplanning the standardized protocol for problem resolution is very important to maintain flow.

Through implementation of learning cycles and pull events we had attempted to create a lean system from a traditional system but we had failed to build in the help chain necessary to keep the process flowing when issues emerged. Manufacturing deals with tangible elements. In manufacturing it is generally easy to see that the line is down, or that product has stopped flowing. Manufacturing has tangible and physical elements that you can touch and feel and see move. Product development is intangible. It is very difficult to see that the development process has stopped flowing.

In the first attempt to instill a pull event, the initial projects had been monitored very closely, so any issues were immediately addressed or escalated. When we did that, we had inadvertently instituted both combat planning and a help chain. As the number of projects increased, the direct connection to each project went away, and both the combat planning mindset and the help chain went away. Forging a help chain first requires defining what constitutes a problem. It is often even necessary to define different types of problems. Once problems are defined, the signal for help needs to be created. Also the specific type of help for each problem needs to be established in addition to defining how quickly the help needs to arrive.

We had not created help chains to support a system that had variability but no slack. The lack of help chains became very evident as problems surfaced at inopportune times. A benefit of the pull events, however, was that they forced problems to the surface. Traditionally, issues were discovered by accident, or were surfaced at launch, so having them surface at pull events was a slight improvement. We needed a way to encourage problems to be highlighted and we needed help chains to resolve problems swiftly and deliberately when they were identified.

Ultimately, the role of leadership is to set direction, make decisions, and solve problems. But knowing what decisions need to be made or what the urgent problems are that need to be resolved are not always immediately apparent. Ken Sutton, the vice president of engineering, once shared his vision with me. "I want to be able to stand at the exit of the building at the end of the day and as people leave to go home, ask them, 'Did you have a good day?'" He went on to say, "After they answer, I want to look them in the eye and ask them 'How do you know?'" Ken was right; how *do* people know if they had a good day? Is a good day getting to all the meetings on time? Is a good day measured by the number of e-mails or phone messages that get a response?

Ken came from manufacturing. In manufacturing everyone always knew if they were having a good day. They didn't even need to wait until the end of the day to figure it out. If the requirement for the plant is to produce 800 parts during an eight-hour shift, at the end of the day it is clear if the goal was achieved or not. The day can even be broken down to know if a specific machine is having a good hour or minute. In product development it is much more difficult to know a good day from a bad day. How do product developers know if they contributed to the objectives for the company as well as they could that day?

Using Visual Management

There is a parking lot that separates the Harley-Davidson technical center from one of the engine plants. Ken ran the engine plants for several years before he came to engineering. In the engine plant it is easy to see if they are having a good day. The plant knows how many engines they need to make every day and every hour. Every department knows how many parts need to be produced and that number is displayed for the entire department to see. Every worker knows their contribution toward the success of the plant. Electronic signs constantly display how the plant is doing. Everyone knows if it's a good or bad day. There are visual displays that track progress and report if the plant is ahead or behind where they need to be. When there is a problem anywhere in the plant, a preestablished help chain is used to alert the appropriate support network to get it resolved quickly and keep the plant on track.

The engine plant also used visual management to broadcast what was happening in the plant. The purpose of visual management is to make status visible at a glance. Visual management creates a work environment where it's simple to see whether every part of the plant is operating normally or abnormally. Visual management creates standard conditions so any abnormalities can be easily spotted and quickly addressed. We needed to find a way to bring that capability to the product development "factory."

Continuous improvement happens through the constant application of P-D-C-A through experiential learning cycles. Sometimes a learning cycle is no more than trying something you think might work in order to uncover the barriers and then find a way around, over, or through them. In trying to improve product development we faced a barrier in not being able to see the work. There had to be a way to make product development visible and instill help chains like the engine plant. Limit and trade-off curves helped to make the knowledge created from the learning cycles visible, but the product development process itself needed to be made visible. Just like in manufacturing, the status of the work and the flow of the work had to be made visible.

The initial answer surfaced during a routine After Action Review. After Action Reviews (AARs) are a learning tool that Harley-Davidson adopted from the U.S. military. AARs are a structured protocol for the "check" and "act" parts of P-D-C-A. It is a way to learn and course-correct by reviewing what was planned and compare it to what actually happened. During a project postlaunch AAR review, the team was discussing how a project had failed to meet certain objectives when someone made an offhand remark. They derogatorily stated, "Well I could have told you *that* was going to happen."

My first reaction was to snap back and ask, "Well then, why didn't you?" But before the words left my mouth I realized that derogatory or not, he was right. This was the barrier we faced. There was no mechanism for people to identify that there was a problem. There were standard project reports, but real escalation of issues only happened by exception. There was no proper protocol for it and the culture discouraged it because it felt like admitting failure. It wasn't a part of the normal business protocol, as it was in the engine plant. Periodically, engineers would take me aside and tell me their concerns, but it was always in confidence. There was a tendency for project teams to hold issues so close to their chest that it was like conducting open heart surgery to uncover the issues. Perhaps it was partly a leadership problem as well. When leadership got involved with a problem it was often a fiasco. It was hard to tell if that was due to the problem or due to the leadership, but it was clear that no project wanted leadership too involved. Regardless of the cause, the result was that there was not a clear way to understand the condition of a project or the overall portfolio in spite of the standard reports. There had to be a way to highlight problems so they could be properly addressed, so that no one would ever say "I could have told you" after a project was over.

Several years earlier, as part of a benchmarking visit to Lotus Engineering in England, we had seen a process called a "boardwalk." The concept was quite simple. All the projects were assigned a board and each project team would post the status of their project on their board. All the boards were lined up in a large room and once a week the leadership team would walk along the boards to review the projects. Each board identified the project status as red, yellow, or green. Since the entire leadership walked the boards together, issues could be immediately addressed.

An executive who accompanied us on this trip later became president of the Buell motorcycle division of Harley-Davidson, and he instituted the red, yellow, and green traffic light concept to their project reports (although they did not adopt the broader concepts of the boardwalk). So at Buell, each project leader identified project status as red, yellow, or green.

Buell gave the colors specific meanings. Green meant, "I'm busy and may have issues, but I am operating within the normal conditions I would expect." Yellow meant, "I have a concern. I have voiced the concern, and there is a plan in place. I have the help I need to get it fixed." Red meant, "I have a problem and need help. Something needs to change. Quality, cost, or timing of the project is expected to be impacted."

In order to make sure that no one at Harley-Davidson would ever again say, "I could have told you," everyone had to have a mechanism to identify status from their perspective and immediately alert the organization if there was a problem. Harley-Davidson's culture also had to change so that everyone was focused on achieving the next pull event and felt obligated to share the status and their concerns in achieving it. Reporting status with respect to the next pull event had to go beyond just the project leader to make sure that reports were not delayed or watered down, and the status report had to accommodate input from everyone associated with the project.

To make the work of product development more visible and to provide everyone a voice, the red/yellow/green report was created. Initially this was a simple Excel spreadsheet but it grew in sophistication over time as we worked with it and added functionality. It began as a matrix of projects and functional areas so that everyone could report their status for the next pull event. All active projects were listed along the side in rows. All of the functional areas associated with product development were listed along the top in the columns. There was a specific person responsible for the intersection of each project and function. It became the obligation of that person to identify the condition for their area for each project with red, yellow, or green to indicate status for the next pull event. After a colorblind member of the leadership team admitted that he could not read the map and we realized that black and white copies of the report were illegible, we supplemented colors with symbols (see Figure 14–1).

The red/yellow/green report provided a visual representation of product development status for the next pull event. Since pull events were the drivers for the system it made it simple to see what part of product development was operating normally and what was not. Visual management creates standard conditions so any abnormalities are easy to spot. The report not only highlighted trouble areas but also provided a temperature map for the product development portfolio. As colors went from green to red in multiple squares in a row, it meant that there were project-related issues that needed to be addressed. As columns went from green to red, it indicated that a functional area needed a closer look and might need help or additional resources.

The red/yellow/green report also highlighted issues that normally occur in the course of product development. However, in the past

Figure 14.1

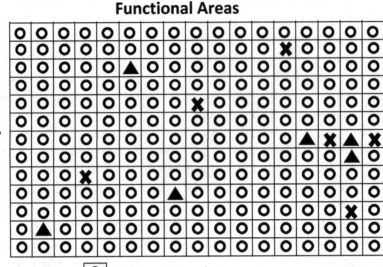

issues were hidden and they tended to surface just before launch. By implementing pull events to pace product development flow, issues began to surface at the pull events. Implementing the red/yellow/green report created improved awareness of issues and allowed them to be addressed even sooner. Each learning cycle made an incremental improvement to the product development system by creating better and faster visibility to the abnormalities in the work flow. Each incremental improvement came from thinking, doing, and learning. Each improvement was the result of having a vision and then finding the obstacles that prevented its implementation. We had to learn to see the obstacles and we had to go through the struggle of overcoming them. Each tool we developed and implemented aided the development process a little.

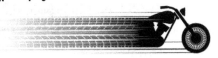

Oobeya

If you can't describe what you are doing as a process, you don't
know what you're doing.

W. Edwards Deming

lthough each of the individual tools we discovered and implemented improved the process incrementally, their effectiveness
was diminished because they operated in relative isolation. The
biggest improvement came in connecting the pieces. As the pieces of
the system came together, the improvement was greater than the individual parts.

Collaboration Using the *Oobeya* Process

Allen Ward had introduced Takashi Tanaka to me about a year after
we started working together. Allen had met Takashi during one of his
research trips to Toyota and introduced us because he thought Takashi
might be able to help in the learning journey.

When we first met, I told Takashi, "Harley-Davidson has a very
special and unique culture. We need to keep that in mind when we
make changes. It is important to know that Harley-Davidson operates
with a cowboy mentality."

Takashi nodded and smiled in admiration. "Yes," he said, "That is something that we Japanese admire very much about America."

Puzzled, I asked him, "What do you mean?"

"Well," Takashi explained, "it is incredible how very few cowboys can herd so many cattle and drive them over such large distances. They are very efficient."

"No, no, no," I contradicted. "By 'cowboy mentality' I mean that everyone is unique. Everyone does things differently. Everyone wants to do things their own way. They like to be rugged individualists."

"Oh," he said. "That is not good."

Takashi is special. He is Japanese, grew up in Japan, and was educated in Japan. With a strong desire to see America, he came to the United States for graduate school. He attended graduate school in Oklahoma, so he spoke English with a mixed Japanese and Oklahoman accent. He has Japanese mannerisms and has acquired an American sense of humor. The American humor served him well in working with Harley-Davidson. He was a joy to learn from—but it almost did not happen.

As for so many things in the product development learning journey, the answer to putting the system together was right under our nose. The solution had been in our grasp but we had rejected it. As was often the case, we had failed to see the obstacle because we were blind to it—we were not ready to see it. We were a band of cowboys who worked in cross-functional teams in a system we called "concurrent product and process development," but we really didn't collaborate very well. Although we had progressed beyond the "throw it over the wall" mentality, product development is a team sport and we still needed to learn to function as a team. Collaboration is critical to winning a team sport.

Takashi had worked with Toyota to develop a concept they called *oobeya*. Oobeya is the Japanese word for "big, open office." It is not the open office but the business philosophy and collaboration process that goes on within the *oobeya* room that is important. The *oobeya* concept has even been credited as the latest and most significant recent improvement to the Toyota development system. Through collaboration, the *oobeya* room changes the way products are developed because it changes with whom, as well as when, where, and how information is shared and discussed. The *oobeya* process uniquely brings together all aspects of the company, including design, engineering, manufacturing, sales, marketing, purchasing, logistics, etc., to focus on development of new products.

The process facilitates collaborative planning and open dialogue across the entire team whether it is to improve quality, reduce costs, or simply to share progress. *Oobeya* is all about collaboration and sharing. Traditional thinking in cross-functional development attempts to break down functional barriers by reassigning people from functional departments to cross-functional teams. In contrast, the *oobeya* process seeks to create open collaboration between functional areas so they can perform within their function better as a team.

When Allen Ward first brought Takashi to Harley-Davidson, Takashi very politely presented the *oobeya* concept to the engineering leadership team. He began his presentation with why Toyota had initiated the *oobeya* concept. He explained that with the sudden increased demand for sport utility vehicles, Toyota had been caught off guard and was late to enter the market. To catch up Toyota significantly increased its number of engineers, but they had seen the profit per vehicle go down dramatically, as efficiency per engineer dropped. To address this problem, Toyota developed the *oobeya* process.

Previous product development improvement efforts at Toyota had been focused on things like computer-aided design tools, creation of standardized work procedures, waste reduction, and improvement of technical knowledge and maintenance. This time it was decided that a completely new method of innovation was required. To dramatically reduce development lead time they had to change their working habits and culture. When Taiichi Ohno established the Toyota production system, he identified two pillars, autonomation and Just-In-Time (JIT). Takashi explained that the *oobeya* process was created as JIT for the knowledge worker.

The process begins with the entire team visualizing the expected output then collaboratively planning the schedule to achieve that output. Visualizing the output is done through team dialogue then the desired output is captured in a picture to make it visual. With the entire team visualizing the output, the exercise serves to create shared vision. When the output is agreed and made visual, the team collaboratively creates a schedule by identifying the key components necessary to achieve the desired output. In creating a schedule, what needs to be done, who needs to do it, and when it needs to be accomplished are all captured. Since all the people responsible for the deliverables are a part of the planning session, there is high agreement and commitment to the schedule, which supports the combat planning attitude.

As Takashi spoke, I looked around at the engineering leadership in the room. I could see that Takashi could have just as well have been making his presentation in Japanese because no one understood what he was saying. He was quickly losing their interest. I could see that the idea of collaboration to establish the output and the schedule, then creating a diagram rather than a report to describe it was too foreign.

Takashi put a slide up on the screen and went on with his description of the *oobeya* process by contrasting the work in manufacturing with the work of a knowledge worker in product development. "In production," he explained, "information exchange is done through *kanban* and progress management is accomplished through visual controls. In product development, visual planning provides both the exchange of information and progress management. This is done through a very simple process of Post-it® Notes," he continued as he put up the next slide (see his figure below) to show what he meant with a picture. He didn't get very far into describing his next slide and how Post-it Notes were used to exchange information or to convey progress status when one of the chief engineers stormed out of the room.

Takashi continued with the meeting and described the rest of the aspects of the *oobeya* process but it was clear that there was too much resistance to the notion of using anything as low-tech as Post-it Notes in a technical center, let alone the idea of making diagrams collaboratively. After the meeting I followed up with the chief engineer who had so abruptly left Takahashi's presentation. He was blunt with his opinion. "There's no way in hell that I'm going to pay some guy to show me how to stick Post-it Notes to a wall," he said. "I have no interest in participating in this experiment."

At that point, the *oobeya* process died for product development.

JIT-Production compared to JIT-Knowledge

	Production	Knowledge-worker
Information Exchange	KANBAN	**Visualized Planning**
Progress Management	Visual Control	
Loss and Waste	• Defects and Repairs • Unnecessary Stock	• Non-value-added Time • Unsolved Problems • Overdevelopment
Automation	• Production Line • Robot	• Autonomous Attitude • Clear Objective/Target
Driver for Change	• Suggestion System • PDCA (Plan-Do-Check -Action) Cycle	Learning Cycles • PDCA Cycle • LAMDA Cycle

Fortunately Don Kieffer, who inherited the engine plant from Ken, saw merit in the *oobeya* system and allowed Takashi to work with his leadership team to try it. Don remarked that he recognized the process was working when he stopped getting e-mails from his plant staff and his voice mail went from always full to only a few new messages per day. The process gave everyone a voice, created shared understanding, and it empowered people to help themselves. Eight months later, when the engine plant had become the best performing plant in the company, there was renewed interest in the *oobeya* process.

The *Oobeya* Process

Even after the *oobeya* process was shown to be effective in the engine plant, product development was still reluctant to try it. Perhaps it was the low-tech aspect of Post-it Notes that turned off the engineers.

Perhaps it was the way it exposed the work and forced leaders into immediate action that scared off the project managers. Or perhaps it was the way it forced everyone to collaborate and keep their commitments that made people reluctant to accept it. But once it was initiated, it became clear that the *oobeya* process changed the working habits and the culture of product development. The *oobeya* process created visibility and allowed the integration of many of the systemic structural changes to the system we had been working to create. The *oobeya* process was not a replacement for the development system we were attempting to build, but rather a vehicle that enabled the system to come together.

The *oobeya* process is a method used to make the contents and status and flow of work visible. The visual management component of the *oobeya* process is specifically intended to make targets, objectives, and progress clearly visible and is oriented toward planning of activities with the inclusion of all related team members and departments. It encourages open collaboration in analysis and finding solutions to issues uncovered during product development. The open availability of information in a visualized format activates a new form of communication, which is based on cooperation between team members and departments. The visual nature of the *oobeya* process also reinforces the active role of management in supporting project teams.

The *oobeya* process has two primary components. The first component is the problem side, the second is the action side. The problem side (the *barashi* side, meaning "to break down into components" in Japanese) is the process of collaboratively defining and agreeing on the problem as well as the decomposition of the problem into actionable elements. The action side identifies the countermeasures that will be taken to resolve each issue and collaboratively schedules actions to specific people to resolve them.

An important element of the *oobeya* process is that everything is done visually, collaboratively, and in the open. Post-it Notes are the primary medium for visual communication and are used because they enable simultaneous input from many people and allow easy modification and adjustment by moving the notes around. Modification of the *oobeya* boards in order to constantly adapt to learning is fundamental to the success of the process. As the process unfolds new problems are uncovered and new countermeasures are developed to address them. The *oobeya* board is often the visual representation of combat planning in action. The figure below depicts the makeup of a typical *oobeya* board, although the figure is much tidier than it would appear in actual use.

Red Post-it Notes are used to denote issues or problems while yellow Post-it Notes signify an answer or a comment. As the visual management aspect of the *oobeya* process evolves, more colors are added to make the process more meaningful. The principles of the *oobeya* process make it scalable from a small team project to oversight of a complete value stream or business function.

The idea of team rooms was not new to Harley-Davidson. Co-

Structure of Visualized Planning

Problem Side

Action Side

BARASHI
Elaboration of Scenario

Expected Output

Decomposition

Process

Long-term Schedule

	Apr.	May	...	Mar.
OOO				
OXO				
XXX				

Clear Output & Key Milestones

Workload Control

Monthly Schedule

	1W	2W	3W	4W
Takashi				
J.Louis				
Unscheduled Jobs				
Load	120%	110%	95%	130%

Activities and Workload

Workload Control

Weekly Schedule

	Mon.	Tue.	...	Fri.
Plan				
Unscheduled Jobs				

Individual Time Management

located teams are not uncommon in product development, and Harley-Davidson often used co-located teams on projects. To reduce project risk for large bin 6 projects, the bin 6 project teams were housed in dedicated team rooms to bring all the functional areas needed for development together. When the Willie G. Davidson Product Development Center was built, it was specifically designed to house a predetermined number of bin 6 team rooms, corresponding with the planned development cadence of bin 6 projects needed to support the business plan. The bin 6 team rooms were designed with a mock-up area and space to accommodate the specific number of people necessary to execute a bin 6 project. But visual management and the *oobeya* process was not something anticipated when the project rooms were designed.

It was difficult to find someone willing to experiment with the *oobeya* process, but after a lot of coercion, a project leader finally stepped forward willing to try it. It was a bin 6 project and the team had been working together for over a year. There was a lot of planning and preparation involved in getting ready to kick off the *oobeya* process in product development. Normally, the *oobeya* process begins with a team "spew-out," but since the team had been together so long it was debated whether it was necessary. Takashi was concerned that there may have been hidden issues or concerns and insisted that a spew out was very important to begin the process.

The spew out refers to a meeting where all team members spew out information and highlight issues or concerns for the entire team to hear. The spew out occurs in a special team meeting where the project leader describes the objectives and expected outcome of the project to all related team members and departments. The project leader (and they may include key members of the team) prepares diagrams in advance of the meeting and posts them on a wall or on a board. Then, the entire extended team stands around the posted information while the project leader describes the expected outcome of the project and the proposed long-term schedule.

This portion of the meeting may take a few minutes or it could take several hours as the team moves from board to board. When the leader finishes sharing the information, it becomes the rest of the team's turn to spew out their issues and concerns, or to raise questions and comments. Each team member is given Post-it Notes and they use the notes to write down their thoughts and then they place Post-it Notes on the picture that refers to the content of their note. When everyone is satisfied that everything that needs to be spewed out has been spewed out, the meeting turns back over to the team leader.

The team leader then reads each Post-it Note aloud and responds to it. If there is a satisfactory answer the original note is removed from the board and placed on a "completed" board. Then a Post-it Note with the response is placed on top of the question to document the solution on the completed board. If a satisfactory answer is not immediately available, the concern is noted and appropriate "countermeasures" are placed on the action side of the management board to ensure that the issue will be addressed by immediately scheduling actions. This portion of the meeting continues until every note is reviewed and it is either agreed that the note can be removed or it becomes an aspect of the project that needs to be addressed. The output from the spew out seeds the top boards of both the *barashi* side and the action side of the *oobeya* process. Depending on the project, the team continues until all the visual management boards are populated, or subsequent smaller meetings are held to populate the remaining portions of the boards. This initiates the *oobeya* process and is then incorporated into the management of the project.

Although the need for a spew out for the initial *oobeya* kickoff had been debated because the team had been together for over a year, in the end we agreed to begin the process with a traditional spew out to start the process. When we planned the event, we had anticipated that the spew out would not take very long and there would not be a lot of input from the team. I was wrong. To my surprise there were over 200 unique Post-it Notes put up by the extended team. I overheard people on several occasions say, "So *that's* what they are trying to do." The initial spew out got the team connected and surfaced a host of issues that the team had been unaware existed. The number of issues and questions that came out during the spew out far exceeded anyone's expectation of the unresolved issues that might be lingering on the project. The number of Post-it Notes the session generated together with the number of people who were enlightened about the project they had worked on for a year ensured the validity of the *oobeya* process. The *oobeya* process and visual management proved to be an important vehicle for driving the implementation of product development improvement efforts.

The Wall

Applying the *oobeya* process in the engine plant first seemed like much less risk than trying it in product development. The engine plant was already using visual management on the factory floor, so using *oobeya* for the plant leadership wasn't as much of a stretch. Watching the plant leadership and what they did would give us a chance to evaluate what *oobeya* was and how we might apply it in product development. So while Takashi worked with Don and his staff at the engine plant, a small group from product development stayed connected to the experiment. Every time that Takashi came to the plant to work with them, he would come across the parking lot and work with us for a while as well. Takashi worked with us as we attempted to learn and better understand what the process was. Admittedly, to the untrained eye it still looked like moving a bunch of Post-it Notes around on a wall.

As a leader, there is no dignified way to stick Post-it Notes to a wall. They do not have the stateliness of a rousing speech or command the authority of giving direction. Perhaps that is part of the power of the process. Communication is largely a function of the medium used to convey thoughts and ideas. Most communication media are exclusionary. A particular medium may be exclusionary because it is one-sided: In a speech, one person talks and many people listen. Or it may be exclusionary because of positional authority: One person gives orders while others take orders. It may be exclusionary due to technology: When an engineer creates a computer-aided model, only other people that know the software can read, manipulate, or modify the model. Post-it Notes on a wall break down all the traditional exclusionary barriers. This communication medium invites involvement and participation once the physiological barrier that "It's not the way things are done" is overcome.

Creating a visual management leadership board in product development was a challenge. We didn't know what we were doing and didn't want 1,000 engineers looking over our shoulder as we tried to figure it out, so we experimented on a wall in the basement of the technical center. It was intended to just be a working experiment so we could learn, but nothing odd stays secret for very long in a technical center. Our little learning experiment soon became affectionately known as "the wall."

The wall began as a large visual representation to figure out who should be working on what projects in order to execute the product plan. It was intended to realign people with project needs as the number of projects with red and yellow flags in the portfolio would spike. Then after a deep dive into the issues it would turn out that it was only one project or one overworked person that had fallen behind and caused a domino effect triggering a bottleneck in the system. The wall was a convenient way to lay out all the projects and who was assigned to each project to figure out the bottlenecks.

But as we realized the usefulness of visually displaying information, the wall grew and the purpose shifted from solving the specific resource allocation problem to understanding and managing the overall product development system. The wall stayed on a basement wall for many months as we worked out what it should look like and what information should be displayed. Over the months as the wall helped us better understood the *oobeya* process, the purpose of the wall was refined as the wall evolved. Although the wall became increasingly useful, we were in no rush to unveil our experiment beyond the small group of people who were working with it. It was meaningful to us, but it was still just "the wall" to everyone else.

The incentive to expose the wall more broadly by moving it out of the basement came from the most unlikely source, Willie G. Davidson. Willie is a man of few words, but he is extremely astute and he has been in the motorcycle business for a long time. As a stylist, Willie is acutely aware of the importance and the impact of visual imagery. He has a knack for understanding how imagery connects to emotion and demonstrates it daily in the styling of Harley-Davidson motorcycles. Even the look and feel of the product development center is strongly influenced by Willie. Color schemes, pictures or the lack of pictures, even clocks on the walls are important in creating the work environment and atmosphere. Willie has a say in it all, and his say has been very insightful and effective.

I noticed that periodically while we were working at the wall, Willie would observe from afar what we were doing. He didn't say anything. He didn't participate. He just observed. I though that he was unhappy about how messy our work looked with large charts plotted out and taped together stuck to a wall. Multiple colors of Post-it Notes were stuck all over the charts and papers. I thought to myself, it won't be long before he's going to make us take this all down. I was not going to incite that decision by asking, so we just carried on.

After observing what we were doing for some time, Willie made the suggestion that it was time to move the wall. He didn't ask us to take it down, as I had feared; instead he asked that it be moved somewhere where everyone could see it. He said, "This work is too important to be hidden in a basement hallway. This work needs to be front and center. But," he said, "This work needs to have the proper placement. It needs to be a focal point and have the proper presence."

On Willie's insistence, "the wall" ended up in a central location along a main corridor where the flow paths from the two entrances to the building come together and not far from the entrance to Willie's styling studio. Some office cubicles were rearranged to make space for it and Willie designed special lights for the wall to make it stand out. The wall became the visual representation for product development. A few minutes at the wall provided a complete perspective of the status, the workflow, and the issues in product development.

The leadership board visually connected the objectives for the company with the innovation objectives and goals for product development. Through the action board and issues board, each employee in product development was able to trace how their work contributed to achieving the company objectives. Whether it was delivery of a project, or resolution of an issue, or installation of new laboratory equipment, each employee was able to see how their contribution was important.

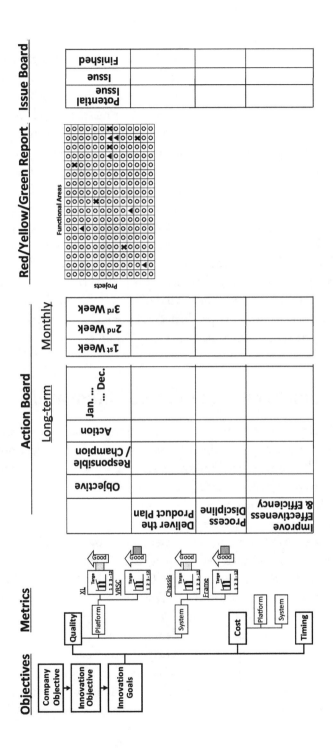

Any work that did not connect could be stopped and the efforts reassigned to something that did connect.

Metrics provided information as to how the organization was doing in achieving goals and objectives. The metrics displayed trends to show if progress was ahead or behind the plan. The red/yellow/green report displayed issues in the portfolio. Both potential issues and actual issues were placed on the issue board with Post-it Notes so they could be addressed. The wall had begun as an experiment in identifying where issues were and how to resolve resource bottlenecks. Through learning cycles, it evolved as a visual representation of the product development system. Just as in the engine plant, now everyone in product development could see how their contribution tied to the objectives of the company. Metrics clearly showed ahead or behind conditions and issues could be escalated to be resolved. The wall provided feedback of how the product development process was running and where the issues were that needed to be addressed.

Quickening the Pace of Innovation

Takashi referred to the process as "quickening through visualization." The *oobeya* process was a vehicle to visualize the product development system and it created the ability to see the work, the flow, and the status of product development, just like parts going down the assembly line in the engine factory. It highlighted the issues and it made it possible to connect each employee to company objectives. But the *oobeya* process itself was not the answer to improving product development. Improving product development came through the struggle of thoughts and seeing beyond the confines of the systemic structures that had until now constrained us. The *oobeya* process was an enabler to accomplish our improvement objectives. The process is generic in the structured approach used to define problems, break down problems, and collectively align team participants to act in creating countermeasures to resolve problems. It is visual, and it brings people together to collaborate by helping to create shared visions and team alignment in an effort to reach common goals. The *oobeya* process was an important vehicle that sped the articulation of the vision that had been created. It brought the systemic structure together by making it possible to see how the elements fit.

With the fundamental elements of the new systemic structure created and a mechanism in place to visualize the product development system, it was time to quicken the pace of product development. It was time to shorten the cadence interval and increase the flow of new products. To reduce time and increase flow, a concerted effort was first placed on reducing the time and improving the consistency of the learning cycles. Improvement efforts focused on the system areas with the longest development cycle times in order to shorten them, while the areas with the shortest cycle times were lengthened in an effort to better synchronize all of the learning cycles. Pull events became the key mechanism used to align and quicken the pace of development.

With visibility of the development system and controls in place, it was possible to set increasingly more aggressive development goals. With increasingly shorter learning cycle targets, monitoring the system for obstacles grew in importance. As the pace quickened and the flow increased, there was less time to react to obstacles. To react to issues quickly, the *oobeya* process operated across three levels. The first level was the leadership board (the wall). The second level consisted of the project boards in the individual team rooms (*oobeya* rooms). The third level was at the system, or departmental level. All three levels were important to properly quicken the pace of product development.

The leadership board decomposed the company objectives into the product development objectives and goals. Product development objectives and goals were further decomposed into projects according to the preestablished cadence and also included a variety of improvement initiatives. The delivery cadence of projects in turn drove the need for support from various system design areas and departments.

To assure that issues were identified and obstacles were addressed, each area prioritized their issues each week. The top two issues recorded on Post-it Notes flowed from the systems and departments to the projects rooms for resolution and the top two issues from the projects flowed to the leadership board on Post-it Notes for resolution.

When the work and issue resolution flow process was first initi-

The Quickening Process

WORK FLOW

WORK FLOW

Leadership Wall

Project Room

System / Department

Issue Resolution Flow

Issue Resolution Flow

Flow: 2 Post-it notes per Week

ated everyone complained that it was not practical. There were far too many issues to address to make resolution of two issues per week practical. But as each area was forced to collaboratively rank their issues and the top two were escalated for resolution, it wasn't long before the flow of issues slowed to a trickle. By forcing prioritization of concerns, it forced each area to identify what was most important and focus on getting it resolved. With only two issues escalated, it was manageable to actually address them and get them resolved at the next level. By clearly and concisely defining the problem, many times the team realized that they were able to resolve the problems themselves and did not need to escalate the issue. When issues were escalated, a clear problem definition made it more feasible to address.

With a systematic approach to shortening development times and increasing flow while monitoring issues and addressing them quickly, the throughput of the development system increased. With improved effectiveness and efficiency of the development system, more projects were able to move from the swirl into the development stream for delivery. For the first time the bow wave of projects that we had pushed out each year due to resource constraints began to diminish, and before long it was gone altogether. The improvements to the development system allowed reaching further up stream to pull projects ahead rather than delay them, as had typically been the case in the past. The new systemic structure created a development system that produced new products according to a set development cadence. The vision of a predictable product development system based on the new mindsets of learning cycles was operational.

Knowledge-Based Product Development

Whether you believe that you can do a thing or not, you are right.

Henry Ford

J erry burst through the door of Ken's office beaming from ear to ear and waving the latest issue of *Easy Rider Magazine*. Jerry was the vice president of sales, a tall lanky man who had been riding motorcycles since he was a kid. He never left the sport and managed to turn his passion of motorcycles into a long career with Harley-Davidson. Most of his career had been in sales or marketing at Harley-Davidson, but he spent a stint as the president of the Buell Motorcycle Company when Buell was first acquired by Harley-Davidson. As a new company, Buell struggled to be relevant in a very competitive sport bike market. To motivate the sales team as they struggled to sell bikes, Jerry had plenty of stories to tell about the tough times at Harley-Davidson in the 80s when he was trying to move Harleys and no one wanted to take them.

Over the years Jerry learned to move a lot of iron by becoming very well tuned in to the motorcycle market. He understood the importance of promotion and rarely missed the opportunity to leverage publicity. He must have run down the hall in his excitement as he strode through the doorway out of breath. He tossed the magazine on the table where Ken and I sat reviewing the latest product development operating metrics. Most of the elements of knowledge-based product development were in place and the product plan had been revised based on the more aggressive development cadence that the system had been designed to deliver. The wall provided visibility to the development system highlighting progress, flow, and issues. Many other tools had been created to ensure delivery of the product plan as we attempted to change the working habits and culture of the development organization. Ken Sutton, vice president of engineering, and I met regularly to review progress and discuss concerns in maintaining flow in order to stay in tune with the pulse of the development organization.

"Have you seen this article?" Jerry asked in excitement, as the magazine landed on the top of the table with a thud. Ken and I looked at each other in surprise. The puzzled look on Ken's face indicated that clearly neither of us had seen the article that Jerry was so worked up over.

"There's a great article in here about the amount of new product we've been putting out." Jerry continued, *"Easy Rider* may be the first to recognize the increase to the number of new products we've been introducing."

Ken picked up the magazine and leafed through the pages past the pictures of scantily clad girls straddling custom bikes decked out in chrome and gleaming paint. I saw his eyes light up when he read the headline of the article Jerry was referring to. The grin widened across his face as he begin to read the article, recognizing that all the hard work and effort expended over the past years to transform the product development system was receiving public recognition. The headline of the article proclaimed in big bold print, "The Sleeping Giant Awakens."

The Sleeping Giant Awakens? Harley-Davidson had seen twenty-four quarters of record sales and record profits, how could this be an awakening? But the article referred not to past sales, but to the magazine's assessment of Harley-Davidson's ability to generate new sales in the future. Some business journals had suggested that Harley-Davidson's magic formula would run out and had predicted Harley's demise as the sales of new bikes steadily climbed each year from the investment in manufacturing capability. But *Easy Rider* is an enthusiast magazine, not a business magazine, and they recognized the significance in the drastic increase in quantity and quality of new products from the development center in Milwaukee.

Easy Rider acknowledged that the previous year had been a big year for Harley-Davidson based on the number of changes and new product offerings, but most companies can manage a single big year. They referred to "an awakening" because Harley-Davidson had managed an encore performance. Harley-Davidson had followed up a big year with an even bigger year of product changes and new models, and the article went on to identify all the new products while extolling the virtues of the new products and features.

The article in the November 2005 issue of *Easy Rider* about Harley-Davidson's 2006 new product lineup went largely unnoticed by the larger business community. Certainly few readers recognized the business significance of the article. At a glance it was like every other article in every other magazine. Motorcycle magazines tend to publish articles about the new motorcycles being offered during the winter months as motorcyclists dream of riding—and the new product reviews stimulate magazine sales.

It might have been big news for the motorcyclist who dreamed of a new Softail or Roadking, but to anyone else, it was just another article. After all, *Easy Rider* is not a scholarly journal and it doesn't even have the circulation volume of the larger motorcycle specialty magazines like *Cycle World* or *Motorcyclist*. Best known and often bought for its centerfold, *Easy Rider* is more commonly associated with big bikes and underdressed, overdeveloped women than with groundbreaking news. Nor would I imagine that it was the intent of the author to highlight the business significance, even if he had understood. Perhaps that makes the article that much more meaningful, since it was simply a motorcycle enthusiast writing about something he loved and was passionate about—motorcycles—and when it comes to motorcycles, more cool products is always better.

Indications of Success

The first indication that the new systemic structure of product development we wanted to create was working came well before the article in *Easy Rider* magazine. The new cadence allowed more product to be developed, so a very aggressive schedule for new product introductions had been set. The year before the article was published had been even bigger. The 2005 model year added six additional models to the Harley-Davidson line of motorcycles, the biggest single-year increase in motorcycle models in Harley-Davidson's history. Dealers who attended the annual dealer meeting were treated to an unprecedented number of new models and new features that year. One dealer remarked, "I've attended this show for over twenty years and this is by far the biggest and most impressive introduction of new products I've seen in all my years as a dealer." But even more impressive than the amount of new product was the lack of launch issues and problems late in the development cycle. Harley-Davidson's president, Jim McCaslin, called the 2005 launch the most successful and problem-free launch he had ever witnessed. The success of the new products launch was a result of a carefully planned and monitored system with adjustments made as needed to ensure delivery.

For over thirty years, the Harley-Davidson product development system had averaged an increase in the product portfolio of 0.74 models per year. This introduction rate meant that the company could add a new model to the line of motorcycles three out of four years in a row. (It is important to note that the total development activity is much greater since the rate of portfolio growth is an aggregate number that takes into account the refresh of existing models, addition of new features, retirement of old models, and the introduction of new models.)

Over the thirty-year period, both Harley-Davidson as a company and product development as a whole changed immensely. There were good years and bad years in the organization's ability to introduce new products as personnel changed, leadership changed, and priorities changed. In thirty years people came and left the organization, computer-aided design tools were introduced, the organization grew, and Harley-Davidson changed ownership as it went public during one of the company's most trying times. Yet over thirty years, Harley-Davidson's rate of additional new model introductions and refresh of existing models remained relatively constant at three-quarters of an additional model per year.

The systemic structural changes of knowledge-based product development ushered in a drastic increase in product development effectiveness and efficiency (see Figure 16–1). In contrast to the previous thirty years, the new system was designed to enable the product portfolio to grow at a rate of more than four new models per year while supporting the refresh of existing models and addition of new features through a planned cadence of new product introductions. Pull events created a structured mechanism to drive the system forward and synchronize learning cycles across the development portfolio. Limit curves and trade-off curves are examples of tools used to create reusable knowledge. Visual management provided the means to see the system in action. With a means to monitor the flow, elevate problems, and provide support, knowledge-based development embodies lean development techniques into Western business practices.

The design of a knowledge-based development system evolved during the learning journey as each cycle of learning provided new opportunities in overcoming obstacles. It is a journey that does not end. Knowledge-based development is an amalgamation of principles and practices built upon the learning of many others who have gone before and it still continues to evolve. Each application is different, and change continues to create obstacles that force adaptation and further change. However, the fundamental principles remain the same. The knowledge-based development system that creates reusable knowledge is built on two pillars: (1) cadence and flow and (2) set-based design.

Dr. Allen Ward was the primary influence in the initiation of knowledge-based development principles. Allen had a hypothesis that a design compiler would be a better form of product development than

Figure 16.1

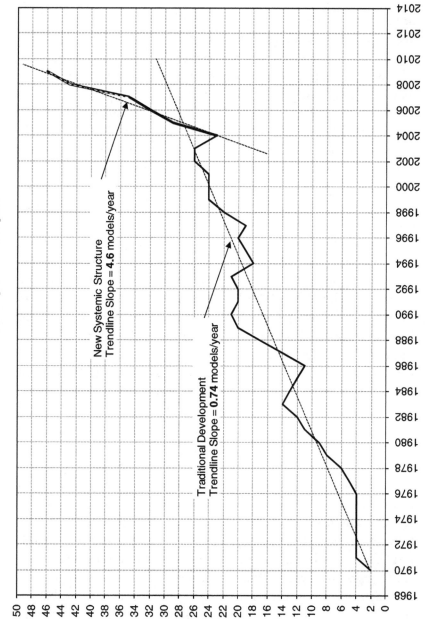

Product Development Output

traditional methods. To validate this hypothesis he studied Toyota's development process as the nearest embodiment of his ideas. With the help of a graduate student, Durward Sobek, who directly conducted much of the on-site research, they modified the idea of a design compiler based on the practices they observed at Toyota. Allen was also influential in bringing the principles to light at Harley-Davidson. First Allen and then Durward (who stepped in to mentor me after Allen passed away) provided guidance in the application of these principles as they were adapted to and merged with the ideas and practices of the Harley-Davidson development process. The journey was truly a struggle of thoughts and ideas as the application of the principles changed the system and forced continual reevaluation of their application.

Allen readily acknowledged that many of the practices he observed at Toyota and even his own ideas for a design compiler had their origins in the work of the Wright brothers and their efforts to conquer the air. Knowledge-based development and the application of the principles is indeed built upon the work of others. The creation of reusable knowledge comes from the Wright brothers, lean principles from Henry Ford and Taiichi Ohno, development cadence from Thomas Edison, learning cycles from John Dewey, and P-D-C-A from W. Edwards Deming. These principles are the beginning rather than the end of improving product development productivity.

The journey to learn and apply these principles and practices resulted in phenomenal improvements in product development output at Harley-Davidson. They greatly improved the effectiveness and efficiency of the development system, yet it is important to realize this effort only scratched the surface of what is still possible to achieve. Just as innovation requires experimentation and inevitable failures for learning to occur, likewise improvement of the product development system requires learning cycles. Every time the learning cycle turns and changes are implemented, new opportunities for improvement and learning emerge. It is the tenacity to overcome obstacles, the ability to see opportunity, and the courage to try something different that enable the continual improvement of the system. As the president of the Council on Competitiveness, Debora Wince-Smith, recently said,

"The only driver for productivity growth for the U.S. is our innovation capacity."

I encourage you to seize the innovation improvement and productivity growth your company is entitled.

Creating Change

There is not one singular perfect solution to improving product development. Each application is different. Some solutions are better or worse than others depending on the environment; however, there are some fundamentally important principles that underlie success. First and foremost, the process of change is a learning journey. When the change process is approached as a learning journey, then the more broadly the journey involves all stakeholders in the process the more effective it can be. It's better to have an imperfect solution created by the users of the system striving to continually improve than to have the perfect solution imposed upon the organization. An organization with clear objectives engaged in the struggle of thought to find a better way and personally vested in the learning process will work much harder to ensure success than an organization forced into practices that are uncomfortable and foreign to their thinking. The Leadership Learning Model has been presented as an effective framework for this purpose. It is the role of leadership to teach their organization. Leaders as teachers is a fundamental aspect of the adoption of knowledge-based development. This does not suggest that leaders have all the answers. On the contrary, "leaders as teachers" is intended to implore leaders to create a culture of discovery and intrigue in their organizations, and to shepherd the learning process.

There are many tools associated with the implementation of lean processes, whether it is in manufacturing or non-manufacturing, and knowledge-based development is no different. Some generic lean tools are adaptable to knowledge-based development and some are not. Some tools are the same, some are similar, yet many are different. Often organizations embark on a journey of change by applying tools. The tools are often the most visible aspect of the process and quickest to copy and implement. But tools are an outcome of the systemic operating structure they support. Applying new tools to a system that has not changed may provide some momentary benefit, but will not change the system itself. When this happens, improvements are subpar and often short-lived.

Introducing new tools to a poor system can also have a negative effect on the change process. When an organization blindly applies tools that are not understood to an ineffective system, the tool may not produce much benefit, resulting in the organization becoming more reluctant to continue the change process. It is important to continuously ask, "What is the problem we are trying to fix," for change must address a problem. Since each company, situation, and application is different there are many unique tools with common principles. If there is not a clear connection drawn for the purpose of the tool it is best to rethink the application of the tool.

Don't get caught in the trap of implementing tools rather than learning through discovery and striving to change the underlying systemic structure of the development system. It is more important to create a shared understanding of the vision, the mental models, and the desired systemic structure than to copy tools. With a shared vision and an understanding of the desired structure, the appropriate tools for the situation will surface as the barriers are uncovered. With a shared common vision, the implementation process becomes sustainable as the organization develops the desire to achieve the shared vision. Embrace the discovery of barriers because the need to break down barriers drives learning and the creation or application of new tools and techniques. With a focus on tools or techniques rather than the systemic structure of the system there may be a momentary improvement, but the change they usher in will not become embedded as a part of the system; the change will just become another fine program. It has been the intent of this book to highlight the importance of the system over the tools.

Product development is a team sport and it is best to have a system that the team collaborates to create even though it may be less than perfect. True learning can only take place through the struggle of thought and shared self-actualization. However, the journey can be aided through the help of a guide. A guide may be a leader who has the desire to drive change, and seeks out the learning and understanding necessary to shepherd the discovery and learning for the organization. To lead change you don't need to know everything. A leader only needs to be a half step ahead of the rest of the organization with the ability to instill a learning environment.

There are some useful external guides. Be leery of the consultants who say they can implement for you or someone who has all the answers. Only you can create the system for your organization. Only you can make the decision to learn and discover, and only you can implement change. There are, however, tremendous benefits in having an experienced guide to help determine the next step, provide encouragement, facilitate, teach, mentor, and help uncover and build connections. I was very fortunate to be mentored first by Allen Ward, then by Durward Sobek and Takashi Tanaka. Any consultant who tells you that they can implement lean principles for you is wrong. Only the people who work in the system can do that. They need to learn and discover and create what works for them in their system.

It is ultimately the combination of a vision and a need that fuels innovation. It is no different in the creation and implementation of knowledge-based development in an organization. There must be a vision for what can be, and it must be connected to the business need. With an understanding of the needs to improve product development in the context of the business tied to a vision to achieve it, the learning journey for knowledge-based development can begin.

Notes

Introduction

1. The term "phase gate" refers to a product development process in which distinct development phases are separated by approval gates ("phase gates") that regulate passage from one phase to the next in an attempt to control risk. Phase gates are also commonly called "stage gates," and this process may also be referred to as a "phased review model." In this text, "phase gate" is used throughout.
2. Product Development Management Association, PDMA Foundation New Product Development Report of Initial Findings: Summary of Responses from 2004 CPAS, PDMA Foundation and Marjorie Adams. http://www.apqc.org/portal/apqc/ksn/PDMAFoundationCPASStudy.pdf?paf_gear_id = contentgearhome& paf_dm = full&pageselect = contentitem&docid = 130180.
3. Economist Intelligence Unit, *Innovation: Transforming the Way Business Creates* (London: The Economist, 2007).
4. www.innovationmetrics.gov/press_releases/04162007.
5. www.compete.org/images/uploads/File/PDF%20Files/Competitiveness_Index_Where_America_Stands_March_2007.pdf.
6. oecd.org/document/26/0,3343,en_2649_34451_37770522_1_1_1_1,00.html.
7. http://www.zdnetasia.com/news/business/0,39044229,61972275,00.htm.

Chapter 1

1. A phase exit review is part of the phase gate approach to the development process, in which distinct development phases are separated by "approval gates" that regulate passage from one stage to the next, intended to control risk.

Chapter 2

1. "What Harley-Davidson learned from GM." February 03, 2007. http://www
.evolvingexcellence.com/blog/2007/02/what_harleydavi.html.

Chapter 3

1. Peter M. Senge, *The Fifth Discipline* (New York: Doubleday, 1990).
2. The basis of organizational learning principles described here comes from the
work pioneered by Peter Senge, John Sterman, and Nelson Repenning. Exposure
to systems thinking came through classes at the Sloan School at MIT, working
directly with Peter, John, and Nelson as well as reading books and articles. A
good text for further information is Senge's *The Fifth Discipline*.
3. Senge, p. 70.

Chapter 5

1. Nelson P. Repenning, Paolo Gonçalves, and Laura Black, "Past the Tipping
Point: The Persistence of Firefighting in Product Development." *California Management Review* (2001), 43, 4: 44–63, or http://web.mit.edu/nelsonr/www/CMR_
PDv4.doc.html.
2. Ibid.

Chapter 6

1. G. David Hughes, "Add Creativity to Your Decision Processes" (1998). http://
www.unc.edu/~gdhughes/ARTICLES.HTM.
2. J. D. C. Little, "A Proof of the Queuing Formula L = ?W." *Operations Research*
(1961), 9: 383–387.
3. Although similar in principle and practice to Toyota's *nemawashi*, the Harley-
Davidson "swirl" was developed entirely independent of Toyota.

Chapter 8

1. James P. Womack, Daniel T. Jones, and Daniel Roos, *The Machine that Changed
the World* (New York: Harper Perennial, 1990).

2. Otto Lilienthal was a German aviation pioneer who became known for his efforts building and flying gliders. He applied an experimentation approach to his development efforts and created the first aerodynamic tables of lift and drag of wing foils. He died on August 10, 1896, one day after breaking his spine in a glider crash when his glider stalled and fell back to earth from a height of over fifty feet. He is reported to have said on his deathbed, *"Kleine Opfer müssen gebracht werden!"* ("Small sacrifices must be made!").

3. The family name is Toyoda, but the car company took an alternate spelling of the name, Toyota.

4. For more information regarding A-3 reports and connection to PDCA (Deming's Plan-Do-Check-Act learning cycle), please see *Understanding A3 Thinking: A Critical Component of Toyota's PDCA Management System,* by Durward K. Sobek II and Art Smalley (New York: Productivity Press, 2008).

5. Allen and Durward went to Japan to look for companies using set-based development practices because they had read reports from Takahiro Fujimoto (See *Product Development Performance: Strategy, Organization, and Management in the World Auto Industry,* Clark and Fujimoto) that the Japanese auto industry used practices that resembled set-based principles. In their efforts to uncover evidence of set-based development they discovered that Toyota was the only company that used development practices anywhere close to set-based principles. As they delved deeper into Toyota's development practices they uncovered trade-off and limit curves as a key mechanism that enables set-based development.

Chapter 11

1. W. Edwards Deming, *Out of the Crisis* (Cambridge, Mass.: MIT Press, 1982), p. 88.

Chapter 13

1. Michael N. Kennedy, *Product Development for the Lean Enterprise: Why Toyota's System Is Four Times More Productive and How You Can Implement It* (Richmond, Va.: Oaklea Press, 2003).

2. The Leadership Learning Change model evolved out of the work of the PDL²T.

Particular thanks and recognition go to John Shibley, the Sloan School of Management at MIT, and the Society for Organizational Learning.

3. A pull event is any carefully planned and orchestrated event coinciding with an integration point that serves to "pull" the work of the development system, in the same way that lean processes pull work in a factory.

Index

AARs (After Action Reviews), 213
acceptance of ideas, 115
action-reflection loop, 170–171
adaptive learning, 47
After Action Reviews (AARs), 213
AMF, 33, 34
"andon" signal, 210–211
assessment, 195
assumptions, underlying business practices, 26
autonomation, 141

balancing loops, 67, 75–76
Beals, Vaughn, 34, 95
Beavertail project, 89–90
bins, 107–113, 164
"boardwalks," 214
brand, 31
budget planning, 105
Buell Motorcycle Company, 214, 234
business process, 35, 39–41

cadence, 98
    application of, 104–107
    and bin designations, 111–113
    in product development, 101–104

CAGR, see compound annual growth rate
Capote, Truman, on conversation, 61
CCPDP (Concurrent Corporate Product Development Process), 4–7
CDC (Create Demand Circle), 36
Center for Innovation in Product Development (MIT), 81
change, 78
    creating, 241–243
    implementation of, 195–196
Channing, William Ellery, on knowledge, 193
China, xvi
Circle Organization structure, 35–37
collaboration, 217–221, 242
combat planning, 208, 209
communication barriers, 226–227
company values, 29–30
compound annual growth rate (CAGR), 119, 122
Concurrent Corporate Product Development Process (CCPDP), 4–7
conference center, 61–62
conflict management, 39

Confucius, on understanding, 145
consensus decision making, 30, 38–39
constructive conflict, 39
conversations, 54, 70–75
Create Demand Circle (CDC), 36
Crosby, Phil, 34
cross-functional product development,
    46–47
customers, manufacturing, 117

Davidson, Willie G., 95–96, 227–228
dealer shows, 105–106
decision making
    consensus, 30, 38–39
    systems thinking for, 48–52
decisions, types of, 38–39
delays, understanding effect of, 50
Deming, W. Edwards, 34, 171, 240
    on learning, xiii
    on what you're doing, 217
derivative products, 109
design compiler, 135, 238, 240
design cycles, 159–166
    and false positive feasibility, 162–164
    and integration points, 164–166
design loops, 85–87, 160, 161, 165–166
design rework (redesign) loops, 152–157,
    168, 169
development throughput, 103–104
Dewey, John, 170, 240
dialogue, 57–59, 74–75
dreams, fulfilling, 31

Easy Rider Magazine, 234–237
Edison, Thomas, 240
    and the art of invention, 102, 171
    on failure, 167
Einstein, Albert, on questioning, 179
Eisenhower, Dwight D., on doing right,
    43
emotion, in product development, 95–96

environment(s)
    evolution of, 25–26
    at Harley-Davidson, 27–30, 41–42
    of Harley-Davidson conference
        center, 61–62
    of industrial-era thinking, 26–27
    of Roaring Motors, 25–27, 29
experiential learning, 170, 178

false positive feasibility, 151, 152,
    162–164
feedback, in systems thinking, 49–50
The Fifth Discipline (Peter Senge), 45,
    50–51
firefighting, 82–91
    and arsonists, 88–90
    leadership in, 84–85
    lessons learned about, 91–93
    in multiple-project organizations,
        87–88
    as necessary skill, 88
    system maps used in, 85–88
five why process, 150–151
FLG, see Functional Leadership Group
flow, 98
    application of, 104–107
    and bin designations, 111, 112
    fed by the "swirl," 113–115
    in non-manufacturing arenas, 93
    in product development, 99–100
Ford, Henry, 240
    on beliefs, 234
    as lean manufacturing pioneer, 34
    as visionary and technical genius,
        141–142
Ford Motor Company, 141–142
Functional Leadership Group (FLG),
    37, 42

Galileo, 53
Gantt charts, 4
Gelb, Tom, 34

generative learning, 47
Gutierrez, Carlos, on innovation, *xvi*

hard dates (schedules), 113
help chains, 210–212
Herbert, Frank, on process, 94
heuristic rules of thumb, 112–113
hiring process, 30
history of Harley-Davidson, 30–35, 95, 96, 98, 117–119
Hutchinson, Ron, 34

ideas, acceptance of, 115
implementing change, 195–196, 241–242
India, *xvi*
Indian Motorcycle Company, 33
industrial-era business practices, 26–27
innovation, *xv–xvii*
    and environment, 42
    quickening pace of, 230–233
integration points, 164–166, 197–199
interdependence, understanding effect of, 50
issues, in business process, 39–41

Jackson, Andrew, on courage, 206
Japanese management principles, 34, *see also specific principles or techniques*

Kennedy, Michael, 194
Kieffer, Don, 221
Knowledge-Based Product Development, 136–138, 168–169
    adapting lean tools to, 241–242
    environment resulting in, 30
    learning cycles in, 169–174
    success of, 237–241

ladder of inference, 72–75
LAMDA cycle, 172, 173
launch assessments, 80–82, 93

leadership, 28, 243
    in Circle Organization, 36, 37
    firefighting by, 84–85
    during turnaround years, 34–35
    for worker empowerment, 27
    see also Product Development Leadership Learning Team
leadership board, 231, 232, *see also* "the wall"
Leadership Learning Change Model, 194–199, 203, 241
lean manufacturing, 34
    adapting tools of, 241–242
    flow in, 93
lean principle(s), 131–144
    adapting, 133–136
    applications of, 209–211
    implementation of, 243
    merits of, 136–138
    as systems approach, 138–143
    working smarter as, 143–144
learning cycles, 169–174, 197, 198
"learningful" conversations, 54, 70–75
learning organizations, 47–59
    building a shared vision in, 55–57
    disciplines of, 48
    mental models in, 53–55
    personal mastery in, 52–53
    systems thinking in, 48–52
    team learning in, 57–60
    see also organizational learning
"left turn" products, 133
Lilienthal, Otto, 137, 138
limit curves, 157
    and false positive feasibility, 162–164
    in set-based design, 179, 183, 191–192
    shape of, 160
Little's Law, 103–104
Luczak, Kerry, 80–82, 93

Machiavelli, Niccolo, on creating a new order, 80

management principles, 33–35
market risks, 110–111
Massachusetts Institute of Technology (MIT), 45, 81–82, 91, 93
McCaslin, Jim, 237
mental models, 53–55, 195, 197, 198
milestone events, 208–209
mission statement, 31
MIT, *see* Massachusetts Institute of Technology
models, increase in, 117–121
The Motor Company, 32
motorcycle market, 120

National Science Foundation, 81
new products
    as bin 6 projects, 108–109
    and creation of dreams, 31–32
    as crucial to business, 42
    and demand—supply ratio, 128–130
    flow of, 99–100
    public introductions of, 106
    rate of introduction for, 103–104
    risks with, 110–111

OCI award, *see* Outstanding Corporate Innovator award
OECD countries, *xvii*
office spaces, 29
Ohno, Taiichi, 34, 219, 240
"100 Years of Great Motorcycles," 94–97
oobeya, 217–233
    application of, 226–230
    collaboration using, 217–221
    as process, 221–226
    as quickening through visualization, 230–233
organizational learning, 41–42, 44–46, *see also* learning organizations
Organization for Economic Co-operation and Development (OECD) countries, *xvii*

Outstanding Corporate Innovator (OCI) award, *xiii*, 97–99, 116
Ozley, Lee, 35

participative organizations, 38–39
patterns of events, 195
P-D-C-A cycle, *see* Plan-Do-Check-Act cycle
PDL²T, *see* Product Development Leadership Learning Team
PDMA, *see* Product Development Management Association
personal mastery, 52–53
phase gate method
    problems in use of, 67–70, 132, 167–168
    and project success, 149, 150
    as risk management protocol, 98
    typical phases and gates in, 145–148
Phillips, Steve, 157
Pilat, Dirk, on China, *xvi–xvii*
Plan-Do-Check-Act (P-D-C-A) cycle, 171–172, 194
point-based development, 146–148, 151, 175
power, dispersion of, 26–27
PPC, *see* Product Planning Committee
Produce Products Group (PPG), 36, 42
product demand, generating, 126–128
product development, *xv*
    cadence in, 101–104
    with CCPDP, 4–7
    cross-functional, 46–47
    current state of, 10–24
    and environment, 42
    flow in, 99–100
    at Harley-Davidson, 67–70
    speed of, 145
    steps in, 145–146
    see also specific topics, e.g.: firefighting
Product Development Leadership Learning Team (PDL²T), 43–47, 61–79, 194

check-in for meetings, 63–64
check-out for meetings, 77
creating shared vision in, 75–78
creation of, 42
dialogue in, 58–59
emotion and passion in, 47
finger-pointing in early days of, 52
learningful conversations in, 70–75
meeting arrangements for, 61–63
meeting process for, 79
organizational learning in, 45–47
phase gate method in, 67–70
secrecy of, 44–45
systems thinking in, 45–47, 64–67
as a "thinking committee," 105
Product Development Management
    Association (PDMA), *xiii*, 94, 97
product life cycle plan, 108, 113,
    120–121
Product Planning Committee (PPC),
    107, 108, 112–114
project management techniques, 102–
    103, 106–107
project portfolio, 108
project risks, 110, 111
Provide Support Circle (PSC), 36
pull events, 199–205
    and help chains, 210–212
    and railroad planning vs. combat
        planning, 207–210

railroad planning, 207–208
redesign loops, *see* design rework loops
red/yellow/green reports, 214–216
Reese, Anthony, 94, 96, 105, 110
reinforcing loops, 66–67, 70
Repenning, Nelson, 81
resource management, 108
rework cycles, 85–87
Riis, Jacob, on stone cutting, 158
risks
    with new products, 110–111

and phase gate method, 98
    predicted by limit curves, 163
Roaring Motors (fictitious company)
    environment of, 25–27, 29
    product development at, 10–24
root cause analysis, 150–151

schedule dates, 113
Senge, Peter, 42, 45, 46, 50–51
set-based development, 174–178
    to avoid late discovery of problems,
        151–152
    design approach in, 179–192
    introduction of, 148–149
shared vision, 55–57, 75–78, 242
Shibley, John, 43, 45–46, 59, 60, 62–67,
    73
Sloan School of Management, 81
Sobek, Durward, 136, 143, 240
spew out, in *oobeya*, 224–226
stakeholders, in business process, 39–41
standardized work, 77–78
Sterman, John, 45
Stevenson, Robert Louis, on planting
    seeds, 116
Stone, Clement, on environment, 25
styling, 95–96
success
    elements of, 31
    environment for, 32
    of knowledge-based development,
        237–241
    from new product development,
        99–100
supply and demand, 117–130
    and generation of demand, 126–128
    and new product development,
        128–130
    and reduction in shipments, 126, 127
    system dynamics model of, 122–126
Sutton, Ken, 212, 235
swirl, 113–115

system dynamics, 45, 65–67, 122
system dynamics model, 122–126
    company revenue in, 123, 125
    data for, 123–125
    for testing potential policy decisions,
        125–126
systems thinking
    in learning organizations, 48–52
    in PDL²T, 44–46, 64–67

takt time, 100–101
Tanaka, Takashi, 217–221, 226, 230
tariff protection, 34–35
Taylor, Charles, 139
team learning, 57–60
Teerlink, Rich, 34–37, 95
tipping point, 83–84, 87–88, 91–92
Toyoda, Kiichiro, 141, 142
Toyoda, Sakichi, 141
Toyota Motor Company
    history of, 140–143
    management principles at, 34
    milestone events at, 208–209
    pillars of production system at, 219
    set-based development at, 175–177
    Ward's and Sobek's research on,
        135–136
    see also lean principle(s)
trade-off curves, 191
turnaround years, for Harley-Davidson,
    33–35, 41, 117–119

values of Harley-Davidson, 29–30,
    39–41

vision(s), 243
    collaborative development of, 195
    shared, 55–57, 75–78, 242
visualization of output, 219–220,
    230–233
visual management, 212–216, 222, see
    also oobeya

"the wall," 226–230
Ward, Allen, 135
    on breaking late discovery cycle,
        151–152
    design compiler hypothesis of, 238,
        240
    initial meeting with, 134–135
    and knowledge-based development,
        148
    and LAMDA cycle, 172
    on limit curves, 157, 164
    and milestone events, 208–209
    on phase gate methods, 152–153, 167
    and set-based development, 168,
        175–177, 186
    and Takashi Tanaka, 217
    Toyota research project by, 136–138,
        140–141, 143, 144
Wilcox, Tony, 158–160, 162, 179–183
Willie G. Davidson Product Develop-
    ment Center, 224
Wince-Smith, Debora, on innovation,
    xvi, 240–241
Womack, Jim, 131–134, 143
Wooden, John, on learning, 131
working smarter, 2, 24
Wright, Orville, on flying machines, 1
Wright brothers, 137–141, 175, 240

CPSIA information can be obtained
at www.ICGtesting.com
Printed in the USA
LVHW081227310720
661997LV00006B/21